GILBERT
AND
SULLIVAN

Caryl Brahms

GILBERT AND SULLIVAN

Lost Chords and Discords

Little, Brown and Company
Boston Toronto

Library of Congress Catalog Card No. 75-4233

First American edition

Designed by Craig Dodd
for Weidenfeld and Nicolson Limited
Filmset by Keyspools Limited, Golborne, Lancashire
Printed in Great Britain by
Tinling (1973) Limited, Prescot, Merseyside

To Margaret Daniel and Shirley Mowbray
who have stayed with this book through a wilderness of sentences, hailstorms
of commas and colons, and, of course, thin and thick.

'Don't distract me with the Facts' – W.C.Fields

Acknowledgements

Photographs and illustrations are supplied by, or reproduced by kind permission of the following: By gracious permission of H.M. The Queen: *38–9*; Nicholas Bentley: 165; The British Library: 25, 46, 105, 126, 127, 198, 206, 251, 252, 254, 257; William Heinemann Ltd: 101; L.E.A. 142, 164, 169; Raymond Mander and Joe Mitchenson Theatre Collection: 18, 26, 29, *40* right, 43, *53, 54*, 56, 61, 69, 73, 77, 78, *79*, 82, 86, 88, 91, 93, 95 right, 103, 108, 109, 112, *117, 118–9, 120*, 121, 132, 134, 138, 143, *146, 147*, 157, *161*, 162, 168, 175, 179, 186, 195, 201, 221, *228*, 230, 231, 234, 242, 243, 248; Mansell Collection: 197, 210, 215; John Murray: 11; National Portrait Gallery: *148*; *187*; *Punch*: 98, 114, 139; Radio Times Hulton Picture Library: 22, 34, 48, 58, 62, 65, 124, 166, 247, 255; Royal Academy of Music: *37*; Ned Sherrin: 40 left and btm; *Sunday Telegraph*: 165; Victoria and Albert Museum: 63, 68, *80*, 101, 115, 128, 141, *145*, 181, *188*, 209, 219, *225, 226–7*.

Numbers in italics refer to colour illustrations.

The author and publishers are grateful to Cassell for permission to quote from *Sir Arthur Sullivan: His Life, Letters and Diaries* by Sullivan and Flower and to the New York Times Company for permission to quote from 'How Stravinsky Became a G & S Fan' © 1968.

Contents

Author's Note

No study of the lives of Sir W. S. Gilbert and Sir Arthur S. Sullivan could be undertaken without consulting the distinguished biographers who have written of them before. And so I have read, learned and helped myself copiously from *Sir Arthur Sullivan: His Life, Letters and Diaries* by Sullivan and Flower (Cassell); *W.S. Gilbert* by Dark and Grey (Methuen); *Sir Arthur Sullivan* by Percy M. Young (Dent); *Gilbert: His Life and Strife* by Hesketh Pearson (Methuen); *The First Night Gilbert and Sullivan* by Reginald Allen (The Heritage Press: New York); and two books by Leslie Baily, *The Gilbert and Sullivan Book* (Cassell) and *Gilbert and Sullivan and their World* (Thames and Hudson). I am grateful to Mr Burton Shevelove for putting his ample theatrical library at my disposal. I have also consulted Raymond Mander and Joe Mitchenson inside the covers of their *A Picture History of Gilbert and Sullivan* (Vista Books), inside their house in Sydenham and inside countless West End theatres on crowded first nights, onslaughts they bore with considerable fortitude. For access to most of these books I am indebted to the Head Librarian and his staff at the London Library; and grateful for their forbearance.

The Stravinsky Estate, through *The New York Times*, has given me permission to quote from an interview with Stravinsky recorded at his home in Beverley Hills in 1968. Mr Nicholas Bentley and *The Sunday Telegraph*, Mr Osbert Lancaster, his publishers and *The Daily Express*, have kindly allowed me to reproduce two cartoons.

I am grateful to the Decca Record Company Ltd, for the benefit of being able to hear constantly and refer to their complete series of recordings of the major operas.

I am particularly indebted to Ned Sherrin for his help throughout the book; and to John Curtis and Celia Clear at my publishers for their advice and assistance.

Furthermore, Sir John Betjeman has endangered his reputation by writing a foreword to this book, an act of gallantry which is characteristic.

CB

Foreword

No one should write a foreword to a book he has not enjoyed. I had thought that everything which could be written about Gilbert and Sullivan had already appeared. That
too-little appreciated and excellent author, Hesketh Pearson wrote well about the lives
and strifes of the pair, Mander and Mitchenson produced a memorable picture history
of Gilbert and Sullivan. They are authoritative biographies. Despite all this, there is
plenty of room for this lavish production by Caryl Brahms. This is because Gilbert and
Sullivan's appeal is perennial because of their operas and because they were such
disparate characters. Sullivan, the handsome choirboy with a bandmaster father, and
Kneller Hall as a background was all his life shy, unmarried, mother-bound and polite.
He was a welcome polished guest at the boards of crowned heads. Only in his music did
he let himself go. All the time he thought of himself as a composer of sacred oratorios and
did not wish to be associated chiefly in the public mind with comic opera. Gilbert had
aspirations to being a country squire with a half-timbered residence. After being at a
good school he went into the Law. As he was always quarrelsome, litigation suited him.
He was happily married and not at all shy or lonely. The only part of himself he did
conceal was his interest in architecture and art and this is evident in the settings he chose
for his opera libretti as well as in the houses where he lived. He thought of himself
chiefly as a serious playwright and not as a composer of words to be set to music by
Sullivan. He did not think much of Shakespeare. Considering that neither Gilbert nor
Sullivan wanted to be remembered after their deaths by what they regarded as their less
important work, it is a happy mystery that they have achieved fame despite themselves.

The rock on which their success was founded was their imaginative producer
D'Oyly Carte. He built for them the Savoy Theatre. He put up with Gilbert's dictatorial methods at rehearsals and with Sullivan's dilatoriness in providing the music. He
was the ideal producer. A C.B.Cochran of his day, and an astute businessman. The
Savoy was the first theatre to be equipped with electric light. It is good to know that the
operas are still run by Miss Brigit D'Oyly Carte so that they are still a family business
which has kept up Gilbert's stage directions and traditions. Indeed to this day the
D'Oyly Carte Company is a world to itself with a vast public crowing class and even
national boundaries.

Caryl Brahms is like an enthusiastic producer: throughout this book she is carrying us along from small beginnings to great triumphs, patting her performers on the back here and there: – Sullivan is always 'swanning' into rooms, Gilbert growls with dissatisfaction but has a soft spot for young ladies. Here and there she steps down from writing the text and puts in a well-chosen phrase in brackets. She is on stage all the time. She never sleeps. She watches and enjoys and so does the writer of this foreword.

JOHN BETJEMAN

Introduction

Gilbert and who?

Ask the question and back will come the full-throated global answer – Sullivan.

When my publisher invited me to write a biography of Gilbert and Sullivan, the quarrelsome collaborators – show me the collaborators who are not? – he made a suggestion that amounted almost to a stipulation; the key, he pointed out, to success in this

'But, surely, dear, no one would DARE to put a bomb in a book about Gilbert and Sullivan.'
A *Daily Express* Pocket Cartoon by Osbert Lancaster, 25 August 1973.

dangerously sensitive area is 'an ideal marriage of an author and his subject'. Further, he begged me to walk delicately – 'to take into account the readers' susceptibilities'.

The challenge was too fascinating to be resisted by the contrary cuss of a writer that I am.

Almost I could see the opening sentence suspended above the view of Regent's Park whence cometh my pertinent or, more often, impertinent adjectives: 'Many of their comic operas are appalling, their plots puerile and their music, of necessity, derivative, but the men are interesting.'

Tempted though I was, I felt it only prudent to reflect on the project. It meant starting from scratch – a very apt metaphor in my case – for I had always taken Gilbert and

Sullivan for granted, in the way that one takes Fortnum and Mason, Beaumont and Fletcher, sausage and mash. I knew nothing about them except that they had quarrelled over a carpet – just the sort of nonsense thing close collaborators would quarrel about – and a strong impression, which subsequent research has suggested I share with Queen Victoria, that Sullivan was forever pulling Gilbert's chestnuts out of the fire with some felicitous twist of tune, an impression which, on the whole, I still retain. I even wondered, during these early hours of pondering whether I would or, indeed, could write the book; if there were any existing biographies I could turn to for facts. Poor chick, I had soon to find myself overshadowed by a mound of books – and all of them adulatory.

Gilbert, I thought, would snatch any word, however remote, on which to turn a rhyme.

> This blind devotion is indeed a crusher –
> Pardon the tear-drop of a simple usher!

or

> For he might have been a Roosian,
> A French or Turk or Proosian.

However I should, I think, also quote out of deference to the susceptibilities of the faithful, an example – and justice insists that it is one of thousands throughout the operas – of some dexterously arranged lines, beautifully turned, from *Princess Ida*. They occur in the Trio at the end of the Prologue, where Arac, Guron and Scynthius deplore their lot:

> For a month to dwell
> In a dungeon cell,
> Growing thin and wizen
> In a solitary prison
> Is a poor lookout
> For a soldier stout
> Who is longing for the rattle
> Of a complicated battle.

Here, the rattle-battle couplet is W. S. Gilbert, the rhyme and rhythm artificer, at his best; though the inversion of 'a soldier stout' is somewhat suspect. But one can forgive it and its irritating onomatopœic chorus,

> Boom! Boom! Boom! Boom!
> Rum-tummy-tummy-tum
> Boom! Boom!

for the jewelled definition of 'complicated battle'. And even I have to admit that these offending syllables when heard with their orchestration make a proud and splendid sound.

Sullivan's music, I thought, was like an ornamental lake such as Gilbert had built at Grim's Dyke, his home on the Harrow Weald, in which ultimately he perished – a placid lake of music throwing back the reflections of other composers, Mendelssohn, Schubert, Brahms, Tchaikowsky – a judgment that a brief listening to some of the few recordings of his serious music confirmed.

After having listened superficially to a few recordings I felt as though, like Macbeth, I had supped full of cream puffs, which is not my habit.

However, to be fair – or fairer – the preponderance of musical opinion has it that Sullivan sacrificed his gifts to those of Gilbert, and certainly much of the musical opinion of his day thought the same.

One great composer who, though he speaks for the angels, I could not but include, was Stravinsky, tape-recorded at his home in Beverley hills, discussing English music and quoted in *The New York Times* for 27 October 1968:

In 1912 ... Diaghilev took me to London. ... We stayed at the Savoy Hotel and went about quite a bit in the evenings when we could get away from rehearsals. One evening when, much against his will, Diaghilev was persuaded to remain peacefully in the hotel, sounds of music seemed to pursue us through the walls and I remember very well that my first impression of those faint strains was 'bouncy'. Further investigation led us to the Savoy Theatre next door which had the D'Oyly Carte in *Iolanthe* on the bill.

It was entirely Diaghilev's idea to go and hear the performance. I demurred. My knowledge of Gilbert and Sullivan was nil. ... I had heard an *a cappella* rendition of Sullivan's 'Onward Christian Soldiers' somewhere and I was unsympathetic. To begin with, I do not like unaccompanied singing, except in music that is primitive harmonically – which 'Onward Christian Soldiers' is far from being. ... Beyond this I had indeed heard how the Stanislavskys had made *The Mikado* the chic-est thing in Moscow. ... Otherwise, Gilbert and Sullivan meant nothing to me. In general my acquaintance with English music was scarcely nodding. ... I vehemently protested Diaghilev's suggestion to see *Iolanthe*. I realise now that my scepticism was probably due to the fact that I did not then speak much English. ... Diaghilev, however, was a strong man and persevered. ... What immediately fascinated me was the way the music adjusted to the rhyme. (No foreigner can be in England more than five minutes without immediately learning two words – 'liberal' and 'conservative', recognisable even when they are pronounced 'li-ber-AL' and 'conser-va-TIVE'.) ... My interest in the technique of the composer increased in the next few weeks. Diaghilev and I went to performances whenever we could. We heard *The Mikado*, *Pirates of Penzance* and *Patience*. Diaghilev became a buff, incidentally, memorising some of the patter songs and making Russian translations of them at the top of his lungs during his matutinal ablutions.

After this initiation, whenever I returned to London I would visit the Savoy Theatre. I believe I heard all of the operas except *The Grand Duke* and *Utopia Limited*. ... But *Iolanthe* has always been the most provocative for me. ... I find here that the composition of the music to the rhyme is a demonstration of the symmetry that requires a special, rare skill at its best.

With Gilbert and Sullivan, words and music are equally important. This is where Sullivan shows an incredibly self-effacing gift. His music is created to Gilbert's words, so that the words survive and have a separate and important existence apart from the music. The values of the words as words – their sounds, their rhythmic qualities, are always apparent.

And having said this, I will now say that while I respect this approach, I cannot go with it. For me the music must be independent of the poetic meaning. ... In all of my works the qualities of the verse, as verse, are sacrificed to whatever I intend in the composition. ...

I heard *Rosenkavalier* for the first time after the war (the first war) and I confess I prefer

Gilbert and Sullivan. The poetry is understandable and the music is not pretentious. Further-more, Sullivan has a sense of timing and punctuation which I have never been able to find in Strauss. And the British team is never boring. The operas gallop along like happy colts, not like cart-horses. They are also moral. The characters are good and bad, and the moral is always clearly drawn, although I do not overlook the sophistication of the satire. They remind me of American Western films. . . .

While they depend on conventions, their attack on conventions is always progressive. This is undoubtedly one of the major reasons for the continued popularity of the operas – they will probably last beyond any sunset on the British Empire. . . .

There is one characteristic of Gilbert and Sullivan, apart from the words and music, that has left a lasting impression on me, and that is their pure, remarkable and consistent tact.

The Gilbert and Sullivan satiric operettas are the great British ethnic folk rite. For a hundred years upper middle-class bathrooms have rung with Sullivan's tunes and a smattering of Gilbert's words sung resoundingly by the amateur baritone voices of early morning celebrants, and those of 'their sisters and their cousins and their aunts'. And the rite has extended to America, which began by pirating and ended by research-ing them. Each time I play a recording of one of the Savoy Operas and, as to the music, decide 'derivative', I feel the censure of million upon million upon millions of the tiled walls and bath-mats of two hemispheres, steaming in mute reproach. A hundred years stand behind their protest, if one ignores their first collaboration – the failure, *Thespis*. Arthur Quiller-Couch, in one of his Cambridge lectures, tells us that he encountered: '. . . two long lines of men on opposite sides of the thoroughfare. The one drawing or seeking to draw, unemployment pay; the other taking, or seeking to take, tickets for Gilbert and Sullivan.'

When *Pinafore* was presented in America soon after its London production in May 1878, 'it was welcomed,' gasped a contributor to *Scribner's Magazine*, 'with an enthusiasm bordering on insanity'.

Together Gilbert and Sullivan wrote fourteen comic operas in twenty-five years. Such a body of work in so short a time would put a strain on any creative partnership. Moreover Gilbert, a quarrelsome man, was also a barrister, and could bring to an erup-tion of complaining correspondence his legal training as well as his natural enthusiasm for irate argument. He flourished his solicitor in the faces of his neighbours, his trades-men and of course Sullivan, and he did in fact take his collaborator and his manager, D'Oyly Carte, to court. He even quarrelled with Shakespeare: 'I was bored by *The Tempest* as I was by *Richard II* and *Julius Caesar*, three ridiculously bad plays. I dare say Shakespeare was a great poet. I am not qualified to express a technical opinion on that point, but I consider myself an authority on dramatic work, and I have no hesitation in expressing a professional opinion that all his works should be kept off the boards.'

'I always had an idea,' wrote a friend, 'that Gilbert did not like Shakespeare's plays.' Surely a classic understatement.

It has been said that the majesty of the law was never far from Gilbert's presence – indeed there were times when he confused it with his own. The trouble was he would invoke it against the wrong people. In 1898 he brought an action based on the suggestion that an American lady journalist had misrepresented him. He wrote afterwards: 'The

Judge summed up like a drunken monkey – he is in the last stage of senile decay and knew absolutely nothing about the case.'

Sullivan, a man of a more patient nature, made heavy calls on his natural tact throughout the period that they worked together. Sullivan was a friend of princes. He pursued the society of men born above his station with an enduring enthusiasm. Not only men. Queen Victoria, with whom he was a great favourite, invited him to 'edit' the musical compositions of the Prince Consort, and accorded him a knighthood in 1883, twenty-four years before Gilbert received the royal accolade – from her successor – in 1907.

Both Gilbert and Sullivan felt their better work had been achieved not in partnership but when they worked alone.

Certainly, the endless war over which should come first, the chicken (the words) or the egg (the music), is still being waged between writers of lyrics and writers of music. An artistic collaboration of any kind has to be a matter of give and take – with each of the collaborators feeling that by giving he is weakening his own work. These necessary adjustments lead to tensions, for both sides have the ultimate aim at heart – the good of the artifact. But they approach the end product down different paths. Trying to admit another, a different approach, is a skill vitally necessary to a successful collaboration. The result when arrived at, more often than not, justifies the means. So long as the dispute is artistic and never financial, bitterness goes with the wings of the morning.

It is a matter of discussion to this day whether both men were right or wrong. One thing is clear. For a composer to have thought that his work was better in 'Seated one day at the organ' than it was in *The Mikado*, and for a librettist to be convinced that a Bab Ballad – written, incidentally, in the train to Folkestone on his honeymoon – excelled the libretto of *HMS Pinafore*, may have been understandable; but it did not make their working relationship easier.

Their days together must be measured against the background of the theatre of their time in England and America. There is no doubt that the literary executors who have mounted guard over their memories have done their best to present a pair of solid Victorian portraits; but a closer study of the letters and diaries of Gilbert, who married early and, with the understanding of his wife, continued to enjoy the companionship of young women – would they be described today as the Victorian equivalent of nymphets? – and Sullivan, who never married but continued throughout his life to enjoy the companionship of men friends as well as not a few women, but who was fundamentally shy, gives Victorian portraiture another dimension.

Sullivan, for years an enthusiastic seeker for better health in all the fashionable European spas, died – before Gilbert – in 1900. Gilbert, of whom it has been said: 'He was a very kind-hearted man, but he did not want anyone to know it,' died of a heart-attack while rescuing a young lady friend from drowning in a weed-entangled ornamental lake at his home in Harrow Weald, in 1911. Their Savoy Operas are given in England and America to theatres packed with the faithful wherever they are played.

Why has their work outlasted so many of the contemporary musical comedies?

Well, why is the music of Offenbach still played? Surely the answer lies in the tunefulness of the music and the happy atmosphere in the gentle satire. And then, in the case of Gilbert and Sullivan the *famille* D'Oyly Carte turned them into a family business, from father to son, and carried on to this day by their niece, Brigit D'Oyly Carte.

As Gilbert and Sullivan grew older and more impossible and I, week by week, with them, it seemed not, as I had supposed before I started out, that it all happened a long time ago, but that, indeed, they lived and squabbled only yesterday. And it became clear to me that I must have invented them in one of the novels I wrote with S. J. Simon – particularly Gilbert.

1
Chorister and Barrister

At number 8, Bolwell Terrace, a self-respecting, unadorned, unpretentious house in a sturdy terrace of what one takes to be two-up, two-down, early nineteenth-century working-class cottages (built on the site of what was formerly Vauxhall Gardens), on 13 May 1842, was born to Thomas Sullivan, an Irish pit-musician, and his wife Maria Clementina, *née* Coghlan, a second son, Arthur Seymour. William Schwenk Gilbert, born on 18 November 1836, at number 17, Southampton Street, Strand, the house of his grandfather, a tea-merchant who could, and probably often did boast of acquaintanceship with Dr Johnson and Sir Joshua Reynolds, was thus already stealing a march on Sullivan, establishing a five and a half years' start, with a birthplace a couple of rungs up the social ladder – an altitude that Sullivan was to clamber to and surpass in maturity, positively swanning past the post of friendship with the future monarch Edward VII. However, Sullivan could hardly have been more conveniently born for the pattern of success in his later life, for although his father earned only a guinea a week playing wind parts at the Surrey Theatre, to which he would walk to work to save the fare, and from where he would trudge back to Bolwell Terrace after the performance, he was destined to rise, even as his second son was born to rise, to become the professor of the clarinet at the military establishment Kneller Hall. 'Thomas Sullivan,' his colonel at this military school of music was to write, 'is one of the most remarkable people we have ever had here – he is what we have lacked – a real musician.' At the age of eight, Arthur Sullivan was familiar with every instrument in his father's band. His mother, too, played a part, though more remotely, in her son's gift for music. 'There are so many things I want to do for music,' he was to write to her later, 'if God will give me two days for every one to do them.'

Sullivan's mother, say his biographers Herbert Sullivan (his nephew) and Newman Flower, had music in her blood, for she was descended from the Italian family of Righi. A Righi had been one of Michelangelo's principal assistants. Also she was said to have had a Jewish grandmother. It was a happy marriage.

Maria, Arthur Sullivan's mother.

Sullivan, who was to die unmarried and, so far as can be discovered, childless, was a loving family man. He adored his elder brother, Fred; loved and honoured his father and, to the last day of her life, idolised his mother. She, in her turn, was equally devoted to her son. Since, in those days, her husband's guinea a week, even with the rent a mere £20 a year, proved inelastic, she put the elder infant, Frederic, born on the second Christmas Day after their marriage, 'out to nurse', and herself took a situation and left her home to become a children's governess.

Gilbert, on the other hand, was the child of an unhappy marriage (an imbalance, moreover, that left its mark for ever on the son), his father being 'tall and choleric, with a strong sense of the ridiculous and a marked tendency to be so', according to Hesketh Pearson. Later, when his son began to make the early beginnings of becoming a writer, his father barked: 'If he can be a writer, anybody can.' However his mother, we are told, in a letter written in 1836, was 'not a little proud of him'.

When Gilbert was two years old, holidaying in Naples with his parents and Nannie, he was carried off by kidnappers and held to ransom for £25, an experience which may have come in handy years later in *The Gondoliers* and *The Pirates of Penzance*. He was sent to the Great Ealing School where Thackeray, Newman, Marriot and Huxley had been educated before him. He was 'clever but lazy, good-looking but unpopular', working in spurts and winning prizes, but distinctly domineering, and stage-managing plays which he probably wrote, too, for his school-fellows. When convalescing in Paris from an attack of typhoid fever, Gilbert saw the Emperor and Empress pass by in procession and recorded in his earliest verses that the sovereigns had observed his shaven head with appreciation. He ended with the immortal couplet:

> And I never saw a phiz
> More wonderful than 'is.

Sullivan's talents were also apparent from an early age. At eight years old he had composed his first anthem, 'By the Waters of Babylon I Sat Down and Wept'. (At the same tender age Mozart was giving lessons at the pianoforte to William Beckford, aged seven. *Autres génies, même mœurs.*) The anthem, if it did not set the Crystal Palace on fire, did have the effect of deciding Thomas Sullivan that this second son should go to a private school rather than a Board school; the family exchequer, though at no time crammed to bursting point, allowing the welcome return of Mrs Sullivan to the nest under the increased salary from Kneller Hall.

Mr William Plees's academy was in Bayswater, quite a trudge from Lambeth, but Mr Plees was soon to discover Sullivan's appetite for music and encouraged it.

The boy wrote home that he had heard he could get a pianoforte by paying 15/6d down, which 'I think is rather dear'. However, a friend warned him that, at fifteen shillings and sixpence – down – the strings would wear out before the purchase was concluded, so the pianoforte vanished from Arthur's schemes and from his dreams.

Meanwhile Gilbert, bored with his Ealing school, called at the theatre where Charles Kean was appearing, unsummoned and unsung. His interview with Kean was not prolonged. Kean sent him back to school forthwith.

At sixteen he was Head Boy with a distinction for translating Greek and Latin verses. When he left school he went to King's College, London, where he made his mark by turning the Scientific Society into the Dramatic Society, and by writing 'satirical verses', and failed to endear himself the more by caricaturing his chums and professors. And so, while Sullivan, smiling son of May, was already making good impressions and friends who would stand him in good social swanning stead in after life, Gilbert, the sardonic, was gathering a good few enemies.

His BA in his knapsack, it being the time of the Crimean War, Gilbert settled down to cram for a commission in the Artillery, and in so doing established for himself a great taste for uniforms of any kind; a taste that was to reap its reward on the roundabouts of time. In 1901 he was to write to Helen Carte: 'We were *quite wrong* in putting the two earls in Act 2 into plain Court dress. ... I should say that it would be best to put them into *Lords Lieutenants' dress* (red coats, silver striped trousers, general's gold belt and cocked hat). ... Plain Court dress would be impossible for such howling swells. ...'

When Gilbert discovered in time that it was the uniforms and not the ballistics which had attracted him to the army (besides, the Crimean War had been concluded without him), he took a competitive examination and, passing, was awarded an assistant clerkship in the Education Department of the Privy Council Office, carrying a salary of £120 per annum, where he remained in exile for four uncomfortable years before being called to the Bar. 'I was one of the worst bargains any government ever made,' he said. He had left the temperamental uncertainties of his parents' home for life as lived in a Pimlico boarding house. Against this background of professional boredom he helped time pass by visits to the theatre, practical jokes, writing verses, drawing cartoons and 'flirting with the girls who took his fancy', writes Hesketh Pearson. 'Convinced,' he says, 'that some day he would be free of his drudgery, he entered himself as a student at the Inner Temple and read for the law.'

Leslie Baily, in his first *Gilbert and Sullivan Book* (Cassells, 1952), had the happy thought to call one of his chapters *Boots and Bouquets*, which clearly defines the next phase of Gilbert and Sullivan. For Gilbert, who eventually had been called to the Bar, the boot was a deadly insult flung at him in Liverpool by his client, an irate Irish woman, questionably sober. What was worse, it was flung on the occasion of his inviting Sir Squire and Lady Bancroft – Mr and Mrs at the time – who happened to be playing Liverpool, to hear him plead.

This success he followed up smartly by defending a lady accused of picking a pocket in an omnibus. Gilbert elicited the facts:

a) she was a regular churchgoer,

b) she was 'on her way to a tea-and-prayer meeting',

c) that she carried in her pocket a hymn-book.

He therefore defended her on the grounds that the purse must have been planted on her.

'You say that you found the purse in her pocket,' he said to the policeman he was cross-examining.

'Yes sir.'

'Did you find anything else?' Counsel asked keenly.

'Yes sir.'

'What?' he pounced.

'Two more purses, a watch, two silver pencil-cases and another hymn book.'

And I shouldn't be surprised if there was laughter in court. Fortunately for him, Gilbert had inherited a few hundred pounds from an aunt, which enabled him, Micawber-like, to wait for two years for briefs to turn up. It was said that Gilbert earned less than £100 as a barrister. 'An unconquerable nervousness prevented me from doing justice to myself or my unfortunate clients.' However, the days of double drudgery were not to pass without one hour of crowded life, the glory of which kept him going. A song from *Manon* he had translated was sung by Madame Parepa-Rosa, wife of the Impressario of Opera, Carla Rosa, at the Promenade Concerts, and off he went to every repetition of it, crowing inwardly with delight at the thought of what the Promenaders would do if they realised that 'standing in their midst was the very man whose translation was thrilling them'.

While Gilbert had a boot thrown at him, for Sullivan it was roses, roses – or perhaps laurels, laurels would be more apt – all the way, and the only disadvantage was that he had to trudge it. Sullivan's progress was less fitful than that of his future collaborator and sparring-partner *malgré lui*. He loved music, and with his clear treble voice was longing to become a chorister, and was clamant to join the Chapel Royal. But careful Thomas Sullivan feared that the fashionable Chapel Royal would distract the boy from a formal education. The stream of vehement letters home followed – concerned entirely with the glory of being a choir-boy – until his father's resistance was quite worn down. 'It means everything to me.' Thomas Sullivan gave in.

And so, in 1854, a period of expansion, while the first stone of the new castle at Balmoral was being laid by Her Majesty and the new electric telegraph was being extended to Osborne; while the Crystal Palace, 'that magnificent structure', was being dismantled at Hyde Park and re-erected in Sydenham, Headmaster Plees of Bayswater trudged up Great Portland Street with the twelve-year-old future chorister, to see Sir George Smart, composer and organist of the Chapel Royal.

'I went to Sir G.Smart yesterday afternoon. He is a funny old gentleman. He read your letter, patted me on the head and told me I must go to Mr Helmore in Onslow Square, Brompton.'

Helmore wasted no time.

'Little Sullivan has called here this evening. I like his appearance and manners [Helmore was not to be alone in this]. His voice is good, and if arrangements can be made to obviate the difficulty of his age being greater than that of the probationers in general, I shall be glad to give him a trial. I shall speak about it to the Sub-Dean tomorrow.'

Sullivan was admitted to the Chapel Royal in Easter week, and two days after he entered, he was singing the solo in Nares's *Blessed Is He*. The star had started spinning on its course.

That dark head 'sunning o'er with curls', as the Poet Laureate was to write in another context and of a fairer head, was to be in for a deal of patting in the next few years, and figuratively for his entire professional career. On one occasion during the early chorister days, the Duke of Wellington went up to him, patted his head and gave him a golden sovereign, which was certainly more rewarding than the legendary half-a-crown and an apple.

Sullivan, born to success as water is to a fountain, lived and breathed music, and was a happy chorister.

'I had to sing a long solo in the Chapel Royal,' he wrote home dutifully, 'The Duchess of Sutherland, Lord Hardinge, Lord Ernest Bruce [the Vice-Chamberlain] and Lord Wilton were present.'

Already he was showing himself to be aware of, and impressed by, people of title – a sure pointer to later halcyon days spent in social swanning in the upper reaches of society made glorious by the sun of grace and favour: 'Watch *The Times* every day,' he urged his father on this occasion, and no doubt not for the last time, 'and most likely you will see it. For there was a reporter from there and he took down my name and a good deal else.'

Twice every Sunday and on every Saint's day, off he trudged in his handsome but heavy scarlet and gold uniform, to St James's Palace and back, a total of ten miles. Many heads must have turned the better to register the young, bravely accoutred, handsome if semitic-looking or at least Italianate boy, as he swung along blithely at the beginning of the pilgrimage, solemn and beautiful music in his head, and perhaps a little

The Chapel Royal, St James's Palace, where Sullivan sang as a chorister.

wearily towards his journey's end. But fortunately in Thomas Helmore, Master of the Chapel Royal, the boy had fallen into strict hands. The Chapel Royal was his whole life. Choristers came and choristers went, and their talent varied, but Helmore never ceased to watch them when they had left, and he was determined that young Sullivan should have no special treatment, as his letters home showed.

'We had the Gospel to write out ten times for not knowing it.'

'M has been thrashed for not knowing the meaning of *fortissimo*.'

'What', he queried, a shade, but only a shade, enviously, 'is Fred [his elder brother] doing cutting capers down in Suffolk, while I am getting cuts for not knowing this and that?'

But on the whole his were happy letters.

'The cake is gone and *I shall soon be in want of another*. I like Mr Goss's new anthem very much; it is very fine. It opens with a fine chorus: "Praise the Lord O my soul." *Very fine.*'

And if the anthem did not win pride of place over the cake, at least it did not sink without trace.

But in spite of his determination not to soften to young Sullivan – an attitude that must have commended itself to his father at Kneller Hall – Helmore could not but be proud of the boy's precocious musicianship, as a letter to his mother shows: 'Arthur sang a very elaborate solo in Church today, with a good many diversions in it requiring flexibility of voice, very nicely, His expression was beautiful, it brought the tears very near my eyes (although the music itself was rubbish), but as I was immediately to enter the pulpit, I was obliged to restrain myself.'

In spite of the many calls on his time and scrutiny, Helmore wrote again to Mrs Sullivan, 'Arthur should do every week about twelve exercises and compose a little something, a song or a sanctus, or an anthem of his own. This is the practical way of testing his industry.'

We can depend on it that Sullivan did all that music required of him as well as one or two extra-curricular chores, such as recommending the March from Ouseley's *The Martyrdom of St Polycarp* for use by his father at the Kneller Hall military establishment – 'It is very much for a band' – and when his father replied with his usual prudence that it was impossible for him to judge its suitability, since it had not been printed, his son sent off the March and all its instrumentation, which he had copied out from memory.

In 1855 Arthur entered for the Mendelssohn Scholarship to the Royal Academy of Music. There were seventeen competitors, all of them older than young Sullivan, but his spinning star was in the ascendant; he was elected a Mendelssohn Scholar.

The gateway was open; and in the eyes of the boy, the vista through it led on to glory.

'I have chosen Music, and I shall go on,' he wrote home, 'because nothing in the world would interest me so much. I may not make a lot of money, but I shall have Music, and that will make up if I don't.'

But he did.

'I went to the Academy this morning at 10 o'clock, and learned that I was to have a lesson a week from Professor Sterndale Bennett. ... I am also under Mr Goss for Harmony.' It was a generally useful meeting, and in it the chorister settled that he should learn to play an orchestral instrument – he plumped for the violin – and learn Italian. In his 'spare time' he scratched together an orchestra. On wet half-holidays, it seems, he persuaded his fellow choristers to stand around the pianoforte at which he presided, each chorister equipped with a comb covered in paper. He had a great facility for taking a comic song and turning it into a hymn tune. A fugal treatment was mother's milk to him – a musical mother, that is. And, said *The Musical Times*, he would often say to the nearest chorister: 'Now be a good chap and sing or whistle something to me,' and would make an excellent fugue of the subject – a facility which is to be found in his comic operas over and over again.

Every time I have made up my mind to sit down and write to you [he wrote in a letter home], some fellow or another is sure to turn me away from it by asking me to come and lead our Band, which, by the bye, consists of two French Squeakers, which, by singing through them, produce a twangy sound like an oboe, two combs, a cover of a book for a drum; I am organist, and go on composing something for it. By the bye, I have sold 22d worth of my songs to different gentlemen. This is very good.

Finance was well above the half-a-crown mark – a bishop tipped him a pound when he learned that the solo he had just heard was by the thirteen-year-old chorister himself.

So, at thirteen years old, in spite of Gilbert's five years' start, young Sullivan was ahead of him, for his feet were already planted on the path of success. Even the warning signs that his voice was breaking were no check to Sullivan for he was re-elected to a second year as a Mendelssohn Scholar and showed such promise that in 1858 it was decided he should be sent to study at Leipzig, the music Mecca of Germany.

It was the benevolent rule at the Chapel Royal that every chorister on leaving should receive £60 from Queen Victoria, and a Bible and a Prayer Book from the Bishop of London, provided that the reason of the chorister's leaving was the breaking of his voice. But Sullivan's pure pipe had not actually descended to his chest when he was due to leave for Leipzig, though it showed signs of doing so any day. The Queen, cautious and thrifty, needed to be assured that the youth's voice had actually broken before she would part with the money, and Sullivan needed that £60. What was to be done? The Bishop also must be assured that the clear voice had actually broken before the routine Bible was taken out of his personal cupboard in the Palace. However in the case of young Sullivan a precedent was, as so often it would be in the future, arranged. The Privy Purse passed over the money; the Bishop produced the Bible, and a Prayer Book.

Meanwhile, though briefs did not precisely bury Gilbert in their luxuriant bundles, he was at least able to while away his days writing, by the time he was twenty-four, fifteen farces and burlesques and the heavens alone knew how many poems, parodies, articles and caricatures. Placing them was quite another matter. None of his early plays found a stage; none of the journalism a journal. Eventually Gilbert lost patience with editors and submitted a humorous article and drawing directly to the proprietor of the penny magazine *Fun*, who issued instructions to the editor (H.J.Byron) to print it. To submit

RIGHT The title page to the first bound volume of *Fun*, 1862.

1862

FUN

VOLO ONE!

LONDON:

PRINTED AND PUBLISHED AT THE OFFICE, 80, FLEET STREET, E.C.

copy over the head of an editor is not a ploy to be recommended but in Gilbert's case it worked. He joined *Fun* as a regular weekly contributor.

For the next ten years Gilbert was to write pieces and poems in *Fun* and all their theatre critiques. (He also wrote a parody based on Rosencrantz and Guildenstern, definitely pipping Tom Stoppard at – or rather long, long before – the post.) He also supplied them with small, *mouvementé* and infinitely economical line-drawings of comical or fanciful figures caught, as it were, in flight. Pay, on 'the Penny *Punch*', was minimal. Prose or poems by established writers was £1 per column, and contributors were paid *pro rata*, every contribution being measured by the cashier with a piece of string (Oh Dickens, where were you then?).

Gilbert, unable to live expansively or expensively on what he earned from his work on the Penny *Punch*, soon began to work, too, for its 'onlie begetter'. Also for *Cornhill* and *The Temple Bar*. And a stream of drama criticism – 'from fair to vitriolic' – was published in *The Illustrated Times*.

The *Bab Ballads* first appeared in *Fun*. Gilbert, uncharacteristically, did not think much of them. Here his estimate and that of the present writer are in complete agreement. 'Were they not composed hastily and under the discomforting necessity of having to turn out a quantity of lively verse' and on a specified day each week? With how much sympathy a fellow writer feels for the author of *Bab Ballads* – feels for him but cannot, in this instance, admire him – even with his disarming admission that 'when they were collected in a (mercifully) little book I ventured to publish the little pictures with them because whilst they are certainly quite as bad as the ballads, I suppose they are not much worse.' However Gilbert returned to them again and again for the seeds of his plots.

And here I must, in honesty, admit my lack of interest in the *Bab Ballads* – that work that is admired by countless of the English, because it appeals to and shares their national dottiness. Quiller-Couch offered sage advice in his Cambridge lectures: 'If you are wise you will treat them as wise men treat *Tristram Shandy*. You will not argue, but you will either like them or leave them alone.'

Fortunately I am not required to assess the verses, which I find appalling rather than appealing: instead I will furnish the reader with a passage from the writings of the ineffable Max Beerbohm to which my loving attention has been drawn by Leslie Baily in his earlier *Gilbert and Sullivan Book*.

The Bab Ballads – how shall I ever express my love of them? A decade ago Clement's Inn was not the huddle of gaudy skyscrapers that it is now; and in the centre of it was a sombre little quadrangle, one of whose windows was pointed out to me as the window of the room in which Gilbert had written those poems, and had cut the wood blocks that immortally illustrate them. And thereafter I never passed that window without the desire to make some sort of obeisance, or to erect some sort of tablet. Surely the Muse still hovers sometimes, affectionately, there where 'Bab's' room once was. Literature has many a solemn masterpiece that one would without a qualm barter for that absurd and riotous one. Nor is the polished absurdity of the Savoy lyrics so dear as the riotous absurdity of those earlier ballads wherein you may find all the notions that informed the plots of the operas, together with a thousand and one other notions, and with a certain wild magic never quite recaptured. . . . Others than Mr Gilbert have been, and others yet will be, Gilbertian; but himself is incomparably so.

27

LEFT W.S. Gilbert in 1868.

But though the mind's eye blinks at the magic image of the easily rhymable Captain Reece 'who was adored by all his men' (and who shall wonder?), for:

> If ever they were dull or sad,
> Their Captain danced to them like mad.

the memory's ear directs me immediately to the dullness, or wilfulness of the early Gilbert's rhyming of the Reverend Hopely Porter of Assesmilk-cum-Worter (yes, really!):

> He plays the airey flute . . .
> Doves round about him hoot.

One wonders what old Polonius would have made of that rhyme.

A writer who selects a name because of the fascinating difficulty of rhyming it, is less peccant than one who, by choosing a name with a myriad rhymes, merely does so to save himself trouble. Take 'Reece' – at a random rummage one can come up with ambergris, altarpiece, cantatrice, caprice, cease, cerise, chimney piece, popping-crease and a dozen other rhymes, thus reducing the honourable chime of rhyme to a labour-saving device.

Even I have to recognise the sheer charm of Gilbert's description of himself in the ballad 'To My Bride':

> You'll marry soon – within a year or twain
> A bachelor of *circa* two and thirty;
> Tall, gentlemanly, but extremely plain,
> And when you're intimate you'll call him 'Bertie'.
> Neat, dresses well; his temper has been classified
> As 'hasty'; but he's very quickly pacified.
>
> You'll find him working mildly at the Bar
> After a touch of two or three professions,
> From easy affluence extremely far . . .
> A pound or two from whist and backing horses
> And say, three hundred from his own resources . . .
> You – only you – can tell me, an' you will . . .
> Will she run up a heavy *modiste* bill?
> If so, I want to hear her income stated.
> This is a point that interests me greatly. . . .

To be fair (an attitude of mind which I have been known to resist) this self-description is a great deal pithier than any of the words I have spilt over Gilbert, kind or unkind. It leaves me wondering if this can be the ballad which Bab, neglecting his bride on their honeymoon journey, penned in the train, and what her emotions may have been toward his seeming neglect.

And just as I am about to forgive Bab for the sake of a witty attitude or well-turned rhyme, I come upon some murderous rhythmic carelessness, such as pairing off the line

> I'm nearly seventy now, and my work is almost done

which is impeccable, with the rhythmically indefensible

> Poll Pineapple's eyes were the standing toast of the Royal Fleet

upon which, had I to write a reasoned critique, I could bear to be rude.

No sooner am I dazzled by, for instance, that part of Annie Protheroe, the Public Headsman's lass: at

> Or if it rained the little maid would stop at home and look
> At his favourable notices, all pasted in a book.

Only a humorist of distinction, I remind myself, could have rummaged the Hangman's Press notices from the recesses of his mind; when wham! I come upon a piece of anapaestic inequality in 'Emily, John, James and I':

> And I think it was time I did
> And I couldn't take my oath.

Lazy, sloppy writing. It is as well I am not required to supply a *critique raisonnée* of the *Bab Ballads*.

Back with, oddly enough, some relief to Sullivan, in 1858. Oddly enough, because composers, it is well known, are recognised to be the *enfants gâtés* if not *enfants terribles* among collaborators if only because they have been at it longer. The first time an infant composer brings both chubby fists down on the keys of the pianoforte, his proud Mamma

Gilbert's sketch on the title page of *The Bab Ballads*; like most of his drawings it is signed with his childhood name.

ups and proclaims that her baby son is a born genius – like Mozart, only better! And your composer, both in infancy and in after life, sees no reason to disagree with her.

But Sullivan, given to a grateful snobbery while still a boy-chorister, has a natural charm as a subject, just as he had as a lad. And how could talent plus charm fail to make its mark in Leipzig?

'I frankly hate the language,' he wrote home; 'but it is so expressive, and one cannot hate what expresses what one feels, for that, after all, is the essence of music.'

Mendelssohn, who founded the Conservatoire, provided a life-long influence on Sullivan's music. Moscheles, a highly-regarded musician, dominated the European music of his day and that of Leipzig and its Conservatoire in particular. A month before Sullivan began to study with him, Moscheles wrote to Klingmann (the Honorary Secretary of the Mendelssohn scholarship committee) in London: 'As you tell me Sullivan has a peculiar talent for composition, it stands to reason that his chief time will be devoted to this branch.'

But when young Sullivan first went to Leipzig, he had not considered earning his living as a composer for at that time his life's ambition was to become a Master of the Pianoforte. Boy-like he had a total belief that he would ultimately beat any professional pianist in London; and though eventually he was to change his mind, there was no record of this in his letters. It was second nature for him to conduct and only natural that little by little conducting should take over.

There was, from the outset, plenty of scope for Sullivan to shine out among the Leipzig luminaries. But money was in short supply and a rigid economy was called for from the sixteen-year-old, as well as a great deal of loving sacrifice from his parents who had to pay for his bed and board.

I am now living in the same house with Taylor of whom I have written you. I have a very nice room with a little sleeping apartment attached to it for which I pay *five* thalers a month. For breakfast *four* thalers a month. I dine at a restaurant with Wright, Taylor, etc for 6½ thalers a month, and a very excellent dinner it is at the price. I mean to be very careful and not spend a *groschen* more than I can help. I began fires today for the first time. I did without them for as long as I could, but it is so very cold now that I thought it right to have one; for I cannot work in the cold, and I am working very hard now. By my living with Taylor we shall both be able to save a good deal. In the evening when I am at home we both write together, and therefore only burn one fire and one light. Supper costs me very little – one evening at Moscheles', one at David's, Barnett's, Oldenbourg's etc.

Further proof that a friend in need is a friend indeed?

Only at Christmas, say his biographers, when in honour bound he was compelled to give presents to a host of acquaintances who had befriended him, was the monthly account hard to balance, and even then he had pinched and scraped and supped with 'the Moscheles, the Davids and the Barnetts' (and how we feel for him) and generally made-do for weeks ahead.

The running battle with the cost of living in Leipzig was waged unintermittently without having the least effect on his buoyant optimism and high spirits, a state we can but envy him.

One can sense the hesitation and indeed reluctance with which, accustomed as he was to scarlet and gold, he wrote to brother Fred: 'Ask Father if I should have a new coat? For having worn this one a whole year almost every day the nap has all worn off and if I want to go for a walk with the Moscheles or Davids [Did the Barnetts not walk?], I am obliged to put on my dress-suit which of course, besides wearing out, looks so absurd in the afternoons.'

At the end of his first year at Leipzig, that substantial fairy godmother, the Mendelssohn Committee, granted him, of its benevolence, a further year's scholarship. Whereupon the gratified Sullivan, to make his gratitude manifest, composed an anthem to the greater glory of God and Sir George Smart – most steadfast and staunch friend of all.

He conducted. He composed. He played the piano. And he never failed to go, albeit in the cheapest seats, to every good concert – and ultimately opera – in sight.

But a glut of food in some circumstances can have much the same effect as no food. For towards the end of the Leipzig days he admitted to his Mamma: 'I get horribly disgusted with music, one hears a little too much of it here. I miss Handel and the Sacred Harmonic Society very much. It will be indeed a treat to hear all that again.' But this must have been a mood, and moods pass.

In June 1860, a birthday letter to his father has all the former zest in it:

I enclose you a programme of our last *Prüfung*. You will doubtless, on looking over it, recognise one of the names. It was such fun standing up there and conducting that large orchestra! I can fancy Mother saying now 'Bless his little heart! How it must have beaten!' But his little heart did not beat at all. I wasn't the least nervous, only in one part where the drum *would* come in wrong at the rehearsal in the morning, but he did it all right in the evening. I was called forward *three* times at the end, and most enthusiastically cheered.

Sullivan trudged the roasting pavements to make his *adieux* to the Moscheles, the Davids and the Barnetts before returning in the autumn to London, as he supposed. His feelings were mixed: the sadness of parting from good friends, the longing for the cheerful hustle and bustle of London, his feeling that London was 'indolent' in matters of music – he blamed London bitterly, for instance, for its petty attitude towards Schumann: 'This new star that blazed across his horizon' (a strong and enduring influence in Sullivan's music, it is particularly interesting to see Schumannesque passages sparkling forth to pull Gilbert's chestnuts out of the fire) – and the special longing for a family reunion.

Came the great storm to break up the torrid heat: Sullivan, of course, wrote home about it.

If you have not heard ahead of the fearful storm, I must tell you about it. At about six o'clock Monday evening the clouds began to blacken, the air became hot and oppressive, and 'a thick darkness' came over the town. Then came the long distant moans of the wind, a few thick large raindrops, and finally the whole storm broke out ... we had to rush for our lives for the hailstones would have killed us ... the average size of the hailstones being that of a *hen's egg* without exaggeration. Chimney pots were falling, tiles rolling down, windows smashing, women and children screaming, horses taking fright and running away.

One wonders how much of the great storm came back to him while he was composing *The Tempest*.

Sullivan already realised that it was time that he 'folded his tent like the Arabs and silently stole away' (though there was likely to be precious little silence surrounding his departure) in July, when he wrote to his father:

I should not have delayed writing so long, but I have been waiting for a letter from Sir George Smart which came yesterday. I enclose it in order that you may read it, and will at the same time explain what he is referring to. I wrote to tell him that my masters, especially Mr Moscheles and

Mr Plaidy, wished me to stay here until Easter, as my execution would by that time be much improved, and I should also probably play in the Grand Public Examinations, besides deriving divers other benefits therefrom. Now read his letter before you go any further. Now you see, to stay here half a year longer would cost £40, from which, subtracting Sir George's kind offer of 5, would leave you the sum of 35 to pay, and which you are in about as good a position to give as I am to fly. Therefore, dear Father, we must give up the Easter plan and look forward to meeting each other in three months in that miniature Paris, Brussels. Polish up your French and Hurrah! for the beefsteaks and porter.

Hurrah! indeed.

... Of course, if one of those mysterious friends one reads of in novels should turn up and send me 50 or 100 pounds anonymously. I have no objection to take it. I would nevertheless, though, if I were you, write and thank Sir George for his kind offer which you cannot accept.

From now on little German farewell parties were to occupy Sullivan the son, while Sullivan the father took up a post at Broadwoods, the makers of the pianofortes, so adding to his earnings at Kneller Hall.

The parental purse still had a lean and hungry snap to it, but by pinching here, scraping there, the Sullivans managed to keep their ewe genius at Leipzig until Easter 1861.

'How can I thank you sufficiently, my dear Father, for the opportunity you have given me of continuing my studies here,' he wrote, 'I am indeed very grateful, and will work very hard in order that you may soon see that all your sacrifices (which I know you make) have not been to no purpose, and I will try to make the end of your days happy and comfortable. ...'

A few days later and another letter went sailing home. The Conservatoire had turned up trumps: 'Mr Schlemitz, the Director, has exempted me from paying for the Conservatorium during the six months I am going to stay here. When I went up to thank him for it, he said to me: "Oh yes, we will let that be entirely. You are a splendid fellow and very useful. We all like you so much that we can't let you go." So you see, that is 40 thalers [£6] less in the expenses.'

Two months later Sullivan started to score his music to *The Tempest*. So little did the significance of this work register, that he wrote of it for the first time only in a postscript: 'I am writing music to *The Tempest*.' But once it took form, it absorbed him and his letters: the music might sound harsh, he warned his father, but it was different and when his father became used to it, he might find he liked it very much indeed. *The Tempest* was performed in April 1861. On the journey home by way of Berlin he wrote: '*The Tempest* was first given in the *Prüfung* last Saturday and was most successful. I was called forward three times afterwards.'

Sullivan reached home full of hope, with his precious manuscript in his bag but no means with which to face the ups, downs, and hiatuses of a nineteenth-century composer's life.

2

Sullivan Acclaimed

Odyssey completed, Sullivan went back at once to his old haunts, the Chapel Royal and the Royal Academy of Music. He described the new Principal, Cipriani Potter, as 'a dear old man, with beetling eyebrows and high stuck-up collars, a fine musician who had known Beethoven very well'. In London the music of Sullivan's household gods, Schubert and Schumann, was hardly ever heard, and he defended Schumann with so much fire that the old gentleman grunted: 'Pity about young Sullivan. Going to Germany has ruined him.'

But young Sullivan, not unexpectedly, held to his opinions:

'Mr Potter,' he said one day four months later, when the perpetual argument was well in its stride, 'have you ever heard any Schumann?'

The Principal of the Royal Academy of Music admitted that he had not, again not unexpectedly.

'Will you play over some of the symphonies with me? I have arranged them for four hands.'

Cipriani Potter was to find that to 'run over' the symphonies was to be won over to the symphonies. Night after night Sullivan played Schumann with him, until, at the end of three months Cipriani Potter became the warmest advocate of Schumann in England.

The Principal of the Royal Academy was in an excellent position to spread the gospel, and this he did with all the fervour of one converted. George Grove, at that time Secretary to the Crystal Palace, was also converted, and the attachment between Grove and Sullivan was cemented over a Schumann symphony.

The meeting was to prove one of several key meetings to the door of Sullivan's future – there were to be a handful of significant meetings in Sullivan's life of which the most highly-prized seem to be with the Duke of Edinburgh, the Prince of Wales, the Monarch, George Grove and, inevitably, W.S.Gilbert.

The meeting with Grove took place in the gallery of St James's Hall during a concert. Grove saw a young man – a darkly handsome young man – staring at him – or so he optimistically thought – through the glass panel of the gallery door, and asked his companion if he knew the name of 'that engaging young man'.

'Him? Oh, that's young Sullivan, just back from Leipzig.'

The introduction was promptly followed by a discussion of Schumann's music – it would be – with the routine result elicited that Grove, though he had heard the name, had never heard the music. So Sullivan appeared, some days later, with Schumann's first Symphony in B flat, which threw Grove into such a state of enchantment with Schumann – and Sullivan – that he programmed it for immediate performance at the Crystal Palace. London deemed him 'a little advanced', but once Schumann's music rang through the Crystal Palace, London soon followed and before long his works entered the concert repertoire.

Settled in, Sullivan went to work on his manuscript of the music to *The Tempest*, revising it and strengthening it, so that the work that was first heard in Leipzig was very different from that which was to be presented at Sydenham in 1862.

'London was not really musical in the sixties,' say Sullivan and Flower. It dreamed to Mendelssohn, threw its shoulders back to Handel's chorus and declared that programmes compounded of the pair of them were the beginning and end of the Art of Music: 'Queen Victoria never played the piano well (Beethoven would have "flustered her fingers" . . .) but she loved a melody – "slow and sweet".'

The Crystal Palace at Sydenham where two performances of Sullivan's *The Tempest* in April, 1862 established his reputation. Sullivan conducted frequently at the Crystal Palace in the years that followed.

While musical society, then, practised its five-finger exercises and defied Schumann, young Sullivan, that humble flower due to set European Society – and not a little American – alight, was pondering how to earn a living. Good friends came to his aid. Helmore passed him a post as tutor to the choristers of the Chapel Royal, not to teach music but to give lessons in the ordinary school curriculum, with music lessons as an extra. Grove created 'the decorative lad' Professor of Pianoforte and Ballad Singing at the Crystal Palace School of Art – small beginnings for one who was destined to swan it with monarchs and princes, but at least a beginning – and a meeting with Jenny Lind, 'the Swedish Nightingale', began a long friendship, and was something of another rung on the professional and social ladder.

Sullivan called Jenny 'the singer with the most beautiful voice I have ever heard'. Already, in his chorister days at the Chapel Royal, her singing had filled Sullivan with near-adoration. Sullivan and all musical London. Ladies bought 'Jenny Lind stockings'. They copied her clothes slavishly. All the gowns she wore were described in the journals of fashion. La Lind scolded him for working too hard; for in addition to his teaching schedules, he worked on his score for *The Tempest* far into the night – a habit that was to stay with him throughout his professional life.

'I am sorry to hear that you have not been well,' she wrote to him. 'Do you give too many lessons ... and [eat] too much indigestible food? ...'

Once finished, the music to *The Tempest* was sent straight off to Grove, and it was decided to give the work at Eastertide 1862.

This was the great day of my life [Sullivan was to write later – subsequent history shows that he enjoyed many great days in his life]. It is no exaggeration to say that I woke up the next morning to find myself famous. The papers, one and all gave me most favourable notices and the success was so great that *The Tempest* music was repeated on the following Saturday.

All musical London came down to the Crystal Palace to hear this second performance. After it was over, Charles Dickens, who had gone with Chorley, *The Times* music critic, to hear it, met me as I came out of the Artists' Room. He seized my hand with his iron grip and said: 'I don't pretend to know much about Music, but I do know I have been listening to a very great work.'

That settled it. Sullivan dedicated his *Tempest* to Sir George Smart, and devoted himself seriously to composing. But of course he had to eat. Fortunately he was appointed to the post of Organist at St Michael's, Chester Square, and was able to give up teaching: 'I hated teaching and nothing on earth would ever have made me a good teacher. The first guineas that I gave up for the work that I wanted to do were those that came from giving lessons.'

The choir at St Michael's provided him with the work that he loved and he rapidly made it into one of the best in the West End.

He himself once said that his music was really intended for the Church, in the context of which it should be remembered that the Victorian era was an age of Church music as Stainer, Gounod and Sullivan understood it.

Of his St Michael's choir he wrote:

We were well off for soprani and contralti, but at first I was at my wit's end for tenors and basses. However, close by St Michael's Church was Cottage Row Police Station, and here I

35

completed my choir. The Chief Superintendent threw himself heartily into my schemes and from the Police I gathered six tenors, and six basses, with a small reserve. However tired they might be when they came off duty, they never missed a practice; I used to think of them sometimes when I was composing the music for *The Pirates of Penzance*.

While Sullivan was borne on the *Tempest* into 'the best musical circles in London'. And while Gilbert was well into 'his punning period' – a taste for which he was not to outgrow – accosting everyone he met with Planche's: 'You're so well bred you ought to be buttered,' and crowing with delight at its effect, he was finding 'the need to mix with his social pen-peers'. He founded a small club or circle called 'The Serious Family'. They met weekly on Saturday nights, at his Chambers in Gray's Inn. The subscription was two guineas, from the payment of which Gilbert was absolved 'in consideration of my undertaking to supply a rump-steak, cold boiled beef, a Stilton cheese, whisky and soda, and bottled ale every Saturday night for the term of my natural life. Although, financially speaking, this was one of the worst bargains I ever made, I have never regretted it.' One of his friends was Tom Robertson, whose plays – *Society*, *Ours*, *Caste* and *School* – were put on by the Bancrofts, and revolutionised the British stage by introducing ordinary people, natural acting and realistic production. Gilbert was given *carte blanche* to attend Robertson's rehearsals, thus collecting a skill that was to stand him in good stead with the Savoy Operas. Robertson advised Miss Herbert to send for Gilbert when she found she needed 'a Christmas Play in a hurry'. His baptism as a dramatist opened in a shower of puns – with an *Extravaganza*.

New friends – even good friends – flocked to the young, promising and good-looking Sullivan, but it seems that he cultivated a few only – Grove of course, Sir George Smart, the ageing Helmore, Otto Goldschmidt and his wife, Jenny Lind.

'Come down on Christmas Eve,' Goldschmidt wrote in December 1862, 'and help to light the tree. We have been playing your *Tempest* and Mrs Goldschmidt has been repeatedly singing the song and duet. She likes the work *very much*.'

And there was Frederick Clay, 'a genial, wandering soul, and a slave to music,' according to Sullivan; they had in turn studied under the same professor in the room where Bach had written some of his greatest fugues. That Clay subsequently wrote 'I'll Sing Thee Songs of Araby' cannot be laid at the good Herr Professor's door. That subsequently Clay sold the copyright of the song for £5 is probably the cause of Clay's still kicking himself in the Shades. Certainly the publishers were shamed by every drawing-room in England into giving him £20, but £25 was all he ever made out of it, a financial trauma from which he emerged with his *bonhomie* unimpaired.

Sullivan had the fun of having his *Tempest* repeated at the Crystal Palace several times throughout the year. In a letter to Mrs Frederick Lehmann he wrote: 'Joachim [the distinguished violinist] is very low-spirited at our being all together in perfect enjoyment without his being able to join us. He asked most affectionately after you and Miss Dickens [daughter of Charles Dickens]. Is he smitten?'

RIGHT Portrait of Arthur Sullivan as a chorister of the Chapel Royal, painted in the late nineteenth century from an early photograph.
OVERLEAF The marriage of Edward Prince of Wales, and Princess Alexandra on 10 March 1863, painted by William Frith. The wedding march which Sullivan wrote for the royal occasion was played all over the country.
Queen Victoria watches the ceremony from the balcony; to the right of the Archbishop of Canterbury stand three of the Queen's daughters, Princess Helena, Princess Louise and the young Princess Beatrice; in the foreground are the two youngest princes, Leopold and Arthur.

Sullivan himself had been semi-smitten during his Leipzig days with a Miss Rosamund Barnett (of the Moscheles, the Davids and the Barnetts ambience), and so was in a receptive mood towards young lovers, wherever they were.

The present writer could shake Sullivan, Clay and all the incompetent Victorian song-composers. For scarcely has one recoiled from the wrath of **realising** that Clay sold 'I'll Sing Thee Songs of Araby', 'The Sands of Dee' and **'She** Wandered Down the Mountainside', all best-sellers, for approximately £5 a piece, when along comes Arthur Sullivan selling six settings to Shakespearean songs for £5 each, and letting his celebrated song 'Orpheus With His Lute', one of the most popular drawing-room (as distinct from bathroom) items of his day, go for £10. Clearly money was not, and probably never would be, everything. It took Grove to convince him that he was selling his songs for a song.

'... I was getting on. But by this time I had come to the conclusion that it was a pity for the publishers to have all the profit. My next song "Will He Come?" went to Messrs Boosey, on the understanding that I was to have a royalty on every copy sold. And oh! the difference to me! I did very well and never sold a song outright afterwards.'

The business side settled, a flood of song poured out. Sullivan was staying a lot of the time at Sydenham, with Grove, who persuaded the, at this period, easily persuadable Sullivan, to ride with the tide, which did not spend itself for eighteen months. 'Sweetheart Let Me Dream Again' and their sixties drawing-room kind, proved a valuable source of income. And of course composers were not the only fruit fit for the publishers' picking in the sixties.

Take Gilbert, who, in the elation of having his first play produced (*Dulcamara, or the Little Duck With The Great Quack*) was to write in *Theatre*: 'The piece, written in ten days, and rehearsed in a week, met with more success than it deserved.' So elated was the neophyte dramatist that he completely forgot to pre-arrange a fee. Asked by the manager, mid-run, how much he wanted, he modestly hoped that: 'since the play was such a success, £30 would not be considered too great a price.' The manager promptly paid up, and only afterwards gave the author a sound piece of advice: 'Never sell so good a play as this for £30 again.'

Nine years later Gilbert went to a revival of *Dulcamara* and hissed it. When the management attempted to reason with him, he turned a surprised face on them: 'May not an author hiss his own play? When first I wrote I thought it good – now I hiss.'

Sullivan's friendship with Dickens flowered, for Dickens declared that he was a genius and that some day London, Europe, the World would discover this for themselves. With Dickens, the Lehmanns and Chorley, of whom more later, Sullivan took a trip to Paris: 'I was never so conscious of the greatness of that man as I was during that Paris visit,' Sullivan was to say some years later.

They passed through all the routine tourist hoops, 'with Dickens as guide', plus all that the *Opéra* offered. They dined at charming little restaurants which Dickens had found, or of which his friends had spoken, and called on all the principal musicians of the day, Dickens arguing with the cab-drivers in bad but voluble French.

Rossini, the amiable and kindly Pappa-Stomache and ageing gentleman, played duets – from *The Tempest*, of course – with Sullivan. 'Rossini', say Sullivan and Flower,

LEFT Three of the many drawing-room ballads which enhanced Sullivan's popularity as a composer.

'would afterwards sit crouched in a low armchair, his face as white as his hair, in the half-light of the ill-lit chamber. There he expounded in his subdued melancholy voice on all that was happening in the world of Music [and Music is a world unto itself] as though he were a returned ghost, who had the power to look down and forecast the changes that Music was to know.'

Rossini, too, gave brilliant parties; musicians, poets, painters, crowded his art-strewn room. 'The babel of conversation would suddenly hush – the Maestro was going to play. He would creep to the piano painfully with his rheumaticky knee-joints, run his fingers over the keys and drop into a minuet or improvise something of quaint delicacy.'

Went with Courtney to see Rossini and were admitted to his bedroom *à la Française* [Sullivan noted]. The old gentleman was very kind and affable. Asked me if I sang, as every composer for the voice ought to be able to sing. Invited me to his Reception the same evening. I found Carl Rosa there, playing a new violin sonata by a young German. . . . Thursday at $9\frac{1}{2}$ a.m. I was at Rossini's house and found him alone, composing a little pianoforte piece for his dog! [Would this be the valse for the poodle in Massine's *Boutique Fantasque*?] He played us a new *Minuet*, very pretty and quaint.

For the first few weeks of 1863 the passion for work blazed in Sullivan, who slaved through night and day. He was now living with his mother and father at Claverton Terrace, Pimlico. He still played the piano for several hours each day, he studied technique with all his old enthusiasm, he conducted and we are not surprised to learn that he continued to hustle his police force. But composition had become the beating heart of his life.

He was offered the post of organist at the Opera House, Covent Garden by his friend Michael Costa, and, once installed, Costa commissioned a ballet – *L'Isle Enchantée*. But Sullivan hated the sheer stage-craft that ballet required. 'I am a musical carpenter, and I like the trade so well that I am going to get out of it.'

He went back to his songs, say his biographers, and Covent Garden knew him no more.

By now he was well-known as a setter of songs, and lyrics were sent to him by almost every post: 'If I were to set all the verses of good quality I receive,' he wrote his mother, 'I should work 24 hours a day, and then half the songs would not have the credit – or discredit – of my notes.'

A visit to Ireland in the late summer of 1863 was to throw a symphonic shadow into the future. He wrote to his mother from Belfast: 'I shall be able to work like a horse on my return. Why, the other night as I was jolting home from Holywood through the wind and rain, in an open jaunting car, the whole first movement of a symphony came into my head with a real fresh flavour about it – besides scraps of other movements.'

Sullivan's first symphony, born in the jaunting car, was first performed at the Crystal Palace in 1866, but was not called the *Irish Symphony* until some years later, and not published until after its composer's death. Fresh it may have seemed to its composer, but even his most enthusiastic fan would have to admit in the light of truth that it owed allegiance to his most admired influences.

On his return to town his friend Chorley gave him a libretto, with a disturbingly embrangled book – he had been working on it with Sullivan the year before in Paris. Sullivan struggled with *The Sapphire Necklace* but to little effect. It was doomed never to clasp itself around the right neck. But much of its music sneaked its way into other works, as time went on.

Sullivan photographed in 1864 at the time of the
Birmingham Festival performance of *Kenilworth*.

Birmingham commissioned a work from Sullivan for their 1864 Festival. Sullivan had no suitable libretto. So Chorley wrote the *Kenilworth Cantata* in a few days. Sullivan then peeled off his figurative coat and went to work with a will.

'This is the fourth day I have worked all night [Irish!]' he wrote. 'Last evening I even forgot my supper, and was painfully reminded of the oversight when my watch conveyed the intelligence that it was 4 am.'

Of all his critics he held one in the highest esteem – his father:

Dear Father,
    I wish so much that I could persuade you to run down tomorrow by the 2.45. You could return the same night, or I would find you a bed somewhere. You see, 1st: You will never have another opportunity of hearing the work performed in such a magnificent style again; 2nd: It is a great event in my career, and one which I should like you to witness. Do come (with Fred) there's a dear.
Yr. affec. son.
Arthur.

The echo of the success of the *Cantata* rippled and ringed its way to London.

Meanwhile Gilbert was barbing one of his earliest arrows aimed at the elderly lady. A gushing spinster of an all too certain age, in a huge crinoline, addresses a swell at the Crystal Palace:

'Oh, Mr Jones, don't you adore the antiques?'

'Ah yes – ' (with deadly venom) 'in marble.'

Another mind-flinching, but admittedly endearing example of Gilbert's wit occurred when his play *Robert the Devil*, or *The Nun, the Dun and the Son of a Gun*, opened at the New Gaiety Theatre in 1868. It was fairly peppered with puns, of which this is a very fair sample:

Bertram: You're in Boulogne – a place all Britons known to!

Robert: A very pretty spot I've been blown to!

Sullivan's symphony in E flat, presented at the Crystal Palace in 1866 completed the conversion of those critics who had doubted him. (It was still a long cry to Gilbert's prolonged attack of gout, on which occasion he christened his left and agonising foot after his most severe critic, Clement Scott.)

Hard on the success of the symphony Sullivan travelled to Manchester, where he had been invited to write the music to a play to be given in Christmas week. It was a night of drizzling rain. The journey, though wet, cold and fruitless, gave him an after-dinner story that he would repeat with great gusto and frequency.

He drove at once to the theatre and asked for the play. It had not been written. Then he must see the author immediately. The author turned out to be an amateur, by profession the lodge-keeper at the local cemetery. Sullivan hired a cab and drove through the, by now, beating rain, for miles in search of the cemetery. Arrived at the lodge, there was no other dwelling in sight for miles around. Neither were there any lights in the lodge windows. Everyone was in bed. He knocked and waited. Almost he might have been Walter de la Mare's traveller:

> 'Is there anybody there?' said the traveller
> Knocking at the moonlit door . . .

but we digress.

An ice-age passed. A candle appeared at a window. An aged, aged man, wearing a night-cap, put his head out and cursed Sullivan with well-chosen, earthy words, before bumbling down to unbolt the door to continue the argument.

Sullivan, wet, and not predisposed to dispense his customary amicability, followed the night-shirted, night-capped figure in the leaping candle-light. He acquainted the grave-digger with his requirements for a Christmas entertainment. He wanted to be given some outline of the plot of the piece. The grave-digger (oh, shades of Hamlet) listened. His jaw fell. They jabbered. Neither understood either. It was no good. Sullivan turned his back on the grave-digger, night-shirt, night-cap, candle and all. Wet, cold, uncomfortable, he returned to Manchester. Next morning he learned that the cabby had decanted him at the wrong cemetery.

On his return to London he found awaiting him an invitation from Norwich to compose a new work for their October Festival.

He settled down to write it. In the morning he would tear up what he had composed the night before, only to go through the same ordeal the next day. He walked the streets but the music he had thought a possibility as he rounded the corner floated nebulously away among the Pimlico chimneypots. August went with its midnight oil; mid-September, with its confetti of torn up MS. Then fate laid a heavy hand on the shoulders of the Sullivan mother and two loving sons. Thomas Sullivan died suddenly at the end of the month. The blow was hard to bear. Thomas Sullivan, who had stinted himself, and had not spared his wife or elder son when need be, to make possible the genius son's amazing progress, was suddenly gone.

All thought of the Norwich Festival passed from Arthur's mind, obsessed with its burden of grief.

Characteristically it was a sentence in a letter from Grove – 'that unfailing friend' – which brought him back to work: 'It was a great thing for him', Grove wrote of the father, 'to have lived to see your triumph. If he had died last year, or even February of this year, before your symphony was due, it would have been quite a different thing to him, and he could not have felt such a satisfaction in your music as he did.' These wise words made their impression on the grief-torn Sullivan. Straightaway he started on his *In Memoriam*. The new and poignant work from the stricken composer drew the crowds, and Sullivan had to buy tickets for friends, although he was conducting. What finer monument could a loving son erect to a loving father?

Now, while Sullivan 'wiped away all tears from his eyes' – presumably on a black-bordered handkerchief and Grove, having sprayed the music of Schumann and Schubert, beloved of Sullivan, pleasantly and frequently through the Crystal Palace, and while the pair of them dashed breathlessly to Vienna in search of Schubert's undiscovered scores: 'We walked to the Schumann's,' wrote Grove '... and saw the Album which Robert Schumann and she [Madame Schumann] kept full of the most interesting letters and portraits and locks of hair of every composer and poet and painter from Jubal and David, downwards.' (Had not Rossini once told Sullivan that his admirers would have shorn him, had he given in to their shears?)

'We went and saw the house Mozart was born and lived in,' Sullivan wrote to Mamma, '... when we wrote our names in the Visitor's Book the librarian asked me if I was the composer of whom he had often read in the "Signaler". I modestly owned that I did occasionally write a little music [oh, the pride in that understatement!] and we bowed and complimented each other.'

And while Sullivan and the librarian are bowing and bowing to each other like a hinged pair of Mandarins, and Grove is smiling benevolently on, Gilbert has allowed himself to be led to the altar, where he wed a calm and piquant, understanding and youthful bride, the seventeen-year-old Lucy Agnes Turner, eleven years his junior, whom in the letters he sent her when absent, he addressed as Kitten, or Kit, or Missus, in defiance of the well-known social dictate: 'In speaking of a wife, a husband may address her by her christian name. In speaking of her to others, it is more proper to style her Mrs and add her surname. To degrade her to a mere initial, to call her Mrs A, or Mrs B, or more especially the Missus, is worse than vulgar, it is heathenish.'

Love must have been in the air in 1867 for Grove introduced Sullivan to the well-to-

Gilbert's sketch of his seventeen-year-old bride, Lucy Turner.
He called her 'Kitten' or 'Missus', according to his mood.

do home circle of Scott Russell in Norwood, not far from the Crystal Palace, and very much the resort of musicians and painters. There Sullivan would accompany Patti at parties and make himself agreeable – too agreeable for her father's liking – to the daughter of the house, Rachel.

If, as we look at him down the years, we fancy that Sullivan could have been bisexual – not that it is our business particularly this late in the day – it would go far to underline his relationship with the Duke of Edinburgh and, over the years, Mrs Ronalds (of whom more later), but if, as the cruel Victorian cartoonists have it, he was homosexual, we have to conclude that while Rachel was in love with Arthur, he was merely flattered by Rachel's interest, and fascinated by her world, and that he allowed himself to go along with her ardent, managing, dream of him. 'We would discuss music, painting, poetry, literature *and even science*, until the clock told us that the last train back to London was nearly due.'

Rachel, certainly a strong influence in Arthur's life during the Norwood idyll, was a determined, not to say down-to-earth young lady, who nonetheless would call a shy kiss on the brow in the moonlight love undying, but wrote to Arthur firmly: 'If you are ready to marry me next year, well and good. I will tell Mama and Papa when you see the project clear before you without a doubt – free of debt – and then there will be no reasonable objection. . . .'

Rachel, in addition to being a determined young woman was a passionate and ambitious girl: 'Will you let Gounod carry off the palm? You have the tools all ready, you have the prizes before you ... will you win for yourself a name and place among the great men who have gone before?'

'Is the Symph. in D getting on? Do write it, my bird. It is the language in which you talk to me. I also want you to write an octet. Mendelssohn's is splendid, and I am sure you could do a glorious thing. Will you?'

But hope deferred maketh the heart – Rachel Scott-Russell's heart, that is – turn to a more likely prospect. Sullivan, like Handel before him, and for the same reason, say his biographers, was forbidden by a Victorian father and, moreover, a father who despised musicians, to marry Rachel. This headstrong young lady gave in to her father's wishes with a docility unexpected in her:

It can have no other ending [she wrote to Sullivan], even in the future, and your young life shall not be dimmed by the nurture of a hope that will never be fulfilled. ... I hear you are changed and ill. God help you and give you strength to bear it all. You have others to work for, and your beautiful genius to live for, and neither I, nor any other woman on God's earth, is worth wasting one's life for.

Sullivan never wrote a second symphony, nor married Rachel.

But Gilbert's Kitten, who never spurred him on to anything – where was the need? – seems to have had wisdom beyond her years; wisdom that grew with the years, the patience of a saint and the blindest eye where her many rivals were concerned, and thus made a harmonious marriage possible through their years together. Gilbert settled himself and Kitten (and we may depend on it, in that order) at 28 Eldon Road, Kensington. Hesketh Pearson, in his biography *Gilbert, His Life and Strife*, gives a penetrating paragraph on the marriage:

She never attempted to impose her will on his, but was clever enough to get what she wanted by making him wish it, first. She quickly realised that his habit of forming attachments to other young women and his admiration for pretty faces sprang from some deep need in his nature.

'The home life of the Gilberts was quiet and relatively free from the discord obtaining in so many households,' says Pearson, yet this he follows with: 'It might be said that the master of the establishment released all his irritability in quarrels with actors, critics, managers and neighbours, and was peaceful at the fireside from sheer exhaustion.'

In the middle of 1876 Gilbert borrowed money from his banker in order to lease No 24 The Boltons, South Kensington, a commodious residence with a tennis lawn.

But the move did little to mollify the rampant Gilbert. No sooner had the last mover's man shaken the straw from his boots than the master of the new establishment sat down in a high old state to write to the decorator, complaining that he had failed to show 'such a personal interest in the matter as I was entitled to expect of you' and refused to pay more than $2\frac{1}{2}\%$ on the builder's account.

A firm that had been briefed to adapt a settee to its new and grander surroundings was the next to draw Gilbert's fire: 'A more clumsily finished piece of work I never saw. It is wholly unlike the sofa which was shown to you as the model for the alteration, and the

Gilbert and 'Missus' in 1867.

quality of the stuffing, the careless manner in which it is finished and its general unsightliness make it impossible for me to allow it to stand in my drawing-room.'

A tempting breach now occurred to this strange, irascible, unlikely and certainly unrepentant former barrister. His coachman made a bid at Tattershalls and the horse was knocked down to him for sixty-two guineas. The firm then discovered that an error had been made and asked for the horse's return. What an opening for Gilbert: 'If there has been a mistake at all, the mistake is yours, not mine, and I must leave you to bear the responsibility thereof. I may add that the peremptory tone of your letter is not calculated to induce me to make any unnecessary concession.'

While puns, poems and burlesques poured from Gilbert, Sullivan, who had not been in Leipzig for five years, returned to give a concert.

He wrote to his mother the next day:

You will like to know about the Overture. It was a great success. Everyone of note came and congratulated me, and I think it has laid a firm foundation to a good reputation in Germany. . . . Grove arrived yesterday and is happy, as the separation was telling on his health. Bosh! . . .

On 20 October his diary records: 'Ran over to Dresden ... saw Wagner's *Rienzi*, which was a great disappointment – a mixture of Weber, Verdi and a touch of Meyerbeer. The whole very commonplace, vulgar and uninteresting.' (That Sullivan, of all composers, should have complained of the plundering!)

A short trip to the Paris Exhibition with Grove, and Sullivan returned to London. There he met Tennyson, and Sullivan decided to set a song-cycle with poems by the Poet Laureate, to be illustrated by Millais, whom he had met recently at the Garrick Club.

Sullivan wrote from Tennyson's house: 'When I got here I had a cup of tea, and then went and smoked with Tennyson until dinner time. He read me all the songs (twelve in number) which are absolutely lovely, but I fear there will be a great difficulty in getting them from him. He thinks they are too light, and will damage his reputation. ...'

'Great difficulty' there was!

Sullivan did finally coax the poems from the Laureate's reluctant grasp. And the old gentleman took the young gentleman into his somewhat crusty friendship. Tennyson, kitted out like a *vie-de-bohème* poet, in a black trilby hat, a guise in which he loved to strut about, called constantly at the house in Claverton Terrace, Pimlico, where Sullivan was still living with his mother, to discuss the songs with his young composer.

Sullivan warned the maid, before one of the poet's visits, that he might seem to be a little eccentric, in which case she was to appear to notice nothing. After the distinguished guest had gone she remarked: 'Well, Mr Sullivan, he *do* wear clothes!'

But no sooner was Sullivan well advanced with the music than the Poet Laureate turned coy again. The scheme would harm his reputation. The time was not propitious. A dozen excuses for backing out were produced. Finally Tennyson offered Sullivan £500 to let him out of their bargain. Sullivan refused. Millais drew one picture, a delicate pencil sketch of a girl at a window. But the Poet Laureate's shilly-shallying exhausted the painter's patience – almost he might have been Gilbert.

'I am very sorry,' Millais wrote to Sullivan, 'as of course I should have liked to have carried out the original idea. You must remember that I did keep the drawings for *months* before they were parted with. One line from him [Tennyson] at the time would have saved the trouble.'

For three years or so the Poet Laureate argued with all-comers that the publication should be dropped. When at last he agreed to publication he wrote an introduction which angered Sullivan.

Four years ago Mr Sullivan requested me to write a little *Leiderkreis*, German fashion, for him to exercise his art upon. He had been very successful in setting such old songs as 'Orpheus with his lute made Trees', and I drest up for him a puppet in the old style, a mere motif for an air, indeed the veriest nothing unless Mr Sullivan can make it dance to his instruments.

I am sorry that my four-year-old puppet should have to dance at all in the dark shadow of these days [the Franco-German war] but the music is now completed and I am bound by my promise.
A. Tennyson

Sullivan tried to reason with Tennyson, and explained that readers would feel he,

49

Sullivan, had taken advantage of him. Tennyson scuttled away like a hermit crab. For a long time he refused to answer letters. Then at last he replied, insisting that the introduction was only 'an expression of my own regret at the unappropriateness of the time of publication, and even that my words were not worthy of your music ...'. This had to serve as the answer that turneth away wrath. Sullivan, if he did not forget, at least forgave. A friendship fated to be life-long was salvaged. But the book of songs with its single illustration by Millais did not appear until 1871.

Meanwhile both Gilbert and Sullivan, though separately, went to work in a spurt which lasted three years, at the end of which they were to meet. Work flowed from them both as one would wish ink to flow from a fountain pen. It was as though both men knew that these were the last years when each would be the sole captain of his ship and were making the most of their independence.

Puns leaped from Gilbert's pen, lively as the little sketches he was wont to scribble in the margins of his notebooks. Journalism showered its squibs. Burlesques found their way to the stage, culminating some years later in *Pygmalion and Galatea*, which had many a revival and in the end netted £40,000 for Gilbert – a sum more substantial than the famous £30 his first play brought him in. Sullivan, too, worked at a fierce pace through 1867 and 1868. He set eleven songs of which 'O fair Dove, O fond Dove' came to roost in drawing-rooms throughout the land. Then there were the thirteen Anthems and Part Songs he composed. These included one, 'O hush thee my babie', which he dedicated to his nephew Herbert Sullivan – that same Herbert Sullivan who grew up to be first his close companion and, later, with Newman Flower, his biographer. In this three-year-long spurt he wrote, too, 'The Long Day Closes', seven hymns and an overture, *Marmion*. Then off he went on an Oratorio (how pleased Rachel would have been), *The Prodigal Son*. He founded the Civil Service Orchestral Society and was appointed its conductor (he was presented with the first keyless watch on his retirement from it). Mr Gladstone sang bass at several performances. Sullivan also composed two comic operettas, *The Contrabandista* and *Cox and Box*.

The Prodigal Son was composed at 'amazing speed'. It took just a little more than three weeks. He sped over to Paris to arrange for Pasdeloup to include his *In Memoriam* at the Cirque Napoléon:

The concert at the Cirque Napoléon startled me. It takes place in a great circus capable of holding 4,000 people, and yesterday, as at all his [Pasdeloup's] concerts, it was crowded. I never saw such a sight. The people sit in tiers rising from the floor half way up to the roof, and everyone can see everyone else. If the people like the things, they applaud vociferously; if they don't, they hiss with equal energy.

Sullivan spent the rest of his Parisian night copying out *In Memoriam* until dawn, because Pasdeloup's string section was very large and he could not find a copyist.

The same frenzy of nervous energy seized him when working on his Oratorio: 'I seemed to work without fatigue, through the day, through the night again, and then well into the next day, till my hand grew shaky with fatigue which I did not otherwise feel.'

Jenny Lind wrote: 'I have just received your note, and hasten to say how *very* sorry I am not to be able to come to your 'Prodigal Son' tomorrow. Saturdays are my Reception days, and I cannot possibly be absent. ...' (O tempora, O mores!)

Perhaps it was as well that Jenny Lind fulfilled her responsibilities to her guests. It was an unsatisfactory performance of *The Prodigal Son* at the Worcester Festival – unsatisfactory because the singers, Tietjens and Sims Reeve, made a nonsense of it with a double booking – almost it might have been the twentieth century with its unrehearsed substitutes. Sir John Goss sent Sullivan a few critical words of wisdom: 'All you have done is most masterly. ... Some day you will, I hope, try at another Oratorio, putting out all your strength – not the strength of a few weeks or months. Show yourself *the best man in Europe*! ... Handel's two or three weeks for the *Messiah* may be a fact, but *he* was not always successful and was not so young a chap as you.'

The theatre in the sixties and seventies was just as trend-ridden as in the 1960s and seventies. Burlesque, which had been drawing all Paris, crossed the Channel on one of the Messrs Offenbach, Meilhac and Halévy's paddle-steamers, as it were, and took possession of the London playhouses in a somewhat raggle-taggle gipsy sort of way. Plays were exiled and burlesques brought in. The music of these shows was, in the main, blatant and dull. Even the comic songs, coarse and raucous, which for a time had been banished from the better theatres, now returned to public favour more coarse, more raucous, more leering than ever.

It was against this background of Continental and indigent burlesque that Sullivan's creative imagination turned to comic operas, in spite of the, by now, lapsed influence of Rachel and the more pompously expressed opinions of Sir John Goss – jolted that way by a bumped-into F.C.Burnand of *Punch*, whom he chanced upon in the street, and who had some friends in an amateur theatrical company. It seemed that they were looking for a musical piece.

Sullivan thought little of the piece at its inception. None the less he hastily reversed the name of Morton's *Box and Cox* to *Cox and Box* (why bother?), dashed off a setting and was pleasantly surprised when after a private performance it was put on for a charity benefit at the Adelphi.

Sullivan himself presided at the pianoforte. *Cox and Box* has a pretty, prattling charm. A pleasantly Rossini-like overture, musicianly and neatly achieved, presages a high-spirited work with Handelian lapses on long vowels, but on the whole, the little opera ripples along pleasantly enough. The score gives Sullivan a chance of a salute to Kneller Hall in the form of a quick-step Military March. The work contains pleasant glimpses of what later was to become his lyrical style. The opera mocks gently at the operatic idiom which, even thus early, Sullivan controlled admirably, and which later he was to make his own. *Cox and Box* bears the same resemblance to a full-throated operetta as a bagatelle to a sonata.

Following the modest success of *Cox and Box*, Sullivan and Burnand pressed on to a second burlesque, *The Contrabandista*, for which the natural shop-window seemed to be the St George's Hall, where Mr and Mrs German Reed had already presented an operetta, by Balfe, whose 'Last Rose of Summer' blossomed in every drawing-room conservatory in the land.

The Contrabandista was ill-starred from the outset. Before the last rehearsals could begin, the *basso* withdrew his deep notes. There was, too, a frantic hunt for a new soprano: 'A Miss H sung to me the other day,' Reed wrote to Sullivan. 'She has a fine voice with rather a coarse Italian style of singing. Short and fat. Not pretty, but with paint and bismuth might be made to look decent.' ('Paint and Bismuth', what a title for a biography.)

But apparently paint and bismuth must have lost its magic, for *The Contrabandista* was withdrawn hard on.

Sullivan, smarting from the unaccustomed blow, turned to his admired Jenny Lind-Goldschmidt for consolation but alas! the socially-conscious Swedish Nightingale was from home, possibly attending someone else's At Home Day.

Sullivan, crestfallen, returned to serious music, to songs and cantatas and church music, and to conducting his work with orchestras up and down the country.

One of his greatest friends at this time – 1870 – was Madame Conneau, lady-in-waiting to the Empress Eugénie, who was taking refuge at Chislehurst from the Tuileries in the 1870 war.

'She was', he wrote of the Empress, 'one of the most brilliant women I ever knew. Her conversation was amazing. Whatever the subject, she knew all about it. I could see this personality swaying an Empire.' Of the Emperor Napoleon he wrote with deep pity: 'In his eyes is a distant stare, as though he saw things that might have been.'

To his mother, who was trying to keep house for a son who disappeared and re-appeared like a Will-o'-the-wisp – even more, one feels, considering his conducting, like a jack-in-the-box – he was a conundrum. Sullivan went swanning, at the drop of a title, in 'the best houses in the land' and wrote her ecstatic letters about them before she had realised where he might be. 'I shall arrive at Paddington at 5.30. Please have a sole and a steak and a half bottle of claret and a good fire.' Or: 'We went shooting yesterday – I am sending you six brace of pheasants.' What was the devoted but puzzled mother to do with six brace? Not until a scribble reached her next morning did her metaphorical brow clear. 'A brace for you *of course*. A brace for the Blanks,' and so on, until the only pucker on the motherly brow was a matter of transport.

He did not give his health a second thought in these days, working through day after day, night after night, without any visible sign of exhaustion. When he was alone, however, he lived very simply and sparely: 'It's time you came home if you are living on fifteen shillings a week,' but he saw no reason to spend more – particularly with sole and steak and claret and a good fire and 'the best mother in the world' waiting for him at the drop of a baton.

And now at last we can set the scene and call the cast on stage for – and at last – the meeting of Gilbert and Sullivan.

'Let battle commence.'

RIGHT Four Edwardian postcards illustrating the popularity of Sullivan's song 'The Lost Chord' written in memory of his brother Frederic.

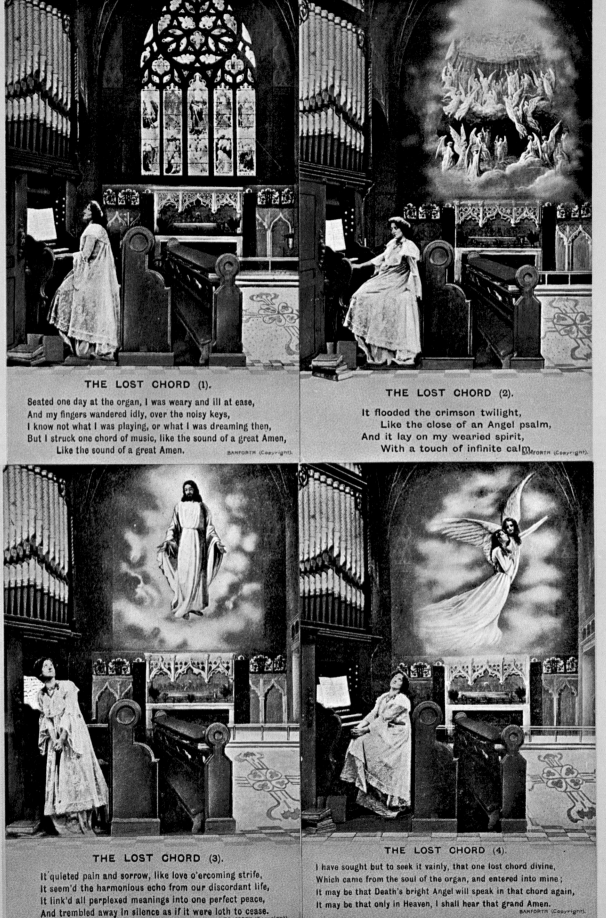

THE LOST CHORD (1).

Seated one day at the organ, I was weary and ill at ease,
And my fingers wandered idly, over the noisy keys,
I know not what I was playing, or what I was dreaming then,
But I struck one chord of music, like the sound of a great Amen,
    Like the sound of a great Amen.

BAMFORTH (Copyright).

THE LOST CHORD (2).

It flooded the crimson twilight,
    Like the close of an Angel psalm,
And it lay on my wearied spirit,
    With a touch of infinite calm

BAMFORTH (Copyright).

THE LOST CHORD (3).

It quieted pain and sorrow, like love o'ercoming strife,
It seem'd the harmonious echo from our discordant life,
It link'd all perplexed meanings into one perfect peace,
And trembled away in silence as if it were loth to cease.

BAMFORTH (Copyright).

THE LOST CHORD (4).

I have sought but to seek it vainly, that one lost chord divine,
Which came from the soul of the organ, and entered into mine;
It may be that Death's bright Angel will speak in that chord again,
It may be that only in Heaven, I shall hear that grand Amen.

BAMFORTH (Copyright).

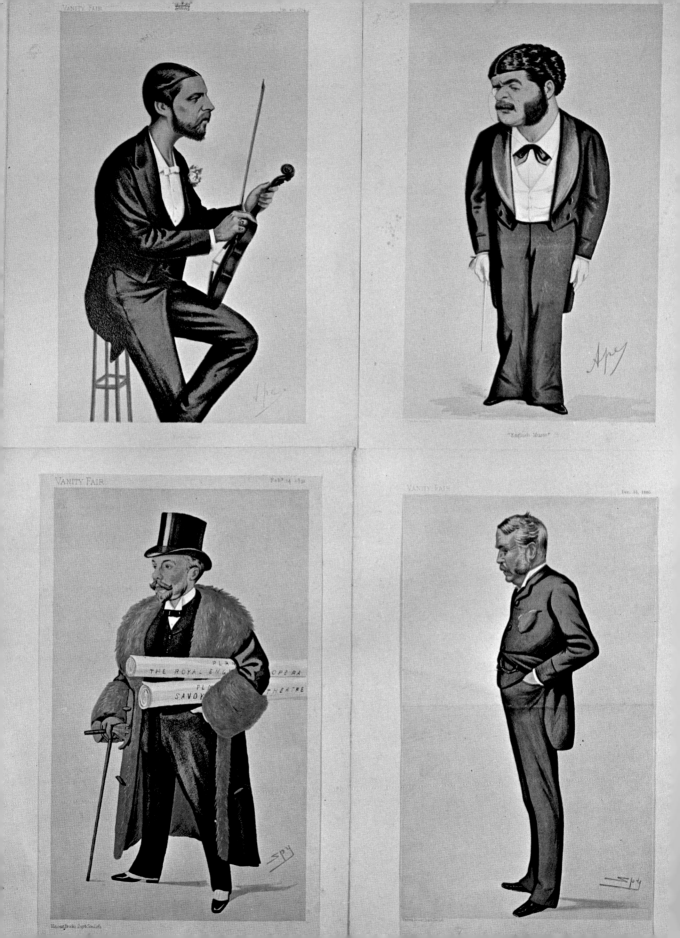

"English Music"

PLAY
THE ROYAL ENG   OPERA
PLA
SAVOY   THEATRE

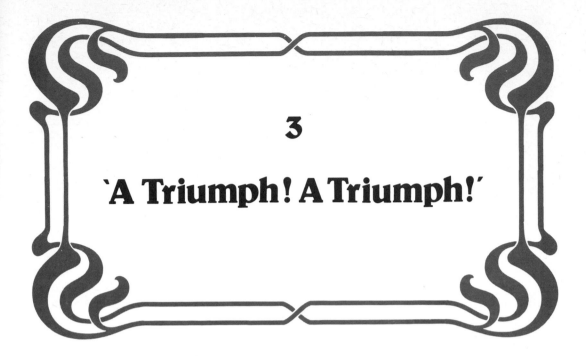

3

`A Triumph! A Triumph!´

Fred Clay, who had invited Sullivan round to watch a rehearsal at the Gallery of Illustration, introduced Gilbert to Sullivan under the tasteful aegis of the impresario German Reed, and Hesketh Pearson tells a characteristic story of Gilbert on that occasion. For his purposes in writing 'a fairy comedy in blank verse', *The Palace of Truth*, founded on a French story, it was essential that one of the characters should display a technical knowledge of music that its author did not actually possess. Gilbert, therefore, read the article on harmony in the *Encyclopaedia Britannica* and then converted a long sentence from it into blank verse:

> Believe me, the result would be the same
> Whether your Lordship chose to play upon
> The simple tetrachord of Mercury
> That knew no diatonic intervals
> Or the elaborate dis-diapason
> (Four tetrachords and one redundant note)
> Embracing in its perfect consonance
> All simple, double and inverted chords!

Gilbert, who could make no sense of it, wanted to find out if it were as impenetrable as it sounded and, at the same time, not unwilling to impress Sullivan with his knowledge of the rules of music, and perhaps subconsciously determined to establish the superiority with which he intended to proceed, put the question to him in prose:

'I maintain,' he said, 'that if a composer has a musical theme to express, he can express it as perfectly upon the simple tetrachord of Mercury, in which (as I need not tell you) there are no diatonic intervals at all, as upon the more complicated dis-diapason (with the four tetrachords and the redundant note) which embraces in its perfect consonance all the simple, double and inverted chords.'

Gilbert paused for breath and a reply.

Sullivan looked at him. 'Say that again,' he suggested.

'The repetition failed to enlighten the composer who,' says Pearson, 'said that he would have to think it over.'

'Gilbert is doing a comic one-act entertainment for me,' German Reed wrote later to Sullivan: 'Soprano – contralto – tenor – baritone and bass. Would you like to compose the music? If so, on what terms? Reply at once as I want to get the piece going without loss of time.'

But German Reed failed to 'get the piece going'. He was not prepared, following the failure of *The Contrabandista*, to risk real money for 'the glory of bringing the Gilbert and Sullivan partnership into being'. Librettist and composer 'never even met to discuss it', writes a disappointed Hesketh Pearson.

John Hollingsworth, who boasted that he kept alight the sacred lamp of burlesque at The Gaiety, was shown Gilbert's libretto of *Thespis* or *The Gods Grown Old*, and

A scene from *Thespis*, the first Gilbert and Sullivan opera, which had a short run at the Gaiety and was never revived.

56

courageously he commissioned Sullivan to write the score. It ran for one month and then vanished from our scene. What the music was like I do not know. Sullivan conducted on the first night. 'The carriage call was for 11 pm, but the yawning truth was that Act II was still playing at midnight.'

The Times came out with a very fair notice: 'The story written by Mr W.S. Gilbert in his liveliest manner, is so original, and the music contributed by Mr Arthur Sullivan so pretty and fascinating, that we are inclined to be rather disappointed when we find the applause but fitful, the laughter scarcely spontaneous and the curtain falling not without sounds of disapprobation.'

No vocal score of *Thespis* was ever published. But one song, at least, 'lived on' in the form of a transference from *Thespis* to *The Pirates of Penzance*: 'Climbing over rocky mountains'.

After *Thespis* had died the death, Gilbert and Sullivan 'shook hands and parted'. Gilbert went on to *Pygmalion and Galatea* via a parody on Tennyson's *Princess*. Sullivan re-embarked on his career as a 'serious' musician. Neither expected to work with either again. But the two men continued to meet socially and, for the time being, happily.

For Sullivan it was a time for unremitting effort. Music societies all over the country were sueing for new works.

Less than a year after the failure of *Thespis*, Sullivan composed one of those Victorian religiosities, *The Light of the World*, scored it 'hastily' – the entire work took less than a month – but Gounod, who came to London later to hear it, declared it to be a 'masterpiece' and Queen Victoria wrote that it was destined to uplift British music.

The first performance took place in Birmingham. The Duke of Edinburgh, himself an amateur violinist and by now a close friend and, if we are to believe the cartoonists, something even closer, travelled to the Midlands for the concert. When Sullivan sank into an armchair in the artist's room, exhausted, HRH was the first to clasp his hand. 'A triumph,' he pronounced. He stood there repeating himself. 'A triumph. A triumph.'

They went from the hall together to a cab, the Duke still murmuring 'a triumph, a triumph'.

Sullivan was never short of music to write or concerts to conduct. Liverpool offered him a directorship of its music, but he could not leave London to live there. And then there was his swanning to fit in. Musical Society showered him with invitations and asked a host of musicians, writers and painters to meet him as an equal:

Dearest Mum

I want quiet – and you. I want to work. The *Overture* last night was a great success; I was recalled, flowers, etc. But I am coming home to work. Better still, I am coming home for your birthday.

By now 'home' was in Albert Mansions, Victoria Street – with 'dearest Mum'.

Between 1871 and 1874, in addition to major works such as the music to *The Merry Wives of Windsor*, the Festival *Te Deum* (first performed at the Crystal Palace) and *The Light of the World*, he composed no fewer than forty-seven additions to the Hymnal (of which he had been appointed editor), including 'the world's greatest marching hymn',

'Onward Christian Soldiers', twenty songs, four choruses and a new scoring of Handel's *Jephtha*.

Meanwhile Gilbert, having launched *Pygmalion and Galatea*, sped the boat with a profusion of delicious squabbles.

Mrs Kendal had a way of her own of playing Galatea, and it was not the way of Gilbert,

Alfred, Duke of Edinburgh with his wife, Marie of Russia. The Duke's love of music brought him into contact with Sullivan and they became bosom friends.

both her author and her director. As a result there were times when they were not on speaking terms except when she was on stage and he was audibly criticising her performance from a box.

At a revival of the piece the actress Janette Steer received a letter from Gilbert: 'If you do not comply with my wishes I give you notice that on Monday I shall apply for an injunction to prevent your playing the piece, or otherwise as I may be advised.'

Janette Steer did as she was bid in the face of Gilbert's threat. But before long she contrived to infuriate him over a further matter.

I understand that you interpolated several exclamations last night while Miss Repton was delivering her important speech at the end of the second act, thereby greatly impairing the effect of the speech, causing it to be indistinct and confused. I have instructed Miss Repton how to deal with the difficulty should it arise again. My instructions to her are to stop short at the first interruption, and to remain silent until that interruption has ceased – then to begin again, and should the interruption be repeated again to stop until the annoyance ceases altogether.

If Miss Steer persisted in her tactics after that, the audience must have had their money's worth.

Looking ahead to the eighties and one of the many revivals of *Pygmalion and Galatea*, we find trouble, not brewing but on the boil, when Mary Anderson, the idol of the many, played Galatea. Miss Anderson, a lady of strong determination as well as talent of a very high order, wished to give her Galatea 'in the classic style', but Gilbert demanded 'modernity', complaining that 'she looked like a Saint in a stained glass window' in the costume designed to her explicit requirements by the painter Alma-Tadema, instead of 'a lively up-to-date girl'. The fact that the audience liked the Saint did not placate his vexation, nor, one fancies, did the increase in his royalties attendant on Miss Anderson's characterisation. With his highly developed sense of situation, he sought for and found a new attacking position. Back in 1872 Gilbert was already asking for larger royalties and a guarantee of a hundred performances from Buckstone, the manager of the Haymarket. Further, he insisted that the piece should not be seen by the public 'until three days after a rehearsal in which all the cast are word perfect'. Before Gilbert's day the text was at risk until a week or so after the opening night; liable to variation owing to fallible memories and insobriety.

The manager replied at once agreeing to the terms but hoping that in the event of further successful productions, Gilbert would not increase his demands and that, if the next piece proved to be a failure, the guarantee of one hundred nights might lapse.

I'm afraid I must stick to the guarantee of 100 nights [replied Gilbert]. If the piece does not succeed it will not be for want of hard and honest work on my part, and all I want is a certainty that my time and thought will not be wasted. At the same time, if the piece is a *dead* failure, you may be morally certain that I shall not have the face to hold you to your bargain. I think you may safely make the arrangement leaving it to my sense of fairness.

Gilbert's 'sense of fairness'?

A success was scored by *The Wicked World* in 1873.

During the run Gilbert brought an action against the drama critic of *The Pall Mall Gazette*, Enoch, who had called it 'vulgar, coarse, offensive and indecent'.

Defending counsel quoted two passages, the second of which suggested 'an immoral exercise of love on the part of the Fairy Queen':

> For six long hours has she retained the Knight
> Within the dark recesses of her bower. ...

Buckstone, well-known as a comedian, gave evidence which reduced the Court of Justice to laughter. Even the Judge was silently convulsed.

The jury found for the defendant and Gilbert was left to pay £60 in costs.

Gilbert was in fine fighting trim and during a performance of this play he came to blows with an actor who was about to appear on-stage through a trapdoor, knocked him down and played his part.

In November 1873 Gilbert set to work on another piece for the Haymarket, when he heard that Buckstone had made arrangements to put on a different piece by a different author, for a limited run over Christmas to give Gilbert time to finish writing his play. There was an explosion: '... I hereby warn you that if my piece is not put into rehearsal forthwith and produced as soon as it is ready I shall place the matter at once in the hands of my solicitor.'

This time Buckstone replied the same day. Gilbert's new comedy, he said, was to have been in his hands on his return to London. He had been back a fortnight and had received no play. 'Since you informed me you had not quite completed it, I presumed I was suiting your convenience by giving you more time.'

Finally Buckstone said that he would present the play on the date agreed, arrange a reading of it in the current week and start rehearsals at once.

Charity was duly mounted, at the Haymarket, in the first week of January 1874. Mrs Kendal played the part of a woman who had 'sinned'. That is, says Hesketh Pearson, a woman who had once enjoyed sexual relations with a man without the consummation of a wedding-ring, and spends the rest of her life atoning for the deed by charitable actions involving self-sacrifice. 'Her "sin" is discussed in language which would be excessive if it had brought about the decimation of the world's population by the wrath of God.'

Gilbert's sentimental two-act piece *Sweethearts* was mounted at the Prince of Wales' Theatre in November 1874 with the distinguished actress Marie Wilton (later Lady Bancroft) playing the leading part.

In December 1875 Gilbert lapsed, once again, into blank verse at the Court Theatre. 'There is more of the *real me* in *Broken Hearts* than in anything I have written.' At the end of the Acting Version these words are printed: 'Finished Monday, 15th November THANK GOD!'

He wrote to John Hare, who was casting the piece: 'I think my opinion as author of the part should go [no doubt Hare thought it "should go", too, but in another sense] not only for *something*, but for a *very great deal*.'

The play gave Gilbert an opening to upbraid the drama critic Clement Scott for his notice: 'I am not by any means a thin-skinned man, but in this case I feel bound to take exception to your treatment of me and my serious work.'

Twenty-six years later, Clement Scott endeavoured to bury the hatchet only to find that his criticism had not been forgotten: 'Your ideas as to the duties and privileges of a dramatic critic are so diametrically opposed to mine that I think we had better let matters rest as they are. Nor do I think that the fact that you will have achieved 60 years on the 6th of October is a reason for a general jubilation. . . .' Yet, when Clement Scott was dying, Gilbert was most solicitous. At the funeral he wept continuously; and, we are told, helped the critic's widow in 'all sorts of ways'.

By the mid-seventies the Crystal Palace concerts, once so popular, were beginning to fail. Even the metropolitan music-lovers were finding Sydenham too far from the centre of London for a concert. In a speech 'filled with ardour and spleen', Sullivan delivered a broadside at the fickle and apathetic public: '. . . You will soon have to pay people to go to a concert, or give them some extraneous attraction – a stall and a packet of White's bubbling soap, for five shillings.'

But while the public were hanging back from Sydenham, the Manager of the Royalty Theatre, Soho, suggested a second work by Gilbert and Sullivan, which, in the event, took the stage. It was the one-act comic opera *Trial by Jury*, which opened in March 1875, and recognisably established the pattern of all the Gilbert and Sullivan works within the canon.

Let us stand back, at this important juncture, from the heat of battle in which creative artists work and squabble and exhaust their nerves to take a look at these two Victorian giants.

Trial by cartoon (Gilbert and Sullivan by Alfred Bryan, 1878).

Gilbert, a broad-framed, bushy-eyebrowed giant, with a down-curved mouth seeking to hide the inner insecurities left in the son by the forever quarrelling parents, with quarrels of his own making. 'I have had many dealings with May [the head of a firm of dressmakers], and on the last occasion of his dressing a piece of mine I told him distinctly that he should never dress another – and with my consent he never shall.'

Gilbert, again the tousled giant, writing to a portrait painter, explained: 'My usual writing dress would hardly do for exhibition, consisting as it does of a night-shirt and dressing-gown, for I only write after 11 pm when everyone has gone to bed. ...' Between 11 pm and three in the morning were Gilbert's regular working hours. 'Then you have absolute peace. The postman has done his worst and no one can interrupt you unless it be a burglar.'

And now, Sullivan, physically a somewhat undersized giant – short, indeed, for a mortal man, but precise in his clothes, with a burnished appearance and never a wavy hair out of place – almost he might have been varnished all over or smoothly painted, like a toy wooden soldier. He had, at this time, an insatiable appetite for making music while keeping his beady eye open for suitable occasions to swan through society, particularly in the upper reaches, urbane, witty, well-liked but, say his biographers, before the morrow's sun broke over the chimneypots of Mayfair, off he had rushed in the earliest possible train to the North to conduct a concert.

He composed in the train in little note-books. What seems less likely is their statement that he 'tramped through the wet streets with the melodies of the future singing in his brain'. Surely, say I, someone would have called a cab to clipper-clopper him to hotel or home.

And the impresario who brought these disparate men with their neat talents together

LEFT Richard D'Oyly Carte, the long-suffering impresario whose business acumen played a large part in the success of the Gilbert and Sullivan operas.

RIGHT A programme from the original run of *Trial by Jury* at the Royalty Theatre in 1875.

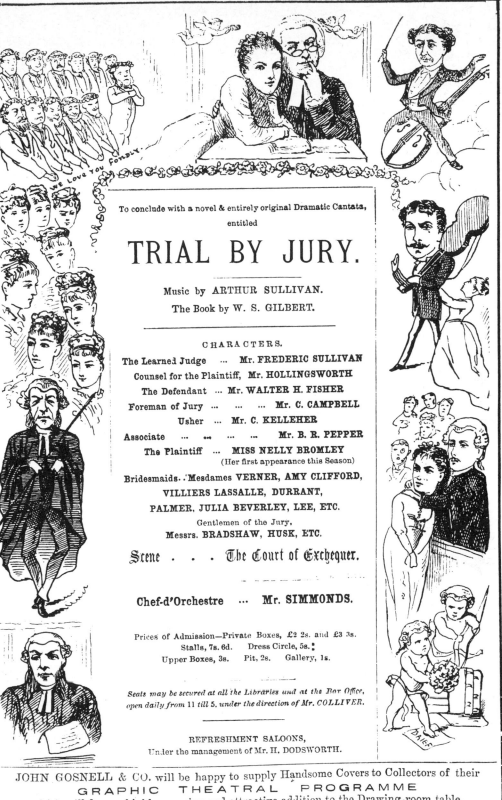

To conclude with a novel & entirely original Dramatic Cantata,

entitled

TRIAL BY JURY.

Music by ARTHUR SULLIVAN.
The Book by W. S. GILBERT.

CHARACTERS.

The Learned Judge ... Mr. FREDERIC SULLIVAN
Counsel for the Plaintiff, Mr. HOLLINGSWORTH
The Defendant ... Mr. WALTER H. FISHER
Foreman of Jury ... ... Mr. C. CAMPBELL
Usher ... Mr. C. KELLEHER
Associate ... ... Mr. B. R. PEPPER
The Plaintiff ... MISS NELLY BROMLEY
(Her first appearance this Season)

Bridesmaids ... Mesdames VERNER, AMY CLIFFORD,
VILLIERS LASSALLE, DURRANT,
PALMER, JULIA BEVERLEY, LEE, ETC.
Gentlemen of the Jury,
Messrs. BRADSHAW, HUSK, ETC.

Scene . . . The Court of Exchequer.

Chef-d'Orchestre ... Mr. SIMMONDS.

Prices of Admission—Private Boxes, £2 2s. and £3 3s.
Stalls, 7s. 6d.   Dress Circle, 5s.
Upper Boxes, 3s.   Pit, 2s.   Gallery, 1s.

*Seats may be secured at all the Libraries and at the Box Office,
open daily from 11 till 5, under the direction of Mr. COLLIVER.*

REFRESHMENT SALOONS,
Under the management of Mr. H. DODSWORTH.

like a dab hand putting together the perfectly fitted pieces of a jig-saw puzzle? By all accounts D'Oyly Carte was – must have been – a man of great courage. Did he not bring the crusty, querulous Gilbert and the sunny, swanning, serious musician Sullivan together after the failure of *Thespis* – an intrepid act in itself. Did he not build the luxurious Savoy Theatre and, later, the Savoy Hotel, and later still the Royal English Opera House, now the Palace Theatre? A man, then, with an eye to the future and the courage to invest in it. He was also the first theatrical manager to light his theatre with electric light.

The son of a flautist, a partner in a firm of musical instruments, he first entered his father's firm, then started a lecture and concert agency of his own, writes Reginald Allen in *The First Night Gilbert and Sullivan*. At thirty-one he was serving as manager of the Royalty Theatre for the divinely named singer Selina Doloro.

The two collaborators had not worked together since *Thespis*. Both had been revolving industriously but in two different worlds. Once, in 1874, their worlds came together for a space long enough to produce the song 'The Distant Shore' with words by Gilbert and music by Sullivan but a permanent collaboration was far from their minds and still on a distant shore.

In 1868 during his days on *Fun*, ex-barrister Gilbert, of whom it was to be said that he could only write about himself – so different from Sullivan who so often wrote like other people – wrote and illustrated a one-page skit of a legal operetta which he called *Trial by Jury*. For his pains he was paid £1.5.6 for the text and £1.5 for the illustrations, 'assuredly a bargain in immortality' observes Reginald Allen.

From this he had prepared a treatment for a one-act Cantata for Madame Parepa-Rosa. She died and the work lapsed for some years. One day he took it along to D'Oyly Carte, still with no thought of reviving the partnership with Sullivan. Carte was himself a desultory composer and probably Gilbert thought that he might set it and find for it some sort of stage. D'Oyly Carte proved himself a true impresario and, conquering the temptation of composing it himself, indicated Sullivan.

A few days later Gilbert went down to Sullivan's flat and read it to him:

He read it through, as it seemed to me [noted Sullivan], in a perturbed sort of way, with a gradual crescendo of indignation, in the manner of a man considerably disappointed with what he had written. As soon as he had come to the last word, he closed up the manuscript violently, apparently unconscious of the fact that he had achieved his purpose so far as I was concerned – I was screaming with laughter the whole time. . . .

The operetta was completed in three weeks. Brother Fred appeared as the Lord Chief Justice, and won golden opinions from Brother Arthur and in the Press, and *Fun* found *Trial by Jury* 'extremely funny and admirably composed'.

Mr Punch's fair-minded Representative Man gave Gilbert a good notice: 'In *Trial by Jury* both Mr Words and Mr Music have worked together and for the first quarter of an hour the Cantata (as they have called it) is the funniest bit of nonsense your representative has seen for a considerable time.'

To the present writer the little dialogueless operetta, while it sets out the pattern of future works very firmly, and since the learned Judge decides, there and then, to marry

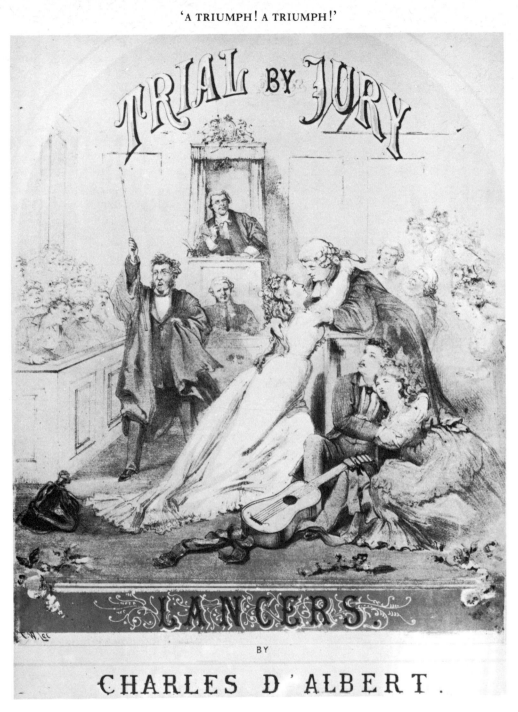

A scene from *Trial by Jury* on a music cover. No set of 'Lancers' was complete without it.

the defendant in a breach of promise case, so paving the way for the description 'Gilbertian', seems to lack the personality that was to come with succeeding pieces. History however relates that the piece ran for a year.

Secure in the box-office receipts for *Trial by Jury*, Sullivan swanned off to Lake Como, that long, hot summer, with Sir Coutts and Lady Lindsay.

'The air is so soft and beautiful,' he wrote to Mamma, 'We are thinly clad, too, with things we bought in Paris, suits of batiste, very light and cool. This morning I got up and bathed in the Lake at 6 o'clock. Then we returned to bed for two or three hours and dozed. Breakfast at 9.30. ... It is all very beautiful and sweetly lazy.'

But energy came back to our 'sweetly lazy' Arthur, and with it work. He wrote five songs in as many weeks. Two of them, we are told, 'Let me Dream Again' and 'Thou Art Passing Hence', sold many thousands in their first three months. He continued to be hag-ridden by work and a conscience that (oh, well-known state) would not let him rest.

Here is my engagement book for this week [he wrote Mama]: Monday, rehearsal. Tuesday, rehearsal and Concert, Glasgow. Wednesday, rehearsal and concert, Greenock. Thursday, rehearsal and concert, Perth. Friday, rehearsal and concert, Dundee (and sleep there). Saturday, return to Glasgow. Rehearsal at 2, concert at 7.

That's pretty well, with travelling. I am dead tired today. Next week I shall be knocked up I fear.

There's a wretched creature on the floor above me who plays a piano a little. He or she has been playing *my* hymn tunes all this afternoon. I hope they don't do it out of compliment to me, for they put their own harmony which, to say the least of it, isn't as good as mine.

A fresh demand on his time came from his friend the Duke of Edinburgh ('a triumph! a triumph!') who, with his elder brother, the Prince of Wales, persuaded Sullivan to accept the Principalship of the National Training School of Music – subsequently the Royal College of Music.

Meanwhile Gilbert has picked a quarrel with, of all people, his postman:

I have to complain of the systematic negligence of the postman who has charge of the early delivery in this district. [Wouldn't we all?] It frequently happens that, through imperfect sorting, or some other cause, he has to return once, and sometimes twice, with letters that *should* have been delivered at eight o'clock. Today, he delivered three letters at eight o'clock [oh lucky William Schwenk!], a small book parcel at 8.45 and two more letters at 10.15. As today's experience is in no way exceptional, I think it is my duty to lay the matter before you.

But although one cannot but shrink at that hypocritical 'I think it is my duty', one sees, over and over again, that Gilbert was a charitable man, although in the following instance he wrecked the good intention with his holier-than-thou ending: 'I am glad the money is likely to prove useful to you, but I am bound to tell you that if I had known as much about you, and your habits, as I have since learned from several excellent authorities, I certainly should not have sent you one penny.'

A desire to be generous while being just, notes Hesketh Pearson, stands comically revealed when someone applied for a testimonial for the character of James Saunders, a man-servant. Gilbert stated that the man's character was admirable but 'a strict sense of justice compelled him to add that Saunders had probably stolen his cigars, worn his linen and attempted to remove his livery'. However, 'I shall be glad to learn that you do not consider my charges against Saunders to be so grave as to render your employing him out of the question'.

He quarrelled over his mess bill (The Royal Aberdeen Militia). He threatened his yacht-builder with his usual swiftness to point out that he would take legal action if his wishes were not carried out. The furnishing and decorations came under the same Damocletian threat. Best and worst of things – best if one takes into account his insatiable appetite for a good quarrel, but worst if one pauses to reflect the subject of his ire – he quarrelled with his father-in-law, General Turner:

Mrs Gilbert has handed me your letters in which you insist on seeing my marriage settlement before paying over the legacy of £150 left to her by the late Lucrezia Turner.

Without stopping to discuss the motive that prompted this demand I will content myself with stating that I have consulted my solicitors [of course] on the subject who inform me that you have no claim whatever to examine the marriage settlements of legatees named in the will of which you are executor.

Acting upon their advice I altogether decline to comply with your request.

By now Sullivan was the most significant figure in music in the country. He would compose up to the last conceivable moment, take a train to the North to conduct a concert and race to the train back while the audience were still filing out of the concert-hall. The strain told on him. Since 1872 he had suffered from stone in the kidney, which afflicted him at intervals with relentless agony. In the train, even while he was conducting his concerts, the long-standing foe would strike: 'I did not hear the applause. I did not see the audience, for the tears rushing out of my eyes in agony.'

In April 1876 he had received a letter from Sir George Macfarren offering him the honorary degree of Doctor in Music at Cambridge. 'The deed is done, and I am Mus. Doc.' Arthur wrote to Mamma after the ceremony.

The winter of 1876–7 found him going zestfully from city to city, travelling in un-heated, bone-shaking trains, snowed-up in the Highlands. Almost he might have been Mrs Siddons, driving in 'wretched horse-cabs' through weather that forced the cold into his bones.

But towards the middle of January his dearly loved brother Frederic was taken ill. Arthur cancelled everything to hasten to his sick-bed. He could not believe that Frederic would indeed die at thirty-nine. Frederic who stood for the fun of life; who 'adorned his letters with sketches of Arthur marching into Paris, monocle, side-whiskers and all, and Arthur marching out. Arthur conducting concerts. ... Letters conceived in a splendid spirit of fraternity,' say Sullivan's biographers.

Frederic, unlike Arthur, had married young and a family of little Sullivans grew up around their youthful father. He had an endearing habit of giving each child a penny to spend, and this done, returning to the child with the best bargain the spent penny.

All through the days and nights Arthur kept watch at the bedside of his brother. In one long night-watch he recalled some lines he had read, some years before, in *Household Words*, a periodical edited by his old friend Charles Dickens. Frederic seemed to have drifted off to sleep, so Arthur drew out some odd sheets of paper he always kept about him, and sketched in the whole of 'The Lost Chord' (the first few bars of which march in perfect counterpoint with the first few bars of 'Onward Christian Soldiers'). It was the last composition he had the heart to write for some months for Frederic died on 18 January, 1878.

Sullivan's brother Fred in the role of the Judge in *Trial by Jury*.

'The Lost Chord' was his *In Memoriam* to his brother. The song, say Sullivan and Flower, swept through England. It exceeded in a few months the sales of any song for over forty years. Inevitably it was parodied.

Sullivan wrote to Soloman, its parodist: 'I wrote "The Lost Chord" in sorrow at my brother Fred's death. Don't burlesque it.'

Almost he might have been Gilbert.

When the shock and sorrow of Frederic's death became manageable, Sullivan turned, not to work, as do most creators finding it the best, the only, way to help them to bear to go on living, but to some fairly high-flight swanning. His mother had departed to live in Fulham by then, with Frederic's widow, when Sullivan wrote:

Dearest Mum

In for a penny, in for a pound. My Princess Louise is coming tomorrow, so I had better do all I can to make her happy! Bring a lot of roses – never mind what it costs – I don't get her here every day. I want nothing but roses about the rooms, masses of them and one in every single thing I've got. Hooray! Blow the expense. I hope neither you nor Charlotte will be late as there is a good deal to do. God Bless You.
Your Affec. A.

(Princess Louise was the daughter of Queen Victoria.)
Sullivan enclosed in 'dearest Mum's' letter a list of guests:

Princess Louise	Mrs Stewart
Lady Sophia – [indecipherable]	Miss Stewart
Duchess of Westminster	Lord Chief Justice
Lady Beatrice Goodwin	Mr Santley
Lady Adela Larkin	Signor Tosti
Mrs Ronalds	Signor Vizetti
Lady Lindsay	Farquhar
Mrs Clay Ker-Seymour	

and along the side of the writing paper, by way of postscript: 'Don't forget the teaspoons.'

From now on, writes Leslie Baily, the name of the American social figure Mrs Ronalds appears almost daily in Sullivan's diary when he was not out of town. Moreover, he notes that 'the timing of his appointments at Cadogan Place' (where Mrs Ronalds had 'a pretty little house', Number 7) and the 'curious symbols he used', suggest she was his mistress. But Mander and Mitchenson, the theatre historians, in one

Mary Francis Ronalds, the American society beauty who was one of the constant factors in Sullivan's life.

of many conversations, seem by no means convinced of this. But be her place in his life what it may, there can be no doubt Mary Ronalds had a considerable influence upon it for many years, and after his mother's death he wrote to her every day of his life when he was out of town.

'The party at Marlborough House', wrote Arthur to his Mamma in April, 'was very small and very swell. The Prince and Princess were both very kind to me, and Mrs Ronalds sang "The Lost Chord" splendidly.'

'I would travel the length of my kingdom to hear Mrs Ronalds sing "The Lost Chord",' said the Prince of Wales.

In fact, some years later, Mrs Ronalds and her 'Lost Chord' were on the first phonograph recording ever to be made in England. 'God gave somebody a brain to invent this instrument', said one of the listeners, on this occasion, 'so that we should never forget your singing.'

So discreetly majestic was that lady's appearance, and so discreetly too did Sullivan behave, for Mrs Ronalds was a married woman, living as *femme seule*, and the composer had much to lose, including the fair esteem of Queen Victoria, so correctly did they behave that their relationship remains a mystery – as such relationships should. Indeed her husband did not bring a divorce suit until 1900, when Sullivan died before the case was heard, and Ronalds dropped it.

When Mrs Ronalds died, in 1916, aged seventy-seven, a manuscript copy of 'The Lost Chord' was buried with her at Brompton Cemetery.

And while Sullivan was listening, rapt, to Mrs Ronalds: 'She brings the tears to my eyes with my own notes', Gilbert was continuing with those *bon mots* which endear him to the present writer but made few friends feel the friendlier. One of the happiest of these crackled forth when a lady said to him: 'Look at that messenger with his package doing a *pas seul* through the crowd!'

'A brown paper *pas seul*,' responded Gilbert.

But a dramatic storm was brewing up in the Gilbertian ever-ready tea-cup.

He had been limbering up, as it were, in a rumpus with a Miss Amy Roselle, an actress who had been in several of his plays and wished not to continue to suffer his barbs and arrows, but was held to the play by a contract. Gilbert threatened her with the inevitable law-suit: 'From your continued impertinent conduct towards me', wrote the poor lady, 'and the gratuitous insults you persist in heaping upon me ... I can only think you wish me to cancel my engagement.' The poor wounded one went on to say that, business apart, she would have nothing to do with him. 'I must refuse to recognise the existence of men who have behaved in such an extremely ungentlemanly manner.'

This, however, was but a ripple in the tea-cup caused by Gilbert's blowing it – though not, in fact, to cool it – compared to the tempest created by the Henrietta Hodson affair.

It started with a rehearsal of his satire *Ought We To Visit Her* in 1874, when the luckless Henrietta thought she was in the act of sitting on a chair and sat on the floor with a bump. Gilbert remarked: 'Very good, very good. I always thought you would make an impression on the stage one day!' They both lost their tempers. At the dress rehearsal a *réchauffée* of the quarrel was introduced by another matter to which Gilbert, this time, took exception. He stormed out of the theatre and made the mistake of describing the episode to a friend of the by no means calm and placid Henrietta in terms that subsequently seemed excessive, even to him.

Dear Miss Litton

I have received a letter from Miss Hodson's attorneys threatening me with an action for slander on the ground that I attributed 'obscene and disgusting language' to her in my conversation with you. . . .

I am prepared to admit that I said Miss Hodson used the ridiculous expression 'floody bool' in reference to me, and that she told me at the last rehearsal 'not to stand growling there, but to go home and go to bed as that was the best place for me'.

Very truly yours

W.S.Gilbert

On hearing what he had said, he wrote to the bruised Henrietta, withdrawing the expression he had used when his temper was out of control.

Henrietta promptly distributed copies of his letter to all the leading members of the theatrical profession in London.

Three years later *Pygmalion and Galatea* was revived at the Haymarket.

Gilbert wrote to the Manager, Buckstone: 'It is impossible to stage-manage a piece when the stage-manager (in this case myself!) and a leading actress are not on speaking terms. . . . If she consents to meet me on an amicable footing, the only objection I have to her appearing in my pieces will be at once removed.'

Rather handsomely, the present writer thinks, Gilbert wrote to the manager:

My conduct towards Miss Hodson at rehearsal will be characterised by proper courtesy and due regard for her professional position, and I shall feel much obliged if you will at once check me if I should happen to be betrayed into any act or word which may smack of discourtesy towards that lady. But, on the other hand, I must be protected from the consequences of any unwillingness on her part to meet my reasonable requests, and in the event of any difficulty arising from such unwillingness, I propose to be guided entirely by your opinion.

What a responsibility on the shoulders of a manager.

But after a few squibs and fireworks Miss Hodson published, in a frenzy of commas, a pamphlet entitled: *A Letter from Miss Henrietta Hodson, An Actress, Being a Relation of the Persecutions which she has suffered From Mr William Schwenk Gilbert, A Dramatic Author, 1877.*

. . . Mr Gilbert told me, that, somehow or other, he had invariably quarrelled with everyone with whom he had been professionally connected and I took the greatest pains to prevent giving him any cause to quarrel with me. . . . When he complained that Shakespeare had statues elevated to him, whereas he, who was in every way Shakespeare's superior, had none, I went so far as to console him with the assurance that, if he would only be patient, there could be no doubt that he, too, would live to see his own statue. When he abused all other dramatic authors, all critics who did not praise him and the numerous actors and actresses with whom he had disputes, I did not defend them. Even when he told me stories, how he had 'humiliated' actresses, who had dared to resent his unprofessional behaviour, I kept my indignation to myself, and uttered no protest. . . .

Feeling sure that our fiery friend would not remain similarly passive and would produce some incandescent answer, I pressed on Bloomsburywards and there in the North Room of the British Museum I found it in a neat little printed but unbound pamphlet entitled: *A Letter addressed to the Members of the Dramatic Profession in reply to Miss Henrietta Hodson's Pamphlet, by W.S.Gilbert*, in which Miss Hodson's charges

71

were refuted. There was an additional letter dated 3 March, sent to Gilbert by Henrietta Hodson:

... I was foolish to believe that you would cease to persecute me after the experience I had already had of your mode of keeping your promises.

As regards the letter of Mr Buckstone of which you send me a copy, YOU ARE FULLY CAPABLE OF EITHER HAVING DICTATED TO HIM OR OF HAVING FORGED IT TO SUIT YOUR OWN PURPOSES. ...

Beneath this epistle Gilbert remarks with a patience unusual in him: 'I assume that there is a limit to the amount of abuse which a Dramatic author is called upon to submit to at the hands of an actress and I take it that in the paragraph that I have printed in capitals, that limit is overstepped.'

While the atmosphere around Gilbert was growing ever more sulphurous, Sullivan made a start on the music for his libretto to *The Sorcerer*. It was not an easy start. Much of the music he tore up or re-composed.

In March 1877 Sullivan, still in trouble with his score to *The Sorcerer* received a letter from C.L.Dodgson (Lewis Carroll) asking him if he would consider setting some words to music, to which, say his biographers, the by now hag-ridden Arthur answered that with so many commitments in hand, and knowing nothing of the work Carroll had in mind, he thought the chances of a collaboration 'were obscure'. But Lewis Carroll wrote again:

... I am the writer of a little book for children, *Alice's Adventures in Wonderland*, which has proved so unexpectedly popular that the idea of dramatising it has been several times started. If that is ever done I shall want it done in the best possible way, sparing no expense – and *one* feature would be good music. So I thought (knowing your charming compositions) it would be well to get two or three of the songs in it set by you – to be kept for the occasion (if that should arrive) of its being dramatised. If that idea were finally abandoned, we might arrange for publishing them with music.

Sullivan replied that the sum he would require to compose the songs would be considered absurdly extravagant, and though Lewis Carroll wrote again asking him to name it, the collaboration failed to take place.

In order to introduce *The Sorcerer* to playgoers, D'Oyly Carte became an independent impresario (his long-time dearest wish) and because of Gilbert and Sullivan's insistence that they be paid a guaranteed advance before they put pen to paper, he formed the *Comedy Opera Company Ltd*, a small syndicate with four directors: Frank Chappell and George Metzler – the music publishers who had published the vocal score of *Trial by Jury* – Collard Augustus Drake – secretary of the company who was also associated with Metzler, and Edward Hodgson Bayly (known as 'Water-cart Bayly', because he virtually held a monopoly on the watering by sprinklers of the London streets). Carte became a director, a year later, in 1877, when he seems still to have been looking for additional capital, and wrote a letter to 'an unidentified nobleman' telling him that he had 'discussed' a new opera comique with Messrs W.S.Gilbert and Arthur Sullivan.

Gilbert had written a short story for the Christmas number of *The Graphic* (1876), *An Elixir of Love* with illustrations by the by-then-seldom-heard-of artist Bab. On 5 June Sullivan wrote:

Music cover from *The Sorcerer*. Another set of Lancers.

My dear Carte

Gilbert and myself are quite willing to write a two-act piece for you on the following terms:
1. Payment to us of two hundred guineas (£210) on delivery of the MS words and music – that is to say before the piece is produced.
2. Six guineas a performance (£6.6) to be paid to us for the run of the piece in London, from this will be deducted the 200 guineas paid in advance, so that the six guineas a performance will not really begin until about the 33rd or 34th performance.
3. We reserve the country right, your right to play it in London on these terms to extend only to the end of your season.

The piece would be of a musical comedy character, and could be ready for performance by the end of September. If this outline of terms is agreed to, we could prepare a proper agreement upon this basis.

The libretto was in Sullivan's hands in April but, as we have seen, he was deep in grief and in no mood to compose a bright piece.

It was not until 1 November that he wrote: 'I am just putting the finishing touches to my opera, and tomorrow begin the scoring. I have been slaving at this work and I hope it will be a success. Everything at present promises very well. The book is brilliant [at least it had got free from Spiffton-extra-Sooper and Assesmilk-cum-water. The theme of the magic pill or potion was one to which Gilbert was often to return, but Sullivan combatted it each time after *The Sorcerer*] and the music, I think very pretty and good. All the company are good and like it very much.' Save for the ballad 'O Love, True Love', which seems the most successful song they were to write for it, and the patter song for John Wellington Wells, which owed nearly everything to Gilbert's expertise in the *mot juste*, *The Sorcerer*, so far as the present writer is concerned, is conspicuously lacking in sorcery. One has an uneasy feeling that Sullivan, master of melody, was not really trying.

Figaro wrote: 'Mr Sullivan has not deemed it worth while to write an Overture, but has, it is said, borrowed his prelude from his *Henry VIII* incidental music [heard in Manchester that August].'

The Times, however, turned up trumps with: 'Messrs W.S.Gilbert and Arthur Sullivan have once again combined their efforts with the happiest result.'

One critic, however, termed Gilbert 'a *poseur* of indifferent merit'.

No sooner had *The Sorcerer* been conjured onto the stage, than off went Sullivan to Paris, where letters from D'Oyly Carte reached him, telling of troubles with 'Water-cart' Bayly and his co-directors, 'who in the afternoon wanted to close down the piece and by the next morning wished to keep it going'. An impresario's lot is not a happy one. *The Sorcerer* ran for 175 performances. On Christmas Day Sullivan wrote from Paris to Mamma:

It is very wet and miserable-looking outside, but my fire and *café-au-lait* tend to give an artificial cheerfulness to my rooms. The Dramatic Profession of London has mustered in great force for Christmas. I meet someone I know at every turning. Of course they all go back for their Boxing Day performance, and a nice crossing they will have, if it is anything like the one I had. I had a cabin and lay down, so kept my balance all the way. Silva [his valet] looked green and yellow when we arrived at Boulogne. '*Ah Monsieur, quelle traversée épouvantable!*' said he. I swaggered and said I had not noticed it – but I was deuced uncomfortable all the way.

I have gone out of mourning today, and shall put it on again tomorrow till the end of the year. But I don't see why I should wear black on dear old Fred's birthday. So I brighten up and shall drink a glass of wine to his memory, bless him, just as I should to his health if he were alive. He would have done the same for me I know. ... I hope I shall come back strong and well, for I have much to do this forthcoming year [1878].
Now goodbye, and God bless you.
Yrs. Affct.
'A'

4

HMS Pinafore and The Pirates of Penzance

While Sullivan was writing home to Mamma from Paris, Gilbert was posting him the outline of *HMS Pinafore*. It arrived in Paris four days later.

Dear Sullivan

I send you herewith a sketch plot of the proposed opera. I hope and think you will like it. I called on you two days ago (not knowing you had gone away) to consult you about it before drawing it up in full. I have very little doubt, however, but that you will be pleased with it. I should like to talk it over with you, as there is a good deal of fun in it which I haven't set down on paper. Among other things, a song (kind of 'Judge's song') for the First Lord – tracing his career as office-boy in a cotton-broker's office, clerk, traveller, junior partner and First Lord of Britain's Navy. I think a splendid song could be made of this. Of course, there will be no personality in this – the fact that the First Lord in the opera is a radical of the most pronounced type will do away with any suspicion that W.H. Smith is intended. . . .

The uniforms of the officers and crew will be effective. The chorus will look like sailors, and I will ask to have their uniforms made for them in Portsmouth.

I shall be very anxious to know what you think of the plot. It seems to me that there is plenty of story in it (*The Sorcerer* lacks story), with good musical situations. Josephine can have two good ballads, and so can Ralph.

I hope you will have fine weather and that the change will do you a lot of good. As soon as I hear from you that the plot will do, I will set to work, sending you the first act as soon as it is finished

Very truly yours

W.S.Gilbert

This letter, say Dark and Grey, is interesting and important because it shows that, certain as Gilbert always was of himself, from the beginning of the collaboration he deferred to the opinions of his collaborator and was anxious for his good opinion and commendation. Clearly, Gilbert was out to allay any possible suspicion on the part of Sullivan, whose friendships in high quarters might have made him nervous of satire at the expense of a Cabinet Minister. (Gilbert must have been getting to know his Arthur Seymour Sullivan.)

On New Year's Day 1878, the 'Tidal train' bore Sullivan and his valet, the green and yellow Silva, back to London, and so far as Sullivan was concerned, to hard work.

Sullivan composed the music of *HMS Pinafore* in agony – some years later he was to say: 'It is, perhaps, rather a strange fact that the music to *Pinafore*, which was thought to be so merry and spontaneous, was written while I was suffering agonies from a cruel illness. I would compose a few bars, and then be almost insensible from pain. When the paroxysm was passed, I would write a little more, until the pain overwhelmed me again. Never was music written under such disturbing conditions.'

While Sullivan was at work on *Pinafore*, Gilbert started a diary. Now a diary is a device by which the diarist records his own reflection, and we need not doubt that Gilbert's early diary mirrored himself (who, but one mirroring a self-portrait in his diary would have dismissed 'Break with Whistler' in three words?), and therefore was contumacious and irascible. It also had reference to whatever nymph was occupying his attention at the time – in this case it was Marion Terry (MT), who often stayed with the Gilberts and appeared in his plays at the Haymarket, for which he would coach her privately.

Hesketh Pearson prints an entertaining selection from his first journal and from it I quote:

Jan. 1st. Lunched Neville and Lord Londesborough. *The Ne'er Do Weel* to be put in rehearsal at once. MT to be offered a part. . . .

Jan. 21st. wrote Captain's song 'I am the Captain etc'.

Jan. 26th. wrote song for 1st Lord.

Jan. 27th. (Sunday) bad headache. Walked out during church time – saw man trying to steal dogs – ordered him off. Short man, reddish whiskers. Met Mrs coming out of Church. Headache lifted about four. Wrote letter to *Observer* but did not send it . . . dined [Marcus] Stone's. Good dinner. Rainy night. Row with cabman – refused to take us – made him – paid him bare fare – abusive – gave him card – Number 8630 . . . played penny bank – lost £2. Left at 12.30.

Feb. 16th. At Brighton. Walked out in morning to Aquarium – then to Mutton's to lunch. Filthy meal – then took carriage and drove along Parade; Home to meat tea – then to Theatre – pantomime very well done. Then drove to lodgings – oysters.

Feb. 18th. At Brighton. Walked out in morning on beach – bought newspaper – home to lunch – then drove out through to Hove and Shoreham – beastly drive. Home to meat tea. . . . Went to Frikell [conjurer] in evening – atrocious entertainment – left when half over – atmosphere putrid – saw *the* Galatea. Evening very warm so we sat on Esplanade. MT in high spirits about nothing – home – oysters – rehearsed with MT.

March 11th. Stopped ten minutes (at shop to buy a cigar case). Then home. Row with cabman – took sixpence away from him. He is going to summons me.

May 25th. Went to Opéra Comique to superintend scene – remained there till 6.30 working at it . . . then went to Beefsteak to dine and dress. To theatre at 8. . . . Rowdy Gallery – singing songs etc. Piece (*Pinafore*) went extremely well . . . enthusiastic call for self and Sullivan.

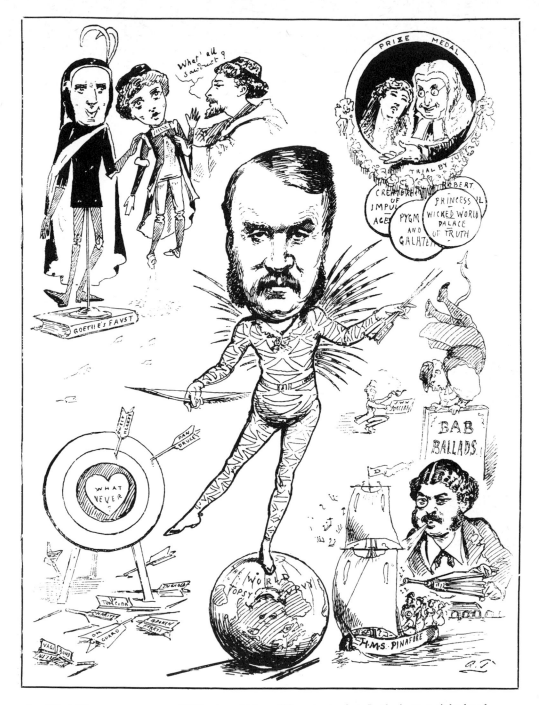

An Alfred Thompson cartoon of Gilbert, and his prolific output, 1879. In the bottom right-hand corner, Sullivan blows *Pinafore* on its money-making course.

In June Gilbert felt ill, but a holiday in Margate revived him sufficiently to take 'Mrs' to Havre and Trouville where they bathed a lot. At the Hôtel d'Angleterre at Rouen, reports the diary, the supper was 'beastly', the wine 'atrocious', the terms 'extortionate' and the hall porter 'churlish', and at this the present writer would not wonder. 'Offered him 3/- – he asked 5/- – refused to give it him – he made me a present of it. ...' At Boulogne 'Parson and wife at St Phillip's, Kensington came up and claimed acquaintance – said they wanted to know me – woman especially offensive – gave them cold shoulder. ...'

How hard it is to tear oneself away from this entrancing diary. But to the voyage of *HMS Pinafore*, the first of the outstanding world-wide, age-long successes of the only too easily parted trio, Gilbert, Sullivan and D'Oyly Carte.

'*The Standard*', reports Reginald Allen in *The First Night Gilbert and Sullivan*, 'was detailed in its enthusiasm: "So perfect a quarter-deck as that of *HMS Pinafore* has

Scenes from *HMS Pinafore* depicted in a leaflet advertising 'Sapolio', a cleaner.

RIGHT A souvenir of the production of the *Pirates of Penzance* by a children's company in the Christmas season at the Savoy, 1884:

assuredly never been put upon the stage. Every block and rope to the minutest detail is in its place, in fact it is an exact model of what it represents. ... Here we find that marvel of marvels, a chorus that acts, and adds to the reality of the illusion."'

The Press swelled a chorus of approval for 'the five or more encores of the various numbers'.

The Times, as always sounder in ear than eye, wrote: 'Few theatres can boast of such a trio of genuine humorists as are Mr G. Grossmith (Sir Joseph Porter), Mr Rutland Barrington (The Captain) and Miss Everard (little Buttercup). The vocal achievements of these are not of the highest order,' continued the old Thunderer, living up to its reputation, 'but their *parlato* style does full justice to the humorous sallies of Mr Gilbert.'

The Daily News commended Mr George Power's light tenor voice, 'of very agreeable quality'. But *The Times* was, as is expected of it, more severe with his intonations: 'A little uncertain' – first night nerves perhaps?

The Era wrote: 'Mr Gilbert and Mr Sullivan have worked together in the true spirit of collaboration.' (But be it not forgotten that these were early days.)

The Times, with considerable insight, said: 'With Mr Gilbert a plot is seldom more than a lay figure which he delights in dressing in the fantastic garb of his wit and imagination. We hardly become conscious of the absence of any kind of human interest. The audience, then, have little reason to complain of Mr Gilbert. But the musician has. His true field of action is, after all, genuine emotion.'

The present writer was fortunate, indeed, to see *Pinafore* in Tyrone Guthrie's production, a very spare, swift and impermissive craft, from which ancient custom had been trimmed to essentials without in any way damaging the romantic Gothic outline of the libretto.

Musically, too, the work holds the years handsomely whenever melody flowers into melody, though it is not entirely free from the kind of wodge-chug-a-chug Sullivan at times allowed himself as a substitute for musical thought, almost permitting his musicianly mind to absent it from felicity a while, leaving Gilbert to get on with it – though, in fairness to him, these lapses from invention occur far less frequently than the many, many occasions when Sullivan came to Gilbert's assistance with unforeseen adroitness and invention, even when he was, as so often, content to be the mirror of other men's music.

But in spite of the indulgent attitude of the press and public, *HMS Pinafore* was no overnight success.

Jimmie Glover, the musical director, in his autobiography *Jimmie Glover, His Book*, lets the cat out of the bag: 'It came out that the second night's receipts were a matter of only £14.' The weather, traditionally the inimical foe to the theatre, was sweltering in May and June of that year. And no sooner had the first night cheers died away than the box office takings dwindled to £100 a night. Water-cart Bayly and his colleagues drove D'Oyly Carte crazy with their repeated orders to withdraw the piece forthwith, only to follow them with orders to withdraw the withdrawals.

Then two favourable currents turned the outgoing tide for *HMS Pinafore*. First, Sullivan, conductor of the Promenade Concerts at Covent Garden, commissioned (from

LEFT The music cover to the 'Pirates of Penzance Waltz' with a picture of Marion Hood in the role of Mabel.

A children's company gave performances of *HMS Pinafore* at the Opera Comique in 1879.

Hamilton Clarke) an arrangement of the music of *Pinafore* as an overture. Having heard it, people went to see it. Soon the word got round. And secondly, another word went the rounds. This concerned the remarkable similarity, in spite of a character make-up designed to cloud the issue, between Gilbert's Right Honourable Sir Joseph Porter KCB, First Lord of the Admiralty, and Disraeli's appointment of W.H.Smith, a news-paper boy who became a publisher, to the position of First Lord. In one of Gilbert's most brilliant list songs Sir Joseph looks back on a career begun 'as office boy in an attorney's firm', rising through the legal profession to a pocket borough in Parliament where:

> I always voted at my party's call
> And never thought of voting for myself at all.
> I thought so little they rewarded me
> By making me the ruler of the Queen's navee.

Disraeli's appointment of W.H.Smith had been opposed by Queen Victoria herself. The Queen was 'prepared to agree if necessary, but she *fears* it may *not please* the Navy in which Service so many of the *highest rank* serve, and who claim to be of equal rank with the Army – if a man from the Middle Class is placed above them in that very high post. ...' (Royal Archives, Windsor.)

Disraeli waxed, as one might foresee, 'persuasive in reply' and Victoria gave in to her Prime Minister's 'unanswerable' arguments, but she added her admonition: Smith must not '. . . lord it over the Navy (which almost every First Lord does) and be a little modest and not *act* the Lord High Admiral which is offensive to the Service'.

Once the news went the rounds, the Prime Minister himself was soon calling him 'Pinafore Smith'. The cartoonists, however, were as soon, if not sooner, drawing 'Pinafore Sullivan'. Years after, Gilbert rewrote the story especially for children, and in it he said:

One of the most important personages in the Government of that day was Sir Joseph Porter, First Lord of the Admiralty. You would naturally think that a person who commanded the entire Navy would be the most accomplished sailor who could be found, but that is not the way in which such things are managed in England. Sir Joseph Porter ... knew nothing whatever about ships. Now as England is a great maritime country, it is very important that all English-men should understand something about men-of-war. So soon as it was discovered that his ignorance of a ship was so complete that he did not know one end of it from the other, some important person said: 'Let us set this poor ignorant gentleman to command the British Fleet, and by that means give him an opportunity of ascertaining what a ship really is.' This was considered to be a most wise and sensible suggestion, and so Sir Joseph Porter was at once appointed First Lord of the Admiralty of Great Britain and Ireland. I daresay you think I am joking, but indeed I am quite serious. This is the way in which things are managed in this great and happy country.

In *Pinafore* the perfect word, placed at the perfect place, flashes out from time to time as though to crown the librettist king of the *mot juste*, as in: 'The British Tar is a soaring soul.' The lyric for this number, incidentally, shows to perfection Gilbert's care for detail and his skill in compiling lists:

> I've snuff and tobaccy and excellent jackey, [plug tobacco]
> I've scissors and watches and knives;
> I've ribbons and laces to set off the faces
> Of pretty young sweethearts and wives.
> I've treacle and toffee and excellent coffee,
> Soft tommy and succulent chops;
> I've chickens and conies and pretty polonies
> And excellent peppermint drops.

If the airs are more inventive and flowing than in any of the earlier collaborations, the best of ballads seem planted in the same soil as eighteenth-century songs:

> Sorry her heart that loves too well,
> Heavy the heart that hopes but vainly,
> Sad are the sighs that own the spell,
> Uttered by eyes that speak too plainly,
> Heavy the sorrow that bows the head
> When love is alive and hope is dead.

There is a nice crack of Gilbert's honeyed-over lash at the British love of ease and the world-wide habit of nepotism – in this case simply social – in the First Lord's song:

> *Sir Joseph:* But when the breezes blow
> I generally go below
> And seek the seclusion that a cabin grants!
> *All:* And so do his sisters and his cousins and his aunts.

Various winds blow reminiscently billowing out the stout sails. For instance, the jolly little hornpipe sets the Captain of the *Pinafore* to a pretty, prancing, piping tune. All pervading, as so it should be, is the salty flavour of the sea, albeit seasoned here and there with a lashing of the fashionable French composer Offenbach. In considering Gilbert's ballads one should not lose sight of the trends of the time in which he lived and worked – all those drawing-room pianos, upright as the Victorian *paterfamilias*, with just a peep of pleated silk showing through the fret-work, waiting to be warbled at.

Nor should one lose sight of the brevity he brings to his lyrics: a brevity he would have done well to apply to his appalling dialogue. He can crystallise an entire romantic predicament in one verse.

> I'd laugh my rank to scorn
> In union holy
> Were he more highly born
> Or I more lowly.

His habit of relating the practical to the romantic is to be found at its happiest outside *The Mikado*:

> Fair moon to thee I sing,
> Bright regent of the heavens,
> Say why is everything
> Either at sixes or sevens?

The months passed, and with them *Pinafore* sailed on to world-wide seas. There were no well-determined copyright laws in America, and before a year was out, eight theatres in New York alone were giving their own version of *Pinafore* at the same time – a version that neither librettist nor composer had ever seen, nor from which did they derive one cent. The music was published over there without consent of either of them, and on the title-page, *Pinafore* was described as 'the reigning sensation throughout all the world'. The London publisher, Metzler, sold edition after edition. One enterprising man in New York who theretofore had been a music copyist, bought a press and printed and sold it in cartloads which left him a rich man. The American managements introduced endless songs of their own devising. One such was a song about a new design in trousers, which was much occupying the sartorial opinions of New York. There was, too, a song inspired by a new supper-dish which, incidentally, had never been tasted by the good ship's creators. One of the pirated productions even interpolated, for no discoverable reason, the 'Hallelujah Chorus'. Thousands of barrel organs churned out the tunes all over New York. Almost Gilbert and Sullivan might have been – and probably were – the contemporary Beatles. 'Such a furore as this opera has created I have never known before, in the history of the American stage,' (American journalist).

They discussed seriously going over to America to put a stop, insofar as they were able, to the piracy.

In a letter to a friend, C.K.Remington, of Buffalo, Sullivan wrote:

It is very good of you to send me so many interesting scraps about the *Pinafore* in America. I am gratified beyond measure at its success there, but there is one matter of great regret to me. Not the money question, although I don't pretend for an instant that I should not prefer to be paid for my work. No, my regret is that my music is not performed as I wrote it. Orchestral colouring plays so great a part in my work that to deprive them of this is to take away from the attraction ... for a very small sum a manager might have had a copy of my score, and my work would have been given to the American public as I wrote it, instead of in a garbled form. ...

Sullivan's illness had, in the meantime, gained ground, and the trip to America had to be postponed. He was forced to refuse an offer to conduct the piece in Philadelphia for a fortnight, for a fee of £1,000: 'I have been suffering a martyrdom.'

Finally he agreed to an operation, and on 18 August 1879, the Duke of Edinburgh wrote:

I cannot tell you how glad I was to read in your letter that you were relieved from your sufferings by a successful operation. The Prince of Wales has asked me to join his congratulations to mine. I hope you will now take great care of yourself, and pick up plenty of strength for your journey to America. ...

Alfred.

"FAIR MOON TO THEE I SING" (PINAFORE)

"THE MERRY MERRY MAIDEN AND THE TAR" (PINAFORE)

For some weeks D'Oyly Carte had been in New York contending with the Pirates and setting up a production of the genuine article. His Board of Directors, Water-cart Bayly and Co, in England, were in their usual dissension over *Pinafore*, but saw in his absence from the country a chance to board and take over the vessel. Their original investment, Leslie Baily reminds us, was £500 each. Since the unprecedented success of the voyage they had been drawing £500 a week, each. But this was not enough for Water-cart Bayly and his grasping gang who no longer wished to stop the run of *Pinafore*. So they sent their hirelings, vans, clipper-clopper dray-horses and all, to the Opéra Comique to snatch the scenery during an evening performance, with the extra-ordinary purpose of erecting it at the Aquarium Theatre, and so setting up a rival pro-duction. A free fight broke out backstage, and they were compelled to lower the Safety Curtain.

Gilbert acquainted his collaborator with the news:

By the way, on Friday night they broke into the theatre with a mob of 50 roughs, during the performance, and tried to carry off the properties. . . . Barker resisted their approach, and was knocked downstairs and seriously hurt. There was alarm among the audience who raised a cry of 'Fire!', appeased, however, by Grossmith who made them a speech from the stage. . . . I hear the performance at the Aquarium was wretched [can one wonder?] and that very few audience were present . . . the soprano is a contralto so has to take her high notes an octave lower. That's all the news.

The rival production ran for only ninety-one performances, but litigation dragged on for over a year. 'We won the case of course,' said D'Oyly Carte, 'but in the meantime the Company had gone bankrupt. We got no damages and had to pay our own costs.'

But the case led to a good practical result – the drawing-up of a contract between the creators and the management, in which Gilbert, Sullivan and D'Oyly Carte put up £1,000 each. The profits were to be distributed in equal shares after all expenses had been paid. Carte was to receive a management fee of £15 a week – Gilbert and Sullivan to be paid four guineas for each representation: 'These salaries to be included in weekly expenses.'

The phrase 'after all expenses had been paid' was to lead to the famous 'carpet litigation' brought by Gilbert – of course – against Carte and Sullivan, later on.

But for the moment it was financial high-tide time all round. Sullivan had his costly operation. Gilbert acquired a sea-going yacht and apparently nurtured a secret ambition to navigate it to America. He called it *The Druidess* after Sir Humphrey Gilbert's barque. (Sir Humphrey was a sixteenth-century navigator whom Gilbert would have liked to believe was one of his forebears.)

Leslie Baily tells another of those sharp-tongued anecdotes with which Gilbert lamentably failed to endear himself to all. When he was building 'a large mansion' in Harrington Gardens, Gilbert had a stone facsimile of *The Druidess* added to the house. A guest, a friendly if curious lady, admiring it, remarked to Gilbert that no doubt it was *HMS Pinafore*. 'Madam,' snapped Gilbert, 'I do not advertise my trade card on my private house.' Gilbert and 'Mrs' nearly came to a watery end when they made their first voyage in *Druidess* – from the Isle of Wight to Ramsgate. They met heavy weather and it took all Gilbert could do to run in to Dungeness. After this he took lessons in navigation, according to his diary.

In spite of the fracas and the temptations of navigation, Gilbert had started work on the outline of the successor to *HMS Pinafore* – not that it showed the slightest signs of needing one. Early in August he wrote to Sullivan:

I've broken the neck of Act II and see my way clearly to the end. I think it [*The Pirates of Penzance*] comes out very well. By the way, I've made great use of the Tarantara business in Act II. The police always say Tarantara when they desire to work their courage up to the sticking point. They are naturally timid, but, through the agency of this talisman, they are enabled to acquit themselves well. When concealed in Act II, and the robbers approach, their courage begins to fail them, but a recourse to Tarantara (pianissimo) has the desired effect. . . . W.S. Gilbert

As soon as Sullivan received the libretto from Gilbert, he began composing, not from Act I, but in the middle of Act II. He might have finished *Pirates* while *Pinafore* was still drawing packed houses, had not Fate, in the form of D'Oyly Carte, intervened with an urgent summons to New York. The impresario had decided that the only way to fight the piracy was to show America what Gilbert and Sullivan's *Pinafore* was, and how it should be played, by dint of setting it up on Broadway.

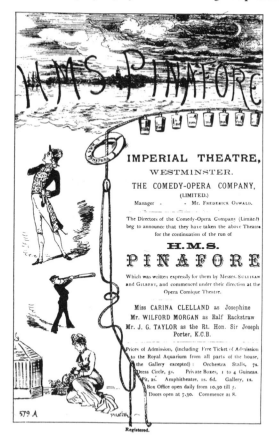

A programme for the rival production of *HMS Pinafore* in 1879, under the management of the former directors of the Opera Comique who had broken with D'Oyly Carte.

The voyage across was not of the easiest. But 'I will not have another libretto of mine produced if the Americans are going to steal it. Not that I need the money so much, but it upsets my digestion,' growled Gilbert. He also made the golden quip that the humours of life were confined to the country he had left behind and not to the seas it was supposed to rule.

Their arrival off Sandy Hook was inspiriting [says Hesketh Pearson]. A large number of steamers, decorated with stars and stripes and union jacks, with bands on board playing their versions of the *Pinafore* airs, came out to greet them; though a rival show of Nigger Minstrels sent forth a tug placarded with the words *No Pinafore!* which did its best to make the music inaudible by means of a powerful whistle.

The Press reported that they were charmed by the famous pair, describing them as simple, amiable and modest, good-natured (one resents this on Gilbert's behalf) and lively. The contrast – or at least a contrast – was noticed: the hearty laugh and quick utterance of the tall, fair-haired, blue-eyed, rosy-cheeked, mutton-chopped whiskered Gilbert; the soulful eyes, mobile face and sensitive expression of the short, dark-haired, gentle-mannered Sullivan.

One deep similarity the reporters may not have recognised at a glance was that both men were disappointed that their more serious work had not achieved the world-wide popularity of a 'frothy' (though perhaps the *mot juste* might be foamy) 'trifle like *Pinafore*'.

Their arrival in America was the talk of New York. Everyone was looking forward to the fray with ill-disguised relish. There would be the devil to pay, said the Press, licking its chops.

Both Gilbert and Sullivan were fêted everywhere, though it soon became apparent that it was Sullivan who was to be the lion of the day. Arthur sent his first letter to Mamma:

On Saturday we dined at the Lotus Club. It was a splendid reception, and although both Gilbert and myself were very nervous, we spoke very well, and I am told, at once gained the goodwill and sympathy of our hearers who comprise the most prominent men in New York. The Judge of the police court in his speech said that, to show his hearty goodwill, and to mark his feeling of gratitude for the many happy hours we had given him, he hoped we might soon be brought before him as drunk and disorderly, so that he might have the satisfaction of letting us off!

We have engaged a first-rate chorus, and the principals are the best who have ever been got together for the immortal *Pinafore* [Sullivan wrote a few days later]. We open on Monday week [1 December] and the rest depends upon the public. ... I must do the Americans the justice to say that they are most wonderfully kind and hospitable. The moment a man sees you, he wants to know what he can do for you, and means it, too.

And again to Mamma: 'Americans for three hours this afternoon. I've talked to more Americans half the night and I'm told there are still more Americans whom I haven't talked to coming tomorrow morning. What I want to know is – when do all these Americans end!!!'

Ungrateful one.

They opened at the Fifth Avenue Theatre. Sensation. For the many and various pirated *Pinafores* had created a limited public who wanted to see the true-blue British article: 'We've seen it as a comedy,' said one American journal, 'we've seen it as a tragedy, but the play these English have brought over is quite a new play to us, and very good it is.'

'Gilbert', says Pearson, 'was told by an American impresario, that he would make a fortune if he were to re-write the piece, changing *HMS* to *USS* and substituting the Stars and Stripes for the British Ensign, anchoring the ship off Jersey Beach and turning the First Lord of the Admiralty into the US Navy boss.'

But soon it became evident that the pirates had purloined the pickings. Gilbert, Sullivan and D'Oyly Carte could see that the quickest way to the American purse-string was to complete *The Pirates of Penzance* (of which, so far, Sullivan had written only part of Act II) and present it in New York before the copyright pirates could plunder it. Sullivan set to work to compose the whole of that piece in his hotel room in New York. He worked at it day and night. Yet Arthur still found time to write Mamma: 'Our houses at the *Pinafore* have fallen off very much this week. All the theatres are doing badly, and we shall have no profits until the new piece comes out – so Gilbert and I are reducing our expenditure. We shall begin by not paying the postage on our letters home! ... I can't help feeling sanguine of success although we ought never to feel sanguine.'

Sullivan recorded his crowded hours of work in his diary, full with the bare facts of rehearsing, conducting, dining and writing music to 4.30 am when not actually writing music until 6.30 am.

His entry for Christmas Day reads: 'Worked all day. Dined at Grants. Came home and worked till 5.30 am.'

On 31 December (first night of *The Pirates of Penzance*):

No rehearsal, except Band at 11 for Overture. Home at 1.35 to breakfast. Too ill to eat. Went to bed to try to get sleep. Could not. Stayed in bed till 5.30. Gilbert came. Got up feeling miserably ill. Head on fire. Dressed slowly and got to New York club at 7.30. Had 12 oysters and a glass of champagne. Went to theatre. House crammed with the élite of New York. Went into the orchestra, more dead than alive, but got better when I took the stick in my hand – fine reception. Grand success. Then home. Could not sleep so did not go to bed till 3.30. Felt utterly worn out.

After each rehearsal the score had been locked in a safe to foil the pirates (of America). So the piece came as a complete surprise to the first night audience. Even so, dotted about in that audience, pirate copyists were making sketchy notes for the soonest possible use. Telegrams from managements all over the United States with offers to mount the new work piled up among the waiting, clamorous reporters. Arthur seized a moment in the middle of the brou-ha-ha, to write to Mamma:

At last I am out of my penal servitude and find a little breathing time to look around me, and write home.

... We had long and wearisome rehearsals, but fortunately our Company and all the chorus are charming people and devoted to us, and spared themselves no pains or trouble to do their work thoroughly well. All except the tenor who is an idiot [almost Sullivan might have been

Sullivan the organ grinder and Gilbert the acrobat
in Alfred Thompson's cartoon of 1880.

Gilbert] ... we took *nine* encores, and could have had more if I liked ... we anticipate immense business for the next few weeks.

What do I think of the piece myself? The *libretto* is ingenious and clever, wonderfully funny in parts, and sometimes brilliant in dialogue – beautifully written for music, as is all Gilbert does, and all the action and business perfect. The music is infinitely superior to *Pinafore* [here the present writer cannot go along with Sullivan, being of the school of thought that holds *The Pirates of Penzance* is *HMS Pinafore* transplanted to the Police Force] funnier and more developed, of a higher class altogether. I think that in time it will be more popular. Then the *mis-en-scène* and the dresses are something to be dreamed about. ... The New York ladies are raving about them. The Policemen's Chorus is an enormous hit and they are cheered tremendously when they march on with their Bull's Eyes all alight, and are always encored. I am sanguine of its success in London for there are the local allusions which will have twice the force they have here. ...

So the New Year opens propitiously for me.

But before, two days before in fact, the auspicious 1880 opened, a single bizarre performance had taken place in England – in Paignton to be exact, refuge of asthmatics even in those days, set on the shore of Torbay. It was a conveniently remote spot, clear, particularly around Christmas-time, from those dangerous chatterers the London first-nighters, and doubly convenient because the D'Oyly Carte company was giving *Pinafore* at nearby Torquay. Paignton was a tiny coastal town in 1879, but it did rejoice in a bijou theatre – *The Royal Bijou* in fact. The single, almost unbelievable, performance was billed for two o'clock and was given solely for the purpose of copyrighting the play. The *entrepreneur* was Miss Helen Lenoir, Carte's trusty secretary and later his second wife. A pianoforte score was sent over from America, but as it did not arrive in England until the day before the performance, 'rough' must have been an understatement for the manner in which songs and music were performed, since the company had no time to learn their numbers. The one and only full rehearsal took place on the stage of the

Torquay theatre after the evening performance of *Pinafore*. The Company appeared at Paignton in their *Pinafore* costumes augmented by coloured handkerchiefs, says Reginald Allen, worn on the head to suggest they were pirates, carrying their parts on with them, from which they read, extemporising (how else?) their songs before whatever bits and pieces of scenery, props and furnishings *The Royal Bijou* could summon onto the stage – one of the earlier examples of 'The show MUST go on' – must and did.

'We congratulate the talented author and composer on another brilliant success,' burbled *The Paignton and Newton Directory*.

'It was, however, a very different *Pirates* from that heard in New York next night,' observes Reginald Allen, not, one imagines, without a sigh. The audience numbered something like fifty.

The (New York) *Sun*, decided that both libretto and music were better than *Pinafore*.

The New York Times thought that: '. . . whether it will be received with the same favour that (has) been accorded to *Pinafore* is very doubtful.'

The (New York) *Herald* noted: 'The opera was received with marked approval and made a palpable hit last evening, though the question of its permanence in public favour (as compared with *Pinafore*) was not established.'

'*The World*', says Reginald Allen, 'surrendered to the Jolly Roger rather than to the Union Jack of Captain Corcoran's saucy ship.'

The Hour turned its social opera-glasses on the audience, to report that on that New York first night: 'All New York was there, and among those in boxes were Mrs Schlessinger and Miss Jerome, both looking charming and showing the audience how to use the Opera-Glass, and how to look when stared at. . . . Mrs Vanderbilt, without diamonds, and Mrs J. J. Astor in the seventeenth row of the stalls.'

The leading lady was twenty-three-year-old Madame Blanche Rosavella (right in the middle of Gilbert's predatory age-group, one gathers), a name contrived from her mother's maiden name, Roosevelt. She had made her debut at Covent Garden as Violetta in *La Traviata*. Interviewed by *Frank Leslie's Illustrated*, she said she had met Sullivan in Paris and declared to the reporter, quite unblushingly, that *The Pirates* had been specially written for her. 'And oh! the music suits my voice to perfection. . . . I have gotten all my dresses for it from Madame Latreille, of the Rue Lafitte, Paris.' Unfortunately a letter from D'Oyly Carte to Sullivan was to prick la Rosavella's breathless bubble: 'I am inclined to think that Rosavella's voice may be too thin for America. . . . I am to hear her sing tomorrow. They are accustomed to big voices and fine singers. . . .'

Carte's choice would have been Helena Crosmond, but as la Crosmond was asking £100 and Carte was offering £20, la Rosavella got the role. 'Her voice', complained *The Sun*, 'is thin in texture and not always true,' but it allowed that the singer was pretty. *The World* pointed out that she was evidently suffering with a cold; *The Dramatic Mirror*, that a certain awkwardness of action seemed constantly present.

One last glimpse of la Rosavella is vouchsaved us by Reginald Allen. She changed her name and her profession – also her husband – and sought a literary career, 'and became the first fair lady to occupy Guy de Maupassant's guest-room at Etretat'.

A week after the New York opening of *Pirates*, a concert was held at Baltimore in

RIGHT Programme for the authentic *Pirates of Penzance* at the Fifth Avenue Theatre in 1880.

Fifth Ave. Theatre.

JOHN T. FORD .... LESSEE AND MANAGER.

Also of Broad St. Theatre, Philadelphia,   Grand Opera House, Baltimore.   Ford's Opera House, Washington.

CHAS. E. FORD .... ACTING MANAGER.

PROV KING.—"He provoked me into loving him!" was a pretty girl's excuse for engaging herself to a man whom she had always professed to hate.

A GREAT MAN is made so for others, not for himself—to relieve the poor, comfort the afflicted, protect the oppressed, correct the vicious, and deliver the captive.

NOT FAR WRONG.—A little girl, being reproved the other day by her elder sister for using a slang expression, sharply retorted, "Well, if you went into society more you would hear slang."

NEW YORK, FEBRUARY 27, 1880.

THIRTEENTH AND POSITIVELY LAST WEEK (BUT ONE) OF THE

Gilbert & Sullivan Opera Season

—BY—

D'OYLY CARTE'S LONDON OPERA CO.

Seats can now be secured for any of the remaining nights.

First production of the New Melo-dramatic Opera, in Two Acts, by the author and composer of "Pinafore," written and composed expressly for production in the United States, entitled

The Pirates of Penzance;

Or, The SLAVE OF DUTY.

WRITTEN BY   COMPOSED BY
W. S. GILBERT.   ARTHUR SULLIVAN

RICHARD, a Pirate Chief .. ..Mr. BROCOLINI

SAMUEL, his Lieutenant ....Mr. NASH

FREDERIC, a Pirate Apprentice ....Mr. HUGH TALBOT

MAJOR-GEN. STANLEY, of the British Army..Mr. J. H. RYLEY

EDWARD, a Sergeant of Police... .... Mr. HODSON

MABEL, General Stanley's youngest daughter,
             Miss BLANCHE ROOSEVELT

KATE, EDITH, ISABEL, } General Stanley's Daughters.
   ....Miss JESSIE BOND
   ..Miss ROSINA BRANDRAM
   ....Miss BARLOW

RUTH, a Piratical "Maid-of-all-work"..Miss ALICE BARNETT

General Stanley's Daughters, Pirates, Policemen, etc.

ACT I.—A ROCKY SEASHORE on the Coast of Cornwall, England.
ACT II.—A RUINED CHAPEL on General Stanley's Estate.

CONDUCTOR...................... Mr. ALFRED CELLIER

The Opera is produced under the personal direction of
THE AUTHOR AND THE COMPOSER.

Elaborate Costumes, imported from Europe (designed expressly for Mr. D'OYLY CARTE'S Company by "Faustin,") made by Mme. LATREILLE, of Paris, Mme. ALIAS, of London, and Messrs. BLOOM, of New York. Uniforms by Mr. NATHAN, of London.

Treasurer.........................Mr. FRITZ HIRSCHY
Chief Usher....................Mr. ALBERT M. KINGSLAND
The Scenery......................by Mr. J. A. THOMPSON
Master Machinist.................Mr. BENSON SHERWOOD
Stage Manager (for Mr. CARTE).........Mr. ARTHUR LECLERCQ
Treasurer (for Mr. CARTE)...............Mr. W. WHITE

Matinee on Saturday at 2 o'clock.

MONDAY EVENING, MARCH 8th, FOR ONE WEEK,

PIRATES OF PENZANCE,

At the BROOKLYN ACADEMY OF MUSIC.

The WEBER Celebrated Pianos are used at this Theatre.

Opera Glasses to hire in the Lobby.

Doors open at 7.30.   Commences at 8 precisely.

Carriages can be ordered at 10.

This Programme is published and printed at A. S. SEER's Show Printing Establishment, 26 Union Square, where all orders for advertisements are received.

Sullivan's honour. That night, after the applause and enthusiasm had died away, Arthur settled down to write to Mamma:

Here I am: The Concert is over, and I have to be up at six tomorrow morning to go off by the 7.30 train. So before going to bed I write a line for Saturday's steamer to tell you that all has gone well, and that I am delighted with the Baltimorites. ... *The Pirates of Penzance* is still doing enormous business every night and likely to last, so that at last I really think I shall get a little money out of America. I ought to, for they have made a good deal out of me. ...

And again, towards the end of January:

Although our work is nominally over, and we ought to be resting, yet the very success of the piece keeps us hard at work, for, in order to strike while the iron is hot and get all the profit we can while everyone is talking about it, we are sending out three companies to other towns in America, and these have to be selected, organised and rehearsed ... all this involves a lot of work and constant anxiety. But we don't mind it, we all work like slaves. ...

Sullivan would have done well, with so much extra work on hand, to have shepherded his resources by cutting out all social activities, for the strain of so much work, public speeches and pain, pain, pain, was becoming greater than he could bear. He was found one day lying in his room half-conscious with his agony; but that same evening, there he was, speaking brilliantly at a public dinner held in his honour.

In his speeches Sullivan attacked the American Law which countenanced wholesale piracy. He also had a gentle admonition for the conduct of American ladies in London, which, but for his genial manner, might have given almost Gilbertian offence:

The many charming American women who visit England [he said] have no cause to complain of the welcome they receive in English Society. Their nationality is a passport which opens all doors to them. As this is the case, and no pleasant attractive American can ever complain of being left out (if only fairly accredited), why are they so ill-natured about each other? ... No, dear charming ladies, you will not acquire greater social importance yourself by trying to depreciate others. Don't let me have to speak again, I pray!

and because it was dear Mr Sullivan, the lion of the hour, there was nothing for the ladies of American Society to do but grin and bear it – and never do it again. Or did they?

Before Sullivan's return to England, sermons gave way to swanning, and swanning with no less a personage than Queen Victoria's own daughter – Princess Louise, the Marchioness of Lorne. Arthur travelled to Ottawa via Buffalo and Niagara.

Trouble at Buffalo: 'We arrived there at 8 on Saturday morning in a violent snow-storm. Of course our first thought was "Bad house today!"'

At Ottawa a sleigh met him at the station and took him to Government House to stay with Princess Louise. Then, after a few days tobogganing – 'I wasn't sure whether I had got my body on or left it behind' – he hastened back to New York and set sail for England on 3 March.

To Sullivan, the American trip had been roses – and agony – all the way, culminating in the visit to Government House in Ottawa. But Gilbert, nothing if not human, had the deep thorns of jealousy, as so often where Sullivan was concerned, in his roses. No Queen Victoria's daughter invited him to play tennis and toboggan at Government House; no one gave concerts – why should they – in honour of him. And once back in London and *The Pirates of Penzance* mounted at the familiar Opéra Comique, Sullivan would be off to the Leeds Festival with all that this entailed in preparatory work – for there would be a cantata to compose for it as well as scores to be studied, and all this would entice him away from the light operatic stage he shared with Gilbert – who would have to pick a few good intricate quarrels to occupy his mind.

While Gilbert mulled over the responsibilities of collaboration in general and, in particular, Sullivan's responsibility to him, and was furiously deciding that his work needed Sullivan more than Sullivan's needed him.

And while Sullivan – between bouts of agonising pain – was pondering to whom to turn to write his Leeds Cantata, the London premiere of *The Pirates of Penzance* triumphantly took place. Rehearsals had not been without trauma.

'Mr W.S. Gilbert and Mr Arthur Sullivan have arrived in England flushed with their American success,' wrote Clement Scott in *Theatre*. If our collaborators were flushed, however, it was with something more desperate than triumph. It would have been, in fact, because the score of *The Pirates*, vulnerable as it was, was missing. By the time the

George Grossmith as the Major-General in *The Pirates of Penzance* from *The Theatre*, May 1880 and Richard Temple as the Pirate King in *The Illustrated Sporting and Dramatic News*, 26 June 1880.

precious package came to light, it had travelled the Atlantic four times.

'The anticipation of the treat to be derived from Mr Gilbert's rich vein of satirical humour and Mr Sullivan's genial and tuneful music were fully realised,' wrote the *Daily News*.

'To the inevitable question, Is it as good as *Pinafore*?' said the *Standard* confidently, 'an affirmative answer can at once be given'. *The Times* held the opposite view: 'Of invention there is little or no trace.'

Of Gilbert's humour, after the first performance, Clement Scott wrote in *Theatre*:

It has been called topsy-turvy, deformed, exaggerated caricature, grotesque; it has been compared to the effect of a man looking at his face in a spoon, in a magnifying-glass, or at the world through the wrong end of an opera-glass; but none of these things hit the mark. It is a kind of comic daring and recklessness that makes fun of things. ... In a comical way he shows us all that is mean, and cruel, and crafty, and equivocal even in the world's heroes; and he makes us laugh at them because we are convinced such faults are lingering in the breasts of the best of us.

Of course Gilbert's initial situation is comical:

> When Frederic was a little lad he proved so brave and daring
> His father thought he'd prentice him to some career sea-faring.

But Ruth, the child's nurse, another of those fat, unbeautiful and ageing women Gilbert loved to hold to ridicule, sings:

> A sad mistake it was to make, and doom him to a vile lot,
> I bound him to a pirate – you – instead of to a pilot.

And although the collaborators had a lot of fun with pirates and policemen and well-brought-up young ladies, a snag presents itself to the far-seeing and thoughtful examiner of portents: was not the very success of Gilbert and Sullivan laying its own trap, baited with patter-song and madrigal?

Certainly as piece succeeded piece, their technique grew. But technique is but a shorthand symbol for know-how; and it leads to repetition. And repetition leads to a rut. And list-songs, ballads and madrigals, however ingenious, romantic and tuneful they may be, if they are used in the same way to the same end and, further, bear a family likeness to the work of both librettist and composer, constitute a danger. This danger is one that can be but vaguely discerned in *The Pirates of Penzance*, but it lurks in wait as surely as do those halcyon works *The Mikado*, *The Gondoliers* and the ramshackle *Yeomen of the Guard*. After them the deluge? But for the present the piece settled down to a run of over four hundred performances.

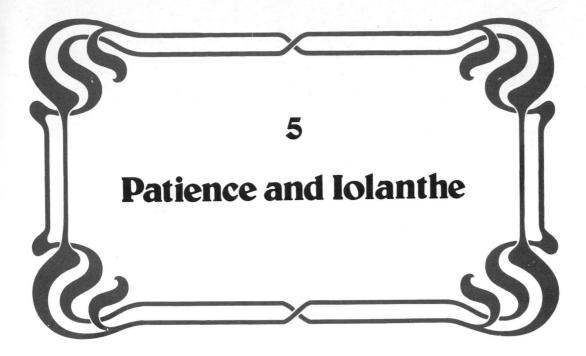

5

Patience and Iolanthe

Sullivan had no intention of neglecting his more serious music. In 1878 he had been elected a Royal Commissioner for the Paris Universal Exhibition, where they were holding a concert consisting solely of his works and those of other English composers – a signal recognition of the musical talent of 'the unmusical English'.

He now settled down to study the Scriptures in search of a subject for his Leeds Cantata, only to decide, each time he picked a passage, that other composers had read their Bible before him. Finally he settled on *The Martyr of Antioch*, a religious drama by Dean Milman of St Paul's. But since the passages were not written to be set to music, he invited Gilbert to work on it with him, so giving him an opportunity 'to prove himself to be a person of culture', as Gilbert himself was to say. The Cantata was a great success.

Gilbert, who had already tempted Sullivan with his idea for *Patience*, did not work with him on a serious subject again. But after the Festival, he wrote:

Dear Sullivan

It always seemed to me that my particularly humble services in connection with the Leeds Festival had received far more than their mead of acknowledgment in your preamble to the *libretti* – and it has certainly never occurred to me to look for any other reward than the honour of being associated, however remotely and unworthily, in a success which, I suppose, will endure until music itself shall die. Pray believe that of the many substantial advantages that have resulted to me from our association, this last is, and always will be, the most highly prized.

Gilbert then returned to his work on the libretto of *Patience*. Originally it was to have been based on his Bab Ballad 'The Rival Curates'.

'I don't feel happy about it,' he wrote to Sullivan. 'I mistrust the clerical element. I feel hampered by the restrictions which the nature of the subject places upon my freedom of action, and I want to revert to my old idea of rivalry between two aesthetic fanatics.'

After a meeting with his collaborator he changed the initial plot, and while Sullivan went swanning in Nice, Gilbert wrote doggedly on.

But, in his luggage, Sullivan had dropped in some songs on which to work. In his diary we find: 'The year 1881 opens when I am still at Nice having brought with me some numbers of the new opera G and I intend doing. I occasionally try to find a few ideas; among others I sketch Bunthorne's song "A good young man", but the sunshine and my natural indolence prevent my doing any really serious work. I enjoy myself doing nothing, with many visits to Monte Carlo.'

Oh, well-earned swanning!

The Gilbert and Sullivan method of collaboration [notes Reginald Allen] appears to have followed the following pattern: First the author described to the composer his idea for a plot, or read him the outline. Then, if Sullivan responded with enthusiasm, Gilbert wrote out a complete story line, without dialogue and without lyrics. Next, working painstakingly through trial and error on copybook pages, he roughed out his libretto, including the lyrics, which he sent to Sullivan for setting as fast as they were finished.

"WHEN ARTHUR FIRST AT COURT BEGAN"——
(*Old Nursery Song adapted to a Pinafore Air.*)

MR. ARTHUR SULLIVAN, MUS. DOC., IS A MASTER OF SCORING FOR AN
ORCHESTRA. AT LEEDS HE HAS JUST SCORED A BIG SUCCESS—
FOR HIMSELF.

A *Punch* cartoon of Sullivan, conducting from the
Duke of Edinburgh's violin case, 30 October 1880.

In an interview with the critic, William Archer, Gilbert explained:

The verse always preceded the music, or even any hint of it. Sometimes – very rarely – Sullivan would say of some song: 'My dear fellow, I can't make anything of this' and then I would re-write it entirely – never tinker at it. But, of course, I don't mean to say that I 'invented' all the rhythms in the operas. Often a rhythm might be suggested by some old tune or other, running in my head, and I would fit my words to it more or less exactly. When Sullivan knew I had done so, he would say: 'Don't tell me what the tune is or I shan't be able to get it out of my head.'

Of course, I plan out the whole stage-management [production] beforehand, on my model stage, with blocks three inches high to represent men, and two-and-a-half inches to represent women. I know exactly what groupings I want – how many people I can have on this bank, how many on that rostrum, and so forth. I have it all clear in my head before going down to the theatre; and there the actors and actresses are good enough to believe in me and to lend themselves heartily to all I require of them. You see I have the exact measure of their capabilities and take good care that the work I give them should be well within their grasp.

He was to say in an interview with Bram Stoker: 'I attribute our success in our particular craft to the fact that Arthur Sullivan and I were in a commanding position. We controlled the stage altogether, and were able to do as we wished, so far as the limitations of our actors would allow of it.'

Leslie Baily quotes a certain 'young good man', a messenger-boy who never looked back until he had become a Director of Chappell's, concerning the printing of the score of *Patience*:

I used to take the proofs with me, and catch a horse-bus to Victoria Street. Mr Sullivan worked in the semi-basement. The Butler would let me in. It was a plainly furnished room. There was a piano, but I don't recollect ever seeing Sullivan playing it. He wrote most of his music at his desk, smoking cigarettes and sipping weak gin-and-water. Very often he would say to me: 'Now you call back to-morrow morning, my boy, and I'll leave the MS with the Butler for you.' I knew this meant he was going to work through the night.

With a mind legally and syllabically trained, Gilbert was to deal in detail with every aspect of mounting the operas. And so, to leap ahead to 8 December 1901, after Sullivan's death, we find:

Dear Mrs Carte

It has occurred to me that it would be good to have *practicable* hands to the clock in Act 2 with *real* clockwork – (to be wound up every night before the act opens) and set to the actual hour of the night – say five minutes past ten (or whatever the hour may be), and let it move on through the act to ten minutes past eleven – or whatever the hour of finishing may be – showing always throughout the act the actual current hour. The clock wouldn't cost above £1 and could be wound up when the scene is lowered.

I think people would talk about it, and it would become a good advt.

Of course the clockwork should be *quite compact* and occupy as small a space as possible in the middle of the clock, so as not to obscure the transparency too much.

Yours very truly

W.S.Gilbert

Sullivan's account of his own effect on Gilbert's outlines was given to his first biographer, Arthur Lawrence:

The first thing I have to decide upon is the rhythm, and I arrange the rhythm before I come to the question of melody. . . . Five out of six treatments are commonplace and my first aim has always been to get as much originality as possible in the rhythm, approaching the question of melody afterwards. . . . It is only after I have decided the rhythm that I proceed to the notation. My first work – the jotting down of melodies – I term 'sketches'. They are hieroglyphics which, possibly, would seem undecipherable. It is my musical shorthand, and of course it means much to me. When I have finished these sketches the creative part of my work is completed.

This stage seems to have included the writing, re-writing and any other rehearsal alterations. After this 'a skeleton score' was achieved. This included all the vocal parts, and the rests for the orchestra, 'but without a note of accompaniment or instrumental work of any kind, although naturally I have all that in mind. Then the voice parts are written out by the copyist and the rehearsals begin. . . . It is not until the music has been thoroughly learned, and the rehearsals on the stage with the action and business are well advanced, that I begin orchestration.'

The libretto of *Patience* is a gentle – very gentle – satire upon Aesthetes, their *mores* and extravagances.

What was known as 'the Aesthetic Movement' was a reaction against the clutter that had become Victorian Art, its neo-Gothic shapes and shrill or deep hues. Morris, Pater, Ruskin, Rossetti, Whistler – we draw them haphazard out of the hat of time. And here comes the wittiest aesthete of all – Oscar Wilde with his velvet jacket and green carnation, a client of D'Oyly Carte's lecture agency who was to spread the gospel when Carte pulled the string, all over America, thus preparing the natives to receive *Patience* and to understand, if a little dimly in the backwoods, what it was all about. Max, the incomparable wit, writer and caricaturist, Max the irreverent, Max the irresistible, who had sketched the elderly, balding and enstomached Prince of Wales standing in the corner, sent there by the angered Queen Victoria, and lived – this accurate and definitive Max made a pale wash drawing of Oscar Wilde, a medieval lily to hand, lecturing to a gathering of embonpointish American businessmen, a harbinger of pleasure to come. There is no doubt that D'Oyly was a wily man.

Leslie Baily quotes a letter from D'Oyly Carte to Helen Lenoire, in America: 'There have been stupid paragraphs in *The Sporting Times*, one saying that I was sending Wilde out as a sandwich man for *Patience*, and another one afterwards saying that he was not going as "D'Oyly Carte found that he could get sandwich men in America with longer hair for half the money".'

A few weeks later, we find Carte writing to Sullivan: '. . . Inscrutable are the ways of the American public and absurd as it may appear, it seems that Oscar Wilde's advent here has caused a regular craze and given the business a fillip up.'

Yes, D'Oyly Carte was a very clever man.

But Aesthetism was in the Piccadilly air, and soon Gilbert was writing to James Albery:

I gather from the notices of your new piece ... that you have made good capital out of the affectations and eccentricities of the modern school of lily-bearing poets. By an odd coincidence, I have completed the greater part of the libretto of a two-act opera (designed six months ago) in which this preposterous School plays a very prominent part. I mention this as otherwise you might reasonably suppose, when the piece comes to be played, that it was in some way suggested by a successful character in your comedy.

Max Beerbohm's impression of Oscar Wilde lecturing on the aesthetic movement to an American audience during his tour of 1881.

Sullivan set off for Paris towards the end of January. He was still in a lazy mood, and did no work on the songs for *Patience*.

He dined at Bignon's on the Avenue de l'Opéra, saw *Divorçons*, at that moment 'the rage of Paris', and pronounced it 'deliciously funny'. Musical Society, seeing him in its midst, 'swept him into a round of gaiety'. On his return to London he had to spend many precious hours in the dessicated atmosphere of his solicitor's office about the lawsuit he, with Gilbert and D'Oyly Carte, was bringing against the Comedy Opera Company (Water-cart Bayly and his colleagues); and digesting Gilbert's new flight of fancy: '... The Hussars will become aesthetic young men (abandoning their profession for the purpose) – in this latter capacity they will all carry lilies in their hands, wear long hair and stand in stained glass attitudes.'

Sullivan did not attack *Patience*, in whatever form, with relish. Yet to the present writer the music seems inventive and musicianly. But then, it is often when work comes hard and has to be hewn out, that the result seems as light as kiss-the-hand. He would write a number or so and then leave them. It is probable that he rejoiced more over the success of *Antioch* than over gold-fingered *Patience* which ran for a year and a half.

Meanwhile the case against Water-cart and Co began on 10 March. All the stars were there, from Irving downwards. Our triumvirate won without calling a single witness. From then on, the Comedy Opera Company went into liquidation. Once litigation was sent flying out of the window, Sullivan went back to his songs. Ten days to score an opera.

April 20th 1881.
Rehearsal at 12, then home to write Tenor Song, afterwards cut out. [Oh, familiar routine!] Duke of Edinburgh came to see me, stayed while I wrote and dined. Went to the theatre at 7.30 to dress-rehearsal. Came home late. Second Tenor song and sketched-out Overture. To bed at 5.30 am. Finished all scoring of the Opera.

And a great relief to the poor gentleman that must have been.

His diary sweats it out with him: 'Crammed house at Opéra Comique. Enthusiastic reception on entering the Orchestra. New piece performed for first time. Went splendidly. Eight encores. Seemed a great success. Called at the Fielding for a lemon-and-soda. Talked a little to Randegger, John Hare etc.'

The Press on the whole was indulgent – even adulatory, though the *Era* did murmur: 'The new production was entitled *Patience* and patience the first-nighters had to have in full measure, as Act I ran an hour and forty minutes.'

Pending the arrival of Dr Sullivan in the conductor's chair [reported *The Sporting Times*], I gazed with furtive curiosity on my neighbours, and confess that the presence of so many representatives of the Good, the Beautiful and the True, filled me with surpassing awe. ... A fierce clamour of screams, yells and hisses which descended from the Gallery signalled the arrival of Mr Oscar Wilde himself. ... There, with the sacred daffodil ... stood the exponent of uncut hair ... Ajax-like defying the Gods.

The Sporting Life recorded: 'End of Act I. General enthusiasm for cigarettes and Chartreuse at the bar. Chorus of delight arises from the audience ... everyone goes about saying "Hey, Willow Waley, O". Nobody knows what this means. ...'

Bunthorne followed by the lovesick maidens; a scene from the first production of *Patience* at the Opera Comique in 1881.

The gentle satire opens with an Overture as expectant as one by Rossini, and at times strongly reminiscent of that Master of Overtures. The first chorus, the present writer thinks, shows Gilbert at his best:

> Twenty love-sick maidens we,
> Love-sick all against our Will.
> Twenty years hence we shall be,
> Twenty love-sick maidens still.

This is followed soon – and inevitably – by one of Gilbert's successful and popular list-songs:

> ... Take all the remarkable people in History
> Rattle them off to a popular tune [Gilbert's own recipe]
> The pluck of Lord Nelson on board of the Victory –
> Genius of Bismarck devising a plan. ...
> The humour of Fielding (which sounds contradictory)
> Coolness of Paget about to trepan.
> The science of Julien, the eminent Musico –
> Wit of Macaulay, who wrote of Queen Anne –
> The pathos of Paddy, as rendered by Boucicault –
> Style of the Bishop of Sodor and Man –
> The dash of a D'Orsay, divested of quackery –
> Narrative powers of Dickens and Thackeray –

> Victor Emmanuel – Peak-hunting Peveril –
> Thomas Aquinas and Doctor Sacheverell –
> Tupper and Tennyson – Daniel Defoe –
> Anthony Trollope and Mr Guizot! …

Almost it might be *The New Yorker*'s *Happy New Year* list.

But Gilbert falls unforgivably from grace with a wilful line showing the sheer effrontery of using the word lily, pronounced broadly as lil-eye to chime with shy or try or why.

And later, oh what another fall was there in a jingle ending, repetitively:

> Sing boo to you –
> Pooh pooh to you –

or

> Bah to you –
> Ha! Ha! to you.

One wonders the national bathroom ceiling does not go on strike. Fortunately for bathrooms country-wide Sullivan, yet again, was at hand to pull Gilbert's chestnuts out of the fire with an Offenbachlike, glittering treatment of the number.

Sullivan's treatment, too, of 'Twenty love-sick maidens we' is very musicianly and wooing, though here, as has been already suggested, Gilbert has minded his own chestnuts – not that it is a chestnut in the accepted second sense.

Again, Gilbert's

> Go breaking heart,
> Go dreaming love requited,

when one has made allowances for the sentimental Victorian phraseology, couples happily enough with Sullivan's drawing-room ballady music; and Sullivan's brassy treatment of 'When I first put this uniform on' has, at many a seaside or urban park bandstand, still proved itself a favourite of Kneller Hall.

Gilbert's persuasive

> Am I alone
> And unobserved? I am.
> Then let me own
> I'm an aesthetic sham,
> This air severe
> Is but a mere
> Veneer.
> This cynic smile
> Is but a wile
> Of guile.
> This costume chaste
> Is but good taste
> Misplaced!

seems to have snatched itself one of Herrick's rhythms, on which it sits charmingly. Not so Sullivan's rough chords, which mar the mood, as, much later on, his music marches foursquare through Gilbert's poetry in 'I might have had to die in June!' (*The Yeoman of the Guard*).

The present writer cannot rob others who, like herself, have a fondness for puns by failing to quote two lines of Gilbert's dialogue:

> *Bunthorne:* Do you ever yearn?
> *Patience:*   I (y)earn my living!

Patience is rich in bathroom ballads of which probably the most often heard floating down the stairs must surely be:

> Prithee pretty maiden will you tell me true
> Hey! but I'm doleful, willow willow waly!

in which the collaborators set one another off, as all good collaborators should.

The introduction to 'Let the merry cymbals sound' would have fitted well in 'The Maid of Arles', while 'O, list while we a love confess' has a delicate Bellini-like treatment.

But 'In the coming bye and bye' displays Gilbert's old grudge against the ageing woman which Sullivan was so fastidiously to deplore, with its

> Fading is the taper waist
> Shapeless grows the shapely limb,
> And although securely laced,
> Spreading is the figure trim!
> Stouter than I used to be,
> Still more corpulent grow I –
> There will be too much of me
> In the coming bye and bye!

Gilbert's allergy to ageing ladies may have sprung from some deep source in his own nature; that same source which had furnished him with his taste for the Edwardian nymph.

From Gilbert's sketchbook.

Gilbert's 'only recorded remark about matronly stoutness outside his writing is: "After all, she's quite nice, only I prefer a woman to be as long as she is broad."' (Baily: *The Gilbert and Sullivan Book*, 1952.)

Patience drew the town, and very soon it was apparent that no further collaboration would be needed for many months. 'Music, that most brutal of all mistresses', as once Sullivan had called it, was beginning to pay off – and pay off handsomely.

In June, the Duke of Edinburgh invited Sullivan and Fred Clay to go with him to St Petersburg, travelling in HMS *Hercules* to the Baltic. Sullivan declared that he would do no more work until Gilbert turned up trumps with a new piece, or until some Festival or other became so importunate for something not heard anywhere else, that he had to compose a work to silence them. But he had not been at sea two days before he was organising concerts and performing at them.

The *Hercules* put in at Copenhagen. The King of Denmark was a keen admirer of Sullivan's music, and apparently the Danish Court orchestra had everything that Sullivan had written 'with standing orders that Sullivan was to figure in the programme at Dinner at least once a week'.

A banquet was given to a hundred people at the Royal Hunting Box, just outside the city: 'The food and wine were without compare,' the music Sullivan's and the speeches of international cordiality:

'The King proposed Queen Victoria's health,' recorded Sullivan's diary, 'and the Duke of Edinburgh's in English. The Duke responded. The Band played "God Save the Queen", repeating each part, which caused some uncertainty about our sitting down.'

On to Kronstadt and an orgy of salute-firing, flag-lowering and all the pomp and circumstance of a Royal Occasion – oh princely swanning!

In a letter to Mamma, Arthur wrote:

This morning we started at nine and went to the Winter Palace to hear the famous Imperial Chapel Choir who were all in full dress – scarlet and gold – waiting for us. The Duke said to me: 'Doesn't it remind you of when you were in the Chapel Royal?' and it did. There were about 80 and, blasé as I am with music, I confess to a new sensation at hearing them. It's like nothing else. ... The Emperor and Empress came on board [the next day] and Oh! my stars! wasn't it splendid to see the yards all manned and the guns all firing Royal Salutes! Then we weighed anchor and here we are in a thick black fog – all the signals going like Blackwater Fair, guns, steam-whistles and bell-buoys. – If we don't all run each other down we shall arrive at Kiel on Thursday.

At Kiel they were entertained by Prince Wilhelm (later Kaiser Wilhelm II) and Prince Henry of Prussia.

'When I got into the carriage,' wrote Sullivan in his diary, 'Prince William bowed to me and sang: "He polished up the handle of the big front door." I burst out laughing and so did every one. It was too funny.'

D'Oyly Carte, whose foresight, cleverness and courage the present writer salutes, had for some time now been dreaming of a newer, larger theatre, and on 10 October 1881 he opened the Savoy in the Strand with a new production of *Patience*. The first night was memorable for D'Oyly Carte's success with electric lighting, used in a theatre for the first time. *The Chronicle* describes the scene:

... Ere the overture to *Patience* commenced, the curtain was parted, and Mr D'Oyly Carte stepped in front of the footlights to make a short explanation. He said that for that night at least, the front of the house only would be illuminated by the electric light, and that this was a mere experiment. ... The experiment might fail, the lamps might go out, but one gas light would be left burning, and, if necessary, the theatre could be at once lighted. ...

The entrance to the newly-built Savoy Theatre, on the Embankment, 1881.

D'Oyly Carte made his exit to 'encouraging applause' leaving behind him 'a feeling of curiosity as to whether the electric light would really be found to work. The sun burner was then lowered, and all eyes were turned towards the pear-shaped lamps. ... As if by the wave of a fairy's wand [Iolanthe's?] the theatre immediately became filled with a soft soothing light, clearer and far more grateful than gas ... the audience gave a cheer. ...' It seems, to the present writer, a remarkable oversight that no one present sang 'Lead Kindly Light'.

Let Sullivan's diary take us through the electrifying event:

October 10th (Monday) 1881. Rehearsal at Savoy at 11. Lasted till 4.30. Lady K. Coke, Mrs R (Ronalds) etc were there. Came home, LW (Little Woman – Sullivan's frequent name for Mrs Ronalds) tea. Dined at home with Smythe [Sullivan's secretary]. Went to conduct first performance of *Patience* in the new Theatre. Great house – enthusiastic reception for all. Went back to sup at Gilbert's – returned home 3 am., changed my clothes – had coffee and drove to Liverpool Street Station to take 5.10 am train to Norwich.

And from our own century floats the refrain: 'Little man you've had a busy day'.

'19th October, Wednesday. Gilbert came, sketched out an idea for a new piece. Lord Chancellor, Commander in Chief, Peers, Fairies, etc, funny, but at present vague.'

Over a year was to pass before *Iolanthe* would be needed.

Sullivan was not in a giving mood. He was busying himself moving into Queen Anne's

A programme for the transfer of *Patience* to the Savoy. The light bulbs symbolise D'Oyly Carte's introduction of electric lighting in the theatre.

Mansions, Victoria Street, which was to be his final home. The move accomplished to his satisfaction, off he went to Egypt, arriving at Port Said on 31 December. The old year went out: the New Year came in. Sullivan welcomed it with a restless, sleepless night. The Casino next to his hotel had an energetic orchestra of German girls who played with a vigour that drove Sullivan straight way out of the town and on to Cairo. 'How I do wish letter-writing was made a crime punishable by death,' he wrote home.

Tell my dear old friend that I am *not* writing an Egyptian Symphony at present, but as soon as I can get an orchestra in London of 'Kanouns', 'Neis', 'Uts', etc with really good players I will see about it.

Egypt held his interest for three months: 'Every day I see something fresh,' he wrote. 'A mosque, an old house, or a bit of characteristic life. . . . I sigh for the good old days of the late Khedive Ismael, who spent money regally [and borrowed it freely, too!], ruined the country, but made the fortunes of his friends and favourites.'

There was some not too bad swanning in Cairo, too. Princes, Pashas, Ambassadors, Financiers and Government Ministers. He made breezy notes in his diary: 'Dined at Blum Pasha's. . . . Took in Miss G (plain and 40) to dinner. Saw the ugliest woman I ever set eyes on – a Miss O – from Hamburg. Left early.'

Almost he might have been Gilbert!

The opening night of *Patience* at the Savoy in 1881, with the exciting lighting at full power.

Gilbert was supervising the building of his new house in Harrington Gardens, South Kensington, while Sullivan was conducting an amateur orchestra in Alexandria, 'very fair, reflecting great credit on their conductor, a successful rag and bone merchant' and sending dearest Mamma colourful little vignettes from the East.

Sullivan returned to London in the middle of April to settle into his new home. But fate was waiting in the wings. Three days after his fortieth birthday (13 May) his dearly loved mother, who had called to see him, felt ill. She went on with her son to a luncheon. But she left the meal unfinished and went back to Fulham and bed.

For two days it was touch and go for the poor, faithful, unselfish and bewildered lady. It is a law of life that if it is hard to be a genius, how very hard it is on the good people surrounding the genius! Then the mother rallied, and the doctors, poor fallible gentlemen, pronounced the danger to be over. Sullivan had been flung into 'a frenzy of anxiety'. 'He remained hour after hour in Fulham and slept – when he could sleep – on the drawing-room sofa. The third night he sat through the hours till dawn, unable to close his eyes. He was numb with fear. The announcement that all danger was past left him inert and stupified.' He returned to Victoria Street. But the next day Sullivan's man, Silva, whom he had sent over to Fulham to see if all was well, came back with news of a sudden relapse. Sullivan hastened to her bed-side. He could see she was sinking. He returned from Fulham at four in the morning. At 8.15 his niece Amy roused him with an urgent summons to return to Fulham at once. 'I knew the worst was at hand if not already over. . . . I was at Fulham before 9. I rushed upstairs and was alone in the room – alone, that is, with dear Mother's lifeless body – her soul had gone to God.'

Sullivan's entry for 1 June 1882 in his diary, reads poignantly: 'Home feeling dreadfully lonely.'

But on 3 June work the infallible, work the one comforter, took him, of its mercy, in stride. Sullivan started one of the most musical of his, as it were, musicals, of which *Punch*, always the most severe of Gilbert's critics, on Ibsen's principle of 'slappings and lullabies', was to say: 'As a musical or dramatic work *Iolanthe* is not within a mile of *Pinafore* or a patch on *Patience*.'

For Sullivan it spelled hard going. He would work half through the night and tear up what he had written in the morning. He was also deeply absorbed in family affairs. His brother Frederic's widow and children were now totally on his hands creating him 'a father by proxy' and in addition to providing for them, he now decided to adopt his nephew Herbert Sullivan, so who has a better title to be his biographer than Sullivan, and his co-biographer Flower? From this decision sprang a companionship 'unspoiled and unbroken. If the composer were out late at night it was the nephew who would wait up for him till the familiar whistle sounded outside the window, and an equally familiar whistle answered it. If the nephew were out late, it was Sullivan who sat up, busy scoring with a J pen, till he heard the familiar whistle . . . and gave reply.'

Then there was his good friend Mrs Ronalds, known to Sullivan's diary as Mrs R or LW – Little Woman. With the death of Sullivan's mother her role was to become more important.

'10th June 1882. LW came at $\frac{1}{4}$ to 3 to lunch, stayed till 5.45.' This, it will be seen, was a few days after Maria Sullivan's death.

Iolanthe progressed slowly but at the Savoy Theatre *Patience* was still holding its own. Not so Gilbert and Sullivan, for the pirates had got to grappling point in America and *Patience* was being played in numerous theatres; its score published by many publishers and the last people to earn money from these infringements were the original creators.

Sullivan met Gilbert and D'Oyly Carte in secret conference and it was decided to give *Iolanthe* a simultaneous opening in London and New York. And for the purposes of rehearsal they would call *Iolanthe*, *Periola*. They agreed, moreover, that Gilbert and Sullivan should receive £1,750 a year each for the 'country and colonial' rights for five years. A good meeting then. So *Periola* she was, up to the morning of the dress rehearsal, still some months ahead. On this occasion the company complained bitterly that they would never remember the new name at such short notice.

'Never mind that,' said Sullivan, 'so long as you sing the music. Use any name that comes to you. Nobody in the audience will be any the wiser except Mr Gilbert, and he won't be there.' Gilbert, says Pearson, cannot have been there when Sullivan delivered this advice.

This assumption was belied, for subsequently we hear of Gilbert's exasperated shout at this same rehearsal to the chorus of The House of Lords: 'For heaven's sake,' he bellowed, 'wear your coronets as though you were used to them.'

The Liberal Party, under Gladstone, had come to power, and just as in *Patience* the collaborators satirised the aesthetes, in *Iolanthe* they took as target the already beginning-to-be-outmoded House of Lords.

Twenty-seven years later the Liberal Party were again campaigning against the House of Lords. Gilbert wrote sharply: 'I cannot permit the verses from *Iolanthe* to be used for electioneering purposes. They do not at all express my own views. They are supposed to be those of the wrong-headed donkey who sings them.'

Towards the end of 1882, added to the strain of grief and of preparing a new work for its premiere, Sullivan was undergoing financial chaos, and a chaos that was none of his making. He had earned a great deal of money in the last few years, and had appointed E.A.Hall as his stockbroker. On 2 October 1882 Sullivan received a note from Hall that made him somewhat apprehensive: 'You shall have your account in a day or two ... the ledger:keeper has mixed up 20,000 dollars of N.Y. Penn and Ohio first Mort. Bonds which I bought a long time ago.'

Two days later Sullivan's mind was put at rest, for the time being. His securities, Hall said, being worth more than £6,000. But on 25 November, the night when Sullivan had to conduct the opening performance of *Iolanthe* at the Savoy, a letter from Edward Hall was delivered to him by special messenger.

My dear Arthur

Perhaps you have learned by this time I am hopelessly [messed?] and that you must for the present look upon your money as lost. God knows how it will all end but I have seen it coming for ages.

Thank God my friends stick to me and believe me honest. I am afraid Cooper [his partner] is not all that we have always thought him. I have been weak and he has exerted a fatal influence and power over me. My mother and family are awfully kind though they have suffered cruelly. Come and see me, my dear boy, though I feel you will hate me.

Sullivan, recovering from the strain of *Iolanthe*, replied next day 'in a more considerate tone than many others would have under similar circumstances':

My dear Edward

I am deeply grieved at the terrible news which I learned first from your letter yesterday. I of course knew from what you had told me that you were passing through critical times, but I did not anticipate such a speedy and lamentable end. As a friend, and one to whom I am so much attached, you have my deepest sympathy, for I know what you must have been suffering.

One question I must ask you. When you speak of my money being lost, do you refer to money I have lent you alone, or to securities of mine which you hold? Money I have lent you would probably include the Galveston and Harrisburg securities. Before I can talk the matter over, I must know this. Send me a line at once, and I will try and see you tomorrow, my poor boy.

One thing I must ask you to do without delay – that is to send me back the securities you hold of mine, or tell me where to send for them. The Galveston and Harrisburg Securities are, I suppose, gone with the thousand pounds. . . .

But back to the genesis of *Iolanthe*.

Dr Sullivan featured in 'Days with Celebrities', from *Moonshine* 1882.

Sullivan was not happy with Act I. He arranged to meet Gilbert in the coffee-room of the Half-Moon Hotel at Exeter, as a kind of half-way house, since Gilbert was yachting. They ate ham and eggs at one o'clock and sat on all through the afternoon, reconstructing the act in the coffee-room, speaking all the time in elaborate whispers as though their ordinary day-to-day voices would be overheard by pirates in America, or their spies in London. So greatly had the habit of secrecy grown on Gilbert that in 1884 – two years on from the whispered planning in the Exeter coffee-room – he arranged, or attempted to arrange, a code for communication between the Savoy Theatre box office and himself.

The collaborators ordered dinner and shared a cab to the station in time for Sullivan to catch the London train. Gilbert had handed over Act II to his partner and Sullivan proceeded to the Beefsteak Club.

Sullivan, a great Club-man, loved the Beefsteak. He usually supped there. Prince Christian had proposed him for the Marlborough Club the year before, and, with the Duke of Edinburgh to second him, he was accepted.

He attended rehearsals at the Savoy and composed more numbers, or scored them, until five or six in the morning, actually rehearsing them two days later – a routine familiar to any composer of a musical but which always seems to astonish the layman. He assured D'Oyly Carte that the music would be ready before the boat that was to carry it to America, and it was – in spite of attendant kidney trouble that lurked waiting to strike.

November 5: Sunday. Tried to write new duet No 5 ['None shall part us from each other'] – but failed. Walked out at 5. Began duet again at 1 am [Oh, that amazing and perpetual self-discipline!] composed and scored it. Finished at 4.10 am.

November 7th: Brighton. Conducted performance of the Martyrs in the evening. Albani, Trebelli (who sang abominably). . . .

Now only the Overture remained. 'The Overture', Sullivan himself said in an interview in *Home News* seven years later, was: 'a quick bit of work, and there was a lot of fresh writing in it, too. I daresay you will recollect the *Captain Shaw* motiv combined with those florid passages for the woodwind.' I daresay.

On 7 November he rehearsed all day, was present for the last performance of *Patience* in the evening, then went back to his home and worked on the Overture until 7 am. Surely enough to exhaust a far stronger man. 'He rehearsed the full company for the last time before the first night until 1.30 am' and then shared a relaxing supper with Tom Chappell, friend and publisher, at Rules, in Maiden Lane. No one knew when he stepped onto the rostrum to conduct the first performance of *Iolanthe* or *The Peer and the Peri*, of the note that he had read just before setting out: his broker had gone bankrupt and had lost Sullivan's savings, £7,000. The entry in the diary was brief and to the point:

November 25th. Saturday. First performance of *Iolanthe* at the Savoy Theatre. House crammed. Awfully nervous, more so than usual on going into Orchestra. Tremendous reception. First Act went splendidly. The second dragged, and I was afraid it must be compressed. However it finished well, and Gilbert and myself were called and heartily cheered. Very low afterwards. Came home.

Five hours later (the difference between British and American time) *Iolanthe* was opening in New York.

Sullivan and Flower tell a charming story:

Early in the run Sullivan's fur-lined overcoat disappeared from the green-room. Clearly it had been stolen. At the end of the week one of the dressers called at Victoria Street. He stood there, looking very wretched as he tried to find the words to tell Sullivan that he had stolen the coat. His wife had just given birth to their seventh son (almost it might have been a Russian folk-tale) and he had pawned the overcoat for £2 to pay the doctor. He held out the pawn ticket. Sullivan put his hand in his pocket and pulled out a fiver. 'I'm sorry you're in trouble,' he said. 'But as it happens I'm in need of that coat now the cold weather has set in. Here's £5. Go and get the coat out of pawn and keep the change to buy something for your wife and baby. And for heaven's sake don't say you're sorry again.'

But to return to the first night of *Iolanthe*:

'The Savoy Theatre, lighted like no other theatre in Europe,' gloated the *Era*.

'In the presence of one of the most brilliant audiences ever attracted to the theatre,' swooned the *People*.

Clearly all the Swans in the Swannery had assembled by Savoy Hill to do honour to one of their number.

A caricature by E. J. Wheeler of D'Oyly Carte with Sullivan and Gilbert from *Punch*, 1882. Not the first time that cartoonists had fantasised Sullivan in feminine dress.

RIGHT Music cover for the Iolanthe Lancers.

But if the first night audience was ecstatic, the Press was – for a Gilbert and Sullivan Press that is – slightly ambivalent. *The Times* said: 'The public once more were indebted to their favourites for an evening of genuine, healthy, albeit not supremely intellectual enjoyment'; words, says Reginald Allen, 'as unlikely to promote a comic opera of the Eighties as they would a musical of today'.

'Same set of puppets as Mr Gilbert has dressed over and over before,' snapped the *Echo*, acutely. Could the critics be beginning to be aware already of the technical rut, the dangers of which the present writer has pointed out already?

On the other hand: 'The composer has risen to his opportunity.' *The Daily Telegraph*. *Bell's Life* attacked Gilbert:

It seems to me that he starts primarily with the object of bringing Truth and Love and Friendship into contempt; just as we are taught the Devil does. ... I have much pleasure in bidding adieu to Mr Gilbert's unwholesome feeling and in calling the attention of my readers to an interesting exhibition of pictures of Venice now on view at the rooms of the Fine Art Society, New Bond Street.

Gilbert and D'Oyly Carte, bent on making the most of the new wonder – they called it '*la Fée Electrique*' in Paris – summoned to their stage 'self-lighting fairies' – instant we would call them these days, 'with electricity stored somewhere about their backs. ... In the Second Act the Fairy Queen and her three chief attendants wear each an Electric Star in their hair. The effect of this brilliant spark of electricity is wonderful.' *The Advertiser*.

'Too dazzling to be pleasant,' growled *Lloyd*'s, 'and in a dark scene obscures the face.' This, we have noticed.

The Savoy's primitive lighting, compared to our own sophisticated streams and lakes of light, prevented a true dimming of the house lights during a performance, and the audience could follow their libretto texts. Clement Scott, reviewing the opening night for *The Illustrated London News*, remarked: 'The whole audience was plunged into the mysteries of the libretto, and when the time came for the turning-over of the leaves of the book, there was such a rustling as is only equalled when musicians are following a score at an Oratorio.'

The first thing to be seen in any analysis is that *Iolanthe* is a closely integrated work wherein both Gilbert and Sullivan are writing at their best in the *genre*. Gilbert's satire, here, is well-honed, and his invention fresh and unflagging; Sullivan's orchestration, at all times masterly, gives the wealth of fluent melodic ideas its particular brilliance.

From the outset one has the feeling that not only are this blessed pair of Sirens very much aware of what they are doing but also each knows what the other is up to – an excellent thing in collaborators, so that the work glitters like a brilliantly cut diamond.

Whatever one may feel about the sun-dappled lake that is Sullivan's music, reflecting what he most admires in the music of Mendelssohn and others, in the Overture there is a brooding passage that is sheer Adolphe Adam, and none the worse for that; who could contradict Sullivan's resonant, flowing or spiced, and exact orchestral effects? To listen attentively to them is to fit pieces in an aural jig-saw.

The opening chorus of fairies with its dotted crotchets sets the creators off in perfect

RIGHT Illustrated music cover from *The Pirates*.
OVERLEAF This design by Alice Havers won first prize in a Christmas card competition in 1882. Gilbert later used it as a programme for a private performance of the second act of Patience at his home in Harrington Gardens.

A DREAM

OF PATIENCE

PATIENCE QUADRILLE

By

CHARLES D'ALBERT.

LONDON CHAPPELL & Cº 50 NEW BOND STREET W.
CITY BRANCH 14 & 15 POULTRY.
Pr 4/-

HANHART LITH

ENT. STA. HALL

dressage as it were. Certainly it finds Gilbert in splendid pizzicato prosody:

> Tripping hither, tripping thither
> Nobody knows why or wither

is a prime Gilbertian throw-away.

There are some who maintain that Gilbert and Sullivan are at their best in their 'serious' songs in the operas (as though every song were not a heart-searchingly serious affair, even, and indeed particularly, in the uproarious list-songs, where they seem only to be word-searching, and oh, what a search is there!). Certainly here, in *Iolanthe*, there is a most persuasive argument in their favour in:

> Thou the tree and I the flower –
> Thou the idol, I the throng,
> Thou the day, and I the hour
> Thou the singer, I the song.

Gilbert's habitual and arguably permanent disenchantment with elderly ladies of *embonpoint* is deployed in his treatment of the plump, short-sighted Fairy Queen, stabbing home barbs in a burst of dialogue.

Fairy Queen: 'Love her? What was your love to mine? Why, she was invaluable to me! Who taught me,' asks the portly fairy, 'to curl myself inside a buttercup? Iolanthe!'

Alice Barnett as the Fairy Queen in the first production of *Iolanthe*, 1882 (see costume design on page 228).

LEFT Illustrated music cover of the 'Patience Quadrille'.

Sullivan proves himself to be a true godson of Kneller Hall, as it were, in the most closely integrated song in the piece and arguably in the whole *genre* with 'Loudly let the trumpets bray', and its clashed out and resounding 'Tantantara! Tzing! Boom!' often repeated, of the scarlet-trained procession of the Peers. I doubt a closer partnership can be found as an exercise in collaboration.

One of my own favourite reflections in *Iolanthe* occurs in a lyric:

> Spurn not the nobly born
> With love affected,
> Nor treat with virtuous scorn
> The well-connected.
> High rank involves no shame –
> We boast an equal claim
> With him of humble name
> To be respected. . . .
> Hearts just as pure and fair
> May beat in Belgrave Square.

Particularly light and Herrick-like is the duet: 'In vain to us you plead':

> It's true we sigh
> But don't suppose
> A tearful eye
> Forgiveness shows,
> Oh no!
> We're very cross indeed –
> Don't go.

It is as though Gilbert throws and Sullivan catches, or like a game of battledore and shuttlecock played in sempiternal sunlight.

And touching it is to think back to a London through which the horse-drawn fire-machines gallop and clatter, a London where every Londoner can be counted on to know the name of the Fire Chief, 'Oh, Captain Shaw!'

Those were the brave days of golden prophecy, and no one more eager to salute them than Gilbert and Sullivan – in their own wayward way:

> And while the House of Peers withholds
> Its legislative hand
> And noble statesmen do not itch
> To interfere in matters which
> They do not understand
> As bright will shine Great Britain's ways
> As in King George's glorious days.

And we are left amidst strike and aftermath to console ourselves with the reflection: *tout lasse, tout casse, tout passe.*

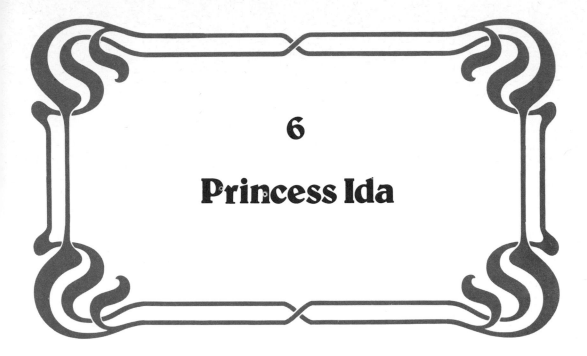

6

Princess Ida

Iolanthe had barely been running for a week when Gladstone went to see it at Sullivan's invitation.

Evidently, Gilbert's satirical attitude to the House of Lords enchanted him:

10 Downing Street
December 6th 1882

My dear Sir

Though I am very sorry that your kind wish to bring me to the Savoy Theatre on Monday should have entailed on you so much trouble, I must thankfully acknowledge the great pleasure which the entertainment gave me. Nothing, I thought, could be happier than the manner in which the comic strain of the piece was blended with its harmonies of sight and sound, so good in taste and so admirable in execution from beginning to end.

I remain, my dear Sir

Faithfully yours

W.E.Gladstone

Six months later Gladstone was writing to Sullivan again:

10 Downing Street
May 3 '83

Dear Mr Sullivan

I have the pleasure to inform you that I am permitted by Her Majesty to propose that you should receive the honour of Knighthood in recognition of your distinguished talents as a composer, and of the services which you have rendered to the promotion of the Art of Music generally in this country.

At the end of that April Sullivan had attended a dinner given by Alfred Rothschild to the Prince of Wales. During the evening the Prince went over to Sullivan, shook hands and said: 'I congratulate you on the great honour we have in store for you.' Sullivan, they say, thought he knew precisely what the Prince had in mind: 'I suppose he meant he is going to place me on the Council of the Royal College of Music,' he wrote in his diary, with misplaced modesty. When the occasion came, the three old friends, Sullivan, Grove and Macfarlane, went down to Windsor together to receive the knighthood at Victoria's hands.

Early in 1883 Gilbert and Sullivan got down to work on a new subject: *Princess Ida*, or *Castle Adamant*, A Respectful Operatic Per-Version of Tennyson's Princess. Or rather Gilbert had got down to writing his outline; and Sullivan had snatched time from delicious swanning to consider it, and considering, too, the offer from Thos. E. Dawes of Victoria Street, which 'respectfully undertook' to supply 'a double Brougham or Victoria Carriage (when you are not using your own Brougham), with Horse, Harness, and Coachman at any time you may require it ... for £20'.

The Princess was, as it so happened, an old friend of Gilbert's. He had first adapted it for the stage in 1870 without success; he now proposed to recast Tennyson's poem as a Savoy Opera.

Sullivan's diary noted: 'February 8th: Went to Stanley's office to meet Carte and Gilbert and signed agreement for five years. Drove Gilbert to Savoy (had a slight breeze and explanation *en route*) and read first Act (or Prologue) of *The Princess*.'

And on 31 July: 'Like the piece as now shaped very much.'

To listen to a play by telephone was a novelty – in fact the first time such an event took place was on Sullivan's forty-first birthday on 13 May 1883 when, having installed a direct line through from Victoria Street to the Savoy, he gave a celebratory dinner party and sprang the surprise on his guests. The Prince of Wales was present, and so, of course, was the Duke of Edinburgh ('A Triumph, dear boy, a Triumph!'). Madame Albani and Tosti took part in the musical programme that preceded the *coup-de-téléphone*. 'Never', the Prince declared, as he presented him with an enamel match-box, 'has Sullivan given a more successful dinner.'

But now came the *pièce de résistance*. Sullivan had arranged secretly for the Savoy Theatre company to go to the theatre (it was Whit Sunday) to sing selections from *Iolanthe* so that the guests who graced his birthday dinner could adjourn from the table and listen at ease to the entertainment offered in another part of the town. One can see the short and by this time plump gentleman secretly watching the clock. At 11.15 he rang the Savoy, and the Prince of Wales, sitting back in his armchair, heard the play from a distance, which must have intrigued him greatly.

It was the year of Gilbert's move to the new house he had built in Kensington; an oasis of luxury. Thickly moulded ceilings crowned the rooms. Richly embossed wall-papers were hung where no oaken panels obtained. Some of the windows were of stained glass. More useful additions were electric light – by no means taken for granted in 1883 – central heating, a telephone and 'a bathroom on each floor'.

All this afforded its owner with several opportunities for icy dissent. 'Several tart letters were sent to one firm who supplied a dado and a chimney-piece.'

LEFT Sir Arthur Sullivan in middle age.

The hall of Gilbert's house at 20 Harrington Gardens in 1884.

The preparation for *Princess Ida* provoked more friction than usual, says Hesketh Pearson, possibly, he hazards, because the blank verse irritated the actors:

'Look here, Sir, I will *not* be bullied! I know my lines!'

'That may be, but you don't know mine!'

It was too easy.

Meanwhile Sullivan had spent two or three days at Leeds, rehearsing for the Festival.

'Only heard five trifling errors', reports his diary after the performance. 'Three wrong notes by the Band, and two entries missed, also by the Band, inaudible and unknown by anyone but myself. . . .'

But the rest of that autumn he reserved for composing *Princess Ida*.

Early in the rehearsal period Sullivan was very much put out by a singer who would not conform to his wishes about a song:

'Mrs Blank,' he said in a pained voice, laying down his baton, 'There is something radically wrong with this song; either you do not understand it, or I don't.'

'I think *I* understand it,' said the singer.

'Perhaps you do,' said Sullivan, deceptively genial. 'That's the worst of being a composer. One always begins at the wrong end of the stick. In future I shall start at the other end. I'll get you to sing my songs first, then I'll compose them after.'

There was an awful silence.

Too easy.

Princess Ida opened on 5 January 1884 at the Savoy. Sullivan, who had been increasingly ill under the pressures of rehearsal, collapsed and had to be given morphine to get him through the ordeal of conducting the first performance:

Gilbert's ironic sketches of his wife viewing her hardworking haymakers in the grounds of Breakspears, a house at Uxbridge which he rented for the summer months.

127

Saturday January 5th 1884: Resolved to conduct the first performance of the opera *Princess Ida* at night, but from the state I was in it seemed hopeless. At 7 pm had another strong hypodermic injection [almost he might have been Sherlock Holmes] to ease the pain, and a strong cup of black coffee to keep me awake. Managed to get up and dress, and drove to the Theatre more dead than alive – went into the orchestra at 8.10. Tremendous house – usual reception. [How blasé can you get?] Very fine performance – not a hitch. Brilliant success. After the performance I turned very faint and could not stand.

He was taken home to bed by nephew Herbert and his old friend and colleague Frank Cellier.

A mixed Press greeted *Princess Ida*. Instead of an Overture the opera began with a short orchestral Prelude – and why not? If Rossini could do it, why then, so could

'First Nighters' at *Princess Ida*, from *The Illustrated Sporting and Dramatic News*, 12 January 1884.

Sullivan. Then the curtains parted on the first of three sets which Beatty-Kingston (*Theatre*) declared were 'among the most beautiful pictures ever exhibited on any stage'. *The Sportsman* however, dipped its 'Esther Brook Relief nib' in acid: 'The girls were dressed with a quaint richness, suggesting Portia after a visit to Swan and Edgar's.' The *Observer* found the opera too long. 'The Prologue, however, which is brief and to the point, is full of spirit.'

Gilbert, growing careless, or possibly forgetful, failed to test the sight-lines of the Gods who, to their somewhat raucous delight, saw clearly the mechanics of stage make-believe when Princess Ida fell into a stream to be rescued by Hilarion. Strange, incidentally, that this found no reflection in Sullivan's diary.

Figaro, keen eyed and alert to other people's faults as ever, found it dragged 'and is from every point of view the weakest'.

On the whole Sullivan fared better at the hands of Press and public than Gilbert, whose libretto placed the public idol, Tennyson, at risk.

From an article signed EY (drama critic Edmund Yates) – 'It was a desperately dull performance ... there were not three and a half jokes worth remembering throughout three and a half hours' misery. ... We are always hearing of Mr Gilbert's wonderful stage management but the tumble of the Princess and her rescue from drowning were so ludicrously mismanaged as to evoke hisses and laughter.'

But from an article signed LE (music critic Louis Engel) '... The rehearsing at this theatre is so conscientious that there is never a hitch in the performance.' To disagree within the same issue must be the prerogative of a free Press, one supposes.

'The success of the opera was never for a moment in doubt last night, and Sir Arthur Sullivan's music, while more ambitious in many of its elements than in his other comic operas, seems sure of gaining speedy popularity ...' – *The Observer*.

Allen tells a nice story of Gilbert:

Contrary to his custom, which was not to remain in the Theatre on a first night, he was sitting in the green-room reading a paper during the last act:

... when this gentleman, who had come over from Paris to enjoy the effect of his armour [it was supplied by a Paris armourer] broke in upon me in a state of wild delight: '*Mais savez vous, Monsieur, que vous avez là un succès solide?*' I replied that the piece seemed to be going quite well. '*Mais vous êtes si calme*' he exclaimed with a look of unbounded astonishment. I suppose he expected to see me kissing all the carpenters!

Paradoxically, I would say that though the general consensus of critical opinion points to Sullivan as the saviour of *Princess Ida* (*Love's Labours Lost* seen through Victorian lenses), it seems to me that Gilbert saves the day with wit and poetry – not, I might add, what I had expected to find, by any means.

Very early in the prologue Gilbert sets a gently humorous tone with Hilarion's charming résumé 'Twenty Years Ago' – a quiet charm that Sullivan carries into his music:

> Ida was a twelvemonth old,
> Twenty years ago!
> I was twice her age, I'm told,
> Twenty years ago!
> Husband twice as old as wife
> Argues ill for married life.
> Baleful prophecies were rife,
> Twenty years ago.
>
> Still I was a tiny Prince,
> Twenty years ago:
> She has gained upon me, since
> Twenty years ago.

Though she's twenty-one, it's true,
I am barely twenty-two –
False and foolish prophets you,
Twenty years ago!

The song foreshadows the gentle humour which plays, like errant sunshine, over the piece.

Soon, we are arrested by King Gama's list song:

I love my fellow creatures – I do all the good I can
Yet everybody says I am a disagreeable man!
And I can't think why!

Here Gilbert might have been writing his own epitaph.

Still in the Prologue we progress to one of the most effective songs in the piece if not in the collaboration:

For a month to dwell
In a dungeon cell;
Growing thin and wizen
In a solitary prison,
Is a poor look-out
For a soldier stout,
Who is longing for the rattle
Of a complicated battle –
For the rum–tum–tum
Of the military drum
And the guns that go boom! boom!

In Act I we come upon a Quartette with strange, somehow unexpected rhythms which might not have put to shame Herrick, Lovelace, T.E. Brown, even Marvell:

The world is but a
broken toy,
Its pleasures hollow –
false its joy,
Unreal its loveliest
hue
Alas!
Its pains alone are true!

Granted iambic pentameter is not the punchiest form of dialogue, what pleasure to come upon the beauty of such broken yet flowing lines as in this number. Over and over again Gilbert shows a mastery of rhythm in the lyrics of this piece though Sullivan, for once, perhaps by reason of increasing illness, or just ordinary fatigue, fails to match invention with invention.

Again we are given a glimpse of Gilbert's way with words, this time making his points with wit:

> ... For I'm a peppery Potentate,
> Who's little inclined his claim to bate,
> To fit the wit of a bit of a chit,
> And that's the long and short of it.

Coming to Act II we come, also, upon another lyric with the echo of Time in it·

> I built upon a rock,
> But ere Destruction's hand
> Dealt equal lot
> To Court and cot,
> My rock had turned to sand!
> I leaned upon an oak,
> But in the hour of need,
> Alack-a-day,
> My trusted stay
> Was but a bruisèd reed!
> Ah, faithless rock,
> My simple faith to mock!
> Ah, trait'rous oak,
> Thy worthlessness to cloak.

By now one has come to look upon King Gama as Gilbert's worser self and his song 'Whene'er I poke', in Act II, does nothing to dispel the illusion:

> Whene'er I poke
> Sarcastic joke
> Replete with malice spiteful,
> This people mild
> Politely smiled,
> And voted me delightful!
>
> Now when a wight
> Sits up all night
> Ill-natured jokes devising,
> And all his wiles
> Are met with smiles,
> It's hard, there's no disguising!

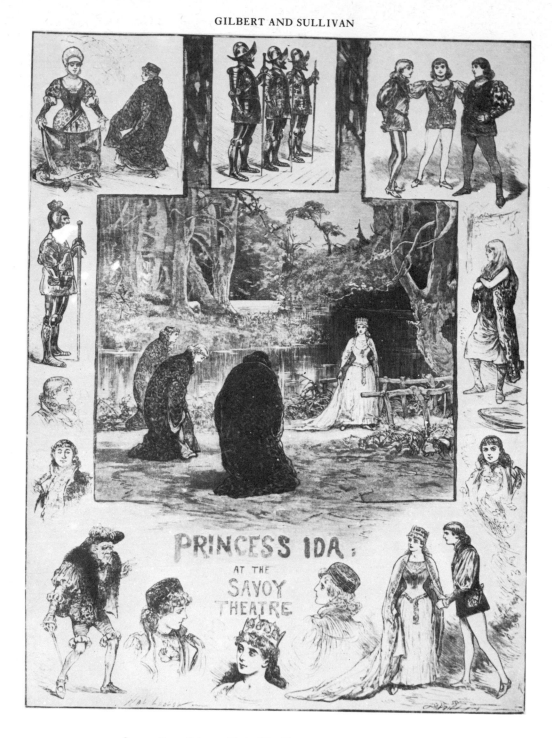

Scenes from *Princess Ida* in *The Illustrated London News*, 1884.

O, don't the days seem lank and long
When all goes right and nothing goes wrong,
And isn't your life extremely flat
With nothing whatever to grumble at!

I offered gold
In sums untold
To all who'd contradict me –
I said I'd pay
A pound a day
To any one who kicked me –
I bribed with toys
Great vulgar boys
To utter something spiteful,
But, bless you, no!
They *would* be so
Confoundedly politeful!

In short, these aggravating lads,
They tickle my tastes, they feed my fads,
They give me this and they give me that,
And I've nothing whatever to grumble at!
(*He bursts into tears, and falls sobbing on a seat*)

Nearing the end of the Opera we come upon one of the best-known satires within the canon; its Handelian treatment endears it in both music and lyrics:

This Helmet, I suppose
Was meant to ward off blows.
It's very hot,
And weighs a lot,
As many a Guardsman knows,
So off that helmet goes.
Yes, yes,
So off that helmet goes!

The short lines are artificially lengthened by the music, in the Handelian mode, and as a collaboration it works beautifully and must have brightened many a bathroom.

In the third week of the new year, 1884, Sullivan wrote to Carte that he would not write any more comic operas. Two things influenced his decision: the tone of the Press for *Princess Ida* and the replacement of the conductor, Costa, at Birmingham, by Hans Richter. 'They should' he observed with unusual sharpness, 'have appointed an Englishman' (but how would hungry young Arthur Sullivan have done in Leipzig if this same extreme nationalism had been adopted by the Moscheles, the Davids and the

Barnetts?) and he was aware that the musical public were saying behind their fans and whiskers, 'what can you expect when the most eminent musician in the country occupies himself with comic opera?'

At least the new appointment gave Sullivan the chance of a *bon mot*: 'Birmingham was a sort of boa-constrictor of music – it devoured a mighty meal of music every three years, and then relapsed into a state of coma to digest it.'

D'Oyly Carte tried to carry the matter off with a high hand by the simple expedient of asking Sullivan formally for a new opera. Sullivan replied: 'It is impossible for me to do another piece of the character of those already written by Gilbert and myself. ... When I return to town, I must, of course, talk the matter over with Gilbert and hear what his views on the subject are.'

Author, Composer, and "the harmless necessary Carte."—*Shakspeare.*

The Savoy trio caricatured by E.J.Wheeler in *Punch*, 1883.

He heard – and sooner than he had supposed:

My dear Sullivan

I learned from Carte yesterday, to my unbounded surprise, that you do not intend to write any more operas of the class with which you and I have been so long identified. ... You are of course aware that by our agreement entered into on the 8th February, 1883, and extending over 5 years, we are bound to supply Carte with a new opera on receiving from him six months' notice and, if for any reason we fail to do so, we are liable with him for any losses that may result from our default.

During your absence I have busied myself with constructing a *libretto*: I have even gone so far as to write some of the numbers and to sketch out portions of the dialogue. . . . In all the pieces we have written together, I have invariably subordinated my views to your own.

It is one of the facts of collaboration that each partner thinks he has subordinated his own talent to that of his partner – it comes up as frequently as a comma on a page.

Sullivan answered Gilbert from Paris:

I will be quite frank. [Surely fatal, with one of Gilbert's awkward temperament?] With *Princess Ida* I have come to the end of my tether – the end of my capability in that class of piece. My tunes are in danger of becoming mere repetitions of my former pieces, my concerted movements are getting to possess a strong family likeness.

I have rung all the changes possible in the way of variety of rhythm. It has hitherto been word setting, I might almost say syllable setting, for I have looked upon the words as being of such importance that I have been continually keeping down the music in order that not one should be lost. [Oh admirable collaborator!] And this suppression is most difficult, most fatiguing and I may say, most disheartening, for the music is never allowed to arise and speak for itself. I want a chance for the music to act in its own proper sphere – to intensify the emotional element not only of the actual words, but of the situation.

I should like to set a story of human interest and probability, where the humorous words would come in a humorous – not serious – situation, and where, if the situation were a tender or dramatic one, the words would be of a similar character. There would then be a feeling of reality about it which would give a fresh interest in writing, and fresh vitality to our joint work. . . . I hope with all my heart that there may be no break in our chain of joint workmanship.

To this letter, Gilbert replied two days later in terms of sharp reproach:

Your reflections on the character of the libretti with which I have supplied you have caused me considerable pain. However, I cannot suppose that you have intended to gall and wound me, when you wrote as you did. I must assume that your letter was written hurriedly.

When you tell me that your desire is that I shall write a libretto in which the humorous words will come in a humorous situation, and in which a tender or dramatic situation will be treated tenderly and dramatically, you teach me the ABC of my profession. It is inconceivable that any sane author should ever write otherwise than as you propose I should write in future.

Sullivan came back to Victoria Street on 9 April. He telephoned Gilbert at once to ask for a meeting.

Thursday April 10th: Gilbert came at 2. Two hours conversation. He proposed to me as subject for new piece the same idea that I had already declined two years ago, based on the notion that by means of a charm – formerly a coin, now a lozenge – a person would really become the character he or she represented themselves to be. Thus a young woman playing an old woman's part would, by taking the lozenge, really become an old woman for the time, and so on. I was obliged to reject the subject, as it makes the whole piece unreal and artificial. Long argument on this point – no concession on either side – complete deadlock, though quite friendly throughout.

Gilbert then offered to retire as a way to unlock the deadlock:

What do you say to this – provided that Carte consents. Write your opera to another man's libretto. I will willingly retire for one term, our agreement notwithstanding. [A handsome suggestion and particularly generous coming from such a stickler as Gilbert.] It may well be that you are cramped by setting so many libretti of the same author, and that a new man with a new style will start a new strain of musical ideas. [If only Gilbert had been content to leave it at that – but he went on more characteristically] . . . Your objections to my libretto really seem arbitrary and capricious. That they are nothing of the kind I am well persuaded – but, for all that, I can't fathom them.

But no other collaborator could take Gilbert's place, it seemed. Sullivan wrote straight back:

I yield to no one in my admiration of your matchless skill and genius . . . your letter of today has just come. Such a proposal as you make therein I could not entertain for a moment. Nor do I see why, because an idea which you propose to me fails in my judgment to afford me sufficient musical suggestion, we should necessarily come to a standstill. [There can be no doubt that Sullivan wanted it both ways – to work with Gilbert, and not to work with Gilbert.] You must remember that you proposed the same idea to me before *Iolanthe* was written, and that I then expressed the same views with regard to it as I hold now.

On the same day Sullivan added, this time in his diary:

Saturday April 12th 1884: Carte came. Then Miss Lenoir joined us, to discuss *modus vivendi* with reference to deadlock with Gilbert. I wrote to Gilbert to mention an insuperable difficulty in his proposed subject, also referred to his letter I had just received. . . . I cannot understand the position he takes – viz.: because I do not like the subject he proposed, he is at a loss to find another.

Oh, poor Gilbert – how well a fellow-writer understands that 'feeling at a loss' when an idea lights a candle in the mind and someone dowses the glim! '. . . I *cannot* do any more of that class of work.'

Gilbert continued to press the lozenge plot; Sullivan continued to refuse it. Imagine Carte's frame of mind. His two talented geese that laid the golden eggs at loggerheads! While Gilbert and Sullivan appeared to be separated by an unbridgable lozenge, he transformed himself into a human pendulum swinging first towards Gilbert's house in Harrington Gardens, then towards Victoria Street and Sullivan's house, to coax, argue, endeavour to persuade, even to tug. Then Gilbert once more wrote to Sullivan: 'May 8th 1884: Gilbert wrote to propose piece on lines I had suggested. Wrote and accepted with greatest pleasure and said under the circumstances I undertook to set it without further discussion.'

My dear Gilbert
    Your letter of today was an inexpressible relief to me, as it clearly shows me that you, equally with myself, are loath to discontinue the collaboration which has been such a pleasure and advantage to us.
    If I understand you to propose you will construct a plot without the supernatural and improbable elements, and on the lines you describe, I gladly undertake to set it without further discussing the matter, or asking what the subject is to be.
Yours sincerely
Arthur Sullivan.

'May 9th 1884: . . . all unpleasantness at an end.'
Peace, perfect peace, or a lull before the storm?

7

The Mikado

Gilbert worked happily, or as happily as it was in his nature to work, on the new script, *The Mikado*. Sullivan, who felt it might lessen the friction if he waited for Gilbert to send him the completed piece before he ruffled the waters with composer's problems, spent the summer on a round of visits. In all, Carte was left for the classic period of nine months before the baby could be delivered.

Sullivan, swanning through Newmarket and Ascot, had a horse of his own. His racing colours were pink and purple.

During the period of gestation Carte revived *Trial by Jury* and *The Sorcerer* on a double bill, to keep the theatre open. Sullivan was able to gather his forces before embarking on the biggest success they were ever to trawl.

In November Wagner's *Parsifal* was performed in London for the first time. This was a tremendous musical event.

'Saturday November 15th 1884: Went to hear *Parsifal* at the Albert Hall [the entire company from Bayreuth was singing]. Finale to 1st Act impressive and noble. Flower scene graceful and scored with delicate charm. But [and one can feel the Diary gathering itself to strike], the whole is heavy, gloomy, dull and ugly. ...' Five days later the collaborators met to work.

What made the becalmed duo turn to Japan? Gilbert himself always said that the idea occurred to him when a Japanese sword (subsequently used as a stage-prop in *The Mikado*) fell from the wall of his study.

It must, too, have chimed happily in his mind with the vogue for *japonaiserie*, started by Whistler with oriental prints on ricepaper, and his beloved 'blue' china, in the sixties, popularised by him and Rossetti in the seventies, and now at its height in the eighties. 'We are all being more or less Japanned,' groaned the *Daily Telegraph*: 'Advertisements tell us every morning that we have Japan in London [there was an important exhibition in Knightsbridge], and the quaint art of a strange people, who are getting rid of their national characteristics as fast as they can, is receiving from us that form of homage which the proverb describes as "the sincerest form of flattery".'

Gilbert was, of course, to stage the opera, and he determined to take the greatest pains with it, following the comparative failure of *Princess Ida*. Weedon Grossmith once remarked that the difference between productions at the Lyceum and at the Savoy was, in the main, that at every rehearsal Irving groped for perfection, while Gilbert arrived at each rehearsal with perfection in his pocket. Irving, Hesketh Pearson explains, saw what he wanted in fitful gleams, Gilbert worked in a hard steady light from the very outset.

Although the critic H.M.Walbrook insisted that there was a remoteness from life in every facet of Gilbert's work; yet his gift for staging their works and his insistence on the correct details in uniforms and orders must be absolved from his whimsical treatments of texts.

The Japanese had, by 1885, taken over every drawing-room in sight, with fans, wickerwork and knick-knacks. And once the background of the piece was confirmed, Gilbert descended on the orientally-minded store Liberty's, and demanded that his costumes should all be made of 'pure Japanese fabric'. Leslie Baily tells us that the costume worn by Miss Brandram, the Katisha, was a genuine Japanese garment, two hundred years old.

At the Japanese Exhibition Gilbert found a geisha girl: 'Her English was limited to "sixpence please", the price of a cup of tea at Knightsbridge.' He took her along to the Savoy rehearsals to teach the cast 'Japanese Deportment'. So while the Japanese were trying to be as English as the English – with varying success – the English were

The Ironmaster at the Savoy.

LEFT Gilbert depicted as a martinet. He was renowned for his strictness with the cast and his close attention to detail.

RIGHT An E.J.Walker cartoon of Gilbert and Sullivan.

The Two Very Fanny Japs at the Savoy.

being enlightened in 'the snapping of fans to denote wrath, delight or homage, the manner of walking of a bunch of Japanese ladies, the giggling and hissing of the girls'. All these oriental manners are preserved (or should it be crystallised?) in the D'Oyly Carte Company's production and date right back to Miss Sixpence Please.

Although unforcedly musical and merry, the writing of the music came slowly, though the first number to be composed was 'Three Little Maids from School are We', which, with a quintet, Sullivan finished in one day – 21 December. But in January he was deeply disturbed by the death of brother Frederic's widow, in Los Angeles. 'Those poor children' was the *cri-de-cœur* in his diary. He resolved, as soon as the *Mikado* was staged, to take a trip to Los Angeles to look into their affairs.

With the coming of February, he became almost a hermit, working, as was his custom, every night until daylight spread about his room.

'March 2nd: All these days since February 21st writing and rehearsing [*Mikado*]. No drives, parties, or recreations of any kind,' mourns the diary.

'March 3rd: Worked all night at Finale, 1st Act. Finished at 5 am. 63 pages of score at one sitting.'

Phew!

He composed 'The Flowers that Bloom in the Spring' one evening between tea and dinner.

Sullivan, it is said, worked best when the calendar stared him in the face.

The partnership was never stronger. What they could not know was that in *The Mikado* or *The Town of Titipu*, they had written a musical piece that was to be accounted the most valuable stage property in the world for the next seventy years. 'Have you noticed', Sullivan was to say of Gilbert, in an interview in the New York *Mirror* in the early autumn, 'what an extraordinary polish there is to his versification? There is never a weak syllable or a halting foot. It is marvellous. He has a wonderful gift, too, of making rhythms, and it bothers me to death sometimes to make corresponding rhythms in music.'

The Mikado opened on Saturday evening, 14 March 1885.

'New opera produced at the Savoy Theatre with every sign of real success,' is the entry in Sullivan's diary. 'A most brilliant House. Tremendous reception. All went very well except Grossmith, whose nervousness nearly upset the piece. A *treble* encore for 'Three Little Maids' and for 'The Flowers that bloom in the Spring'. Seven encores taken – might have taken twelve.'

The *Evening News*, however, was in a carping mood, saying: '... it was not likely to add very much to the reputation of either author or composer.'

But the *Era* stoutly appeared with: 'Messrs Gilbert and Sullivan must be familiar with success by this time, but never in their brilliant partnership of sprightly music and fantastic fun has a more unanimous verdict of approval been passed upon their labours than when the curtain fell on Saturday last.'

'From the moment the curtain rose on the Court swells in Japanese plate attitudes,' wrote Rutland Barrington (Pooh-Bah) in his Memoirs, 'to its final fall, it was one long succession of uproarious laughter at the libretto, and overwhelming applause for the music.'

RIGHT A programme for *The Mikado*, 1885.

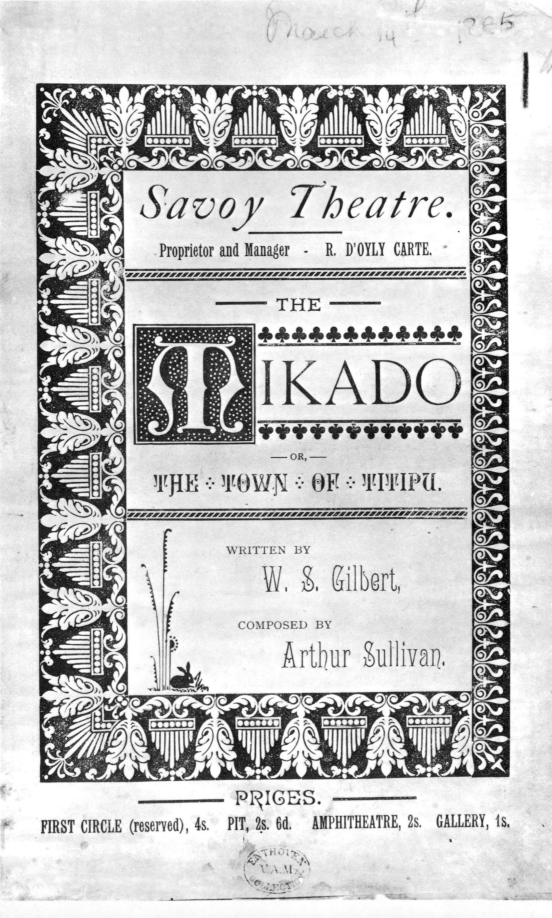

Savoy Theatre.

Proprietor and Manager - R. D'OYLY CARTE.

THE

TIKADO

— OR, —

THE · TOWN · OF · TITIPU.

WRITTEN BY

W. S. Gilbert,

COMPOSED BY

Arthur Sullivan.

— PRICES. —

FIRST CIRCLE (reserved), 4s. PIT, 2s. 6d. AMPHITHEATRE, 2s. GALLERY, 1s.

Figaro reported that: 'Mr Gilbert was not in the house till shortly before the fall of the curtain, when he came to the footlights hand-in-hand with Sir Arthur Sullivan.'

Yes, all was harmony between them, but for how long?

The gilded audience, writes Reginald Allen, included several members of the Royal Family: the Princess Louise and Prince Louis of Battenberg, and the Duke and Duchess of Edinburgh. While Queen Victoria's amateur musician son was enjoying himself – one trusts ('A triumph! A triumph!') – in a box, he was happily unaware that outside the theatre newsboys were shouting the clearly unfounded report of 'Serious Accident to the Duke of Edinburgh'. Among others present, reported *Watch*, was James McNeil Whistler, attracted by the reports of the Willow Pattern nature of the entertainment?

Sullivan with the Duke of Edinburgh, sketched in *The Illustrated Sporting and Dramatic News*, 28 March 1885.

The present writer would like to think that also present, perhaps in the family Circle or up in the Gods, two sales-ladies from a Regent Street Store were excitedly watching the stage. One sales-lady pointed to a particularly Japanese silk gown with a particularly English artist swathed in its kimono shape: the sales-lady drew in her breath. She snorted. 'It's a Liberty!' she exclaimed.

A JAPANESE VILLAGE AT THE SAVOY.

A cartoon by Alfred Bryan, 1885.

The first night was full of conflicting tensions as these affairs mostly must be. First, there was the audience, out to enjoy itself. On the stage the cast were trembling. The dress rehearsal had gone badly. Gilbert had been in a particularly awkward mood: 'Very good, Lily; very good indeed, but I have just come down from the back row of the gallery and there were two or three words which failed to reach me. ... Sullivan's music is, of course, very beautiful and I heard every note without difficulty, but I think my words are not without merit and ought to be heard without undue effort ...,' quotes Baily, not without relish. He all but cut one of the great list songs, 'To make the punishment fit the crime'. It was only when a deputation from the chorus begged him to put it back that it was reinstated.

Gilbert was particularly incensed by Beaty-Kingston's notice, when it came out in *Theatre*: '... unsusceptible of a single kindly feeling or wholesome impulse; were they not manifestly maniacal they would be demoniacal. ... Decapitation, disembowelment, immersion in boiling oil or molten lead, are the eventualities upon which their attentions are kept fixed, with gruesome persistence; what wonder that ... their hearts should be turned to stone. ...'

G.K.Chesterton was to write of the revival in 1907:

In that play Gilbert pursued and persecuted the evils of modern England till they had literally not a leg to stand on; exactly as Swift did under the allegory of *Gulliver's Travels*. Yet it is the solid and comic fact that *The Mikado* was actually forbidden in England because *it was a satire on Japan*. ... I doubt if there is a single joke in the whole play that fits the Japanese. But all the jokes in the play fit the English. ... The great creation of the play is Pooh Bah. I have never heard, I don't believe, that the combination of inconsistent functions is specially a vice of the extreme East. I should guess the contrary; I should guess that the East tends to split into steady and inherited trades or castes, so that the torturer is always a torturer and the priest a priest. But about England Pooh Bah is something more than a satire; he is the truth. It is true of British politics, probably not of Japanese, that we meet the same man twenty times as twenty different officials.

While considering the felicities of *The Mikado*, the wit of its libretto and the fresh invention welling up in its music as from some invisible well, let us keep the words of Thomas F.Dunhill, that sensitive musician who set W.B.Yeats' 'Had I the heavens' embroidered cloths', whether we agree with him or not: 'If a man's masterpiece is the work which appeals to the largest number of people of all nationalities and shades of thought, then it must be said that *The Mikado* was Sullivan's *chef d'œuvre*.'

The overture – which Sullivan himself did not score, though no doubt he gave indications as to possible instrumentation in some passages, and one can imagine how the sharp beat of the composer's baton would increase the excitement of the rushing figures of the strings – sparkled and tingled, and the brass resounded at the first performance.

We can take it that the town of Titipu is the mirror in which Gilbert's England holds a tilted reflection – tilted, because satiric. At the very outset of the piece both librettist and composer state the style:

> If you want to know who we are
> We are gentlemen of Japan

and the male chorus sing in unison:

> On many a vase and jar –
> On many a screen and fan –

The Japanese craze, like the aesthetic movement, is to meet its musical come-uppance. It is strange, then, that having started to establish an atmosphere and a manner:

> If you think we are worked by strings,
> Like a Japanese Marionette,
> You don't understand these things:
> It is simply Court Etiquette:

Sullivan, in one of his most popular songs, 'A wandering minstrel', throws idiom and style over the zany moon and settles for the kind of tune to introduce his hero, Nanki

RIGHT Two characters from *Iolanthe* by Jack from *Society*, 1882: Leonora Braham as Phyllis and George Grossmith as the Lord Chancellor.
OVERLEAF LEFT A calendar for 1890 illustrated with scenes from the Savoy operas.
RIGHT The bottom and side of a box of writing paper picturing the Three Little Maids and Ko Ko from *The Mikado*.

"And in my court I sit all day,
Giving agreeable girls away."—IOLANTHE.

Yours faithfully
Geo: Grossmith

PRINTED BY ALFRED GIBBONS, 172, STRAND, W.C.

Poo, that might be found in any other of his comic operas, so pricking the bubble, or should it be jarring the jar?

In this, the very first sentimental number, Gilbert typically stops by to touch in a very British Japanese army:

> Our warriors in serried ranks
> Never quail – or conceal it if they do
> And I shouldn't be surprised if nations trembled
> Before the mighty troops of Titipu:

And more than a touch of the British Sea Shanty:

> And if you call for a song of the sea,
> We'll heave the capstan round,
> With a yo-heave-hò, for the wind is free
> Her anchor's a-trip and her helm's a-lee:

so harvesting the best of both worlds, or rather confirming that Japan is the looking-glass – and a very looking-glass Japan it is we see – and England the reflection. It is typical of the humour of the work that the important hinge of the plot should be placed within a song:

> Our great Mikado, virtuous man,
> So he decreed in words succinct
> That all who flirted, leered or winked
> (Unless conubially linked),
> Should forthwith be beheaded.

When the chorus hails the Lord High Executioner, Ko-Ko, Sullivan proclaims himself if not a son, at least a godson, of Kneller Hall with his use of sonorous brass, in what one might be forgiven for considering rather barren ground:

> With beat of drum
> And a rum-tum-tum. ...

Gilbert again shows us his flashing taste for the *mot juste* with his:

> She'll toddle away as all aver
> With the Lord High Executioner,

toddle being a very apt description for the Japanese shuffle used throughout the piece.

Enter procession of Yum-Yum's school-fellows, heralding Yum-Yum, Peep-Bo and Pitti-Sing: 'Comes a train of little ladies'. A recent television production quite literally brought them on in a crazy little Japanese train. Gilbert writes a precise, lyrical song with just a tang of wit:

> Comes a train of little ladies
> From scholastic trammels free;
> Each a little bit afraid is
> Wondering what the world can be!

PREVIOUS PAGE A supplement to *The Ladies Pictorial* entitled '*The Mikado* by our Japanese artist', May 1885.
LEFT A portrait of Gilbert painted by Frank Hall in 1886.

Is it but a world of trouble
Sadness set to song?
Is its beauty but a bubble
Bound to break ere long?

Are its palaces and pleasures
Fantasies that fade?
And the glory of its treasures
Shadow of a shade?

Schoolgirls we, eighteen and under,
From scholastic trammels free,
And we wonder, how we wonder,
What on earth the world may be!

This leads into the well-loved:

Three little maids from school are we
Three little maids who, all unwary,
Come from a ladies' seminary
Freed from its genius tutelary
Three little maids from school!

Sullivan found a pretty highly vocalised treatment that makes it almost a classic copy-book manner of handling a song – here two neat talents coincide to everyone's comfort.

Another charming lyric well matched by sensitive musical collaboration is Yum-Yum's song, which held audiences spell-bound a century ago, and still does:

The sun, whose rays
Are all ablaze
With ever-living glory,
Does not deny
His majesty –
He scorns to tell a story!
He don't exclaim
'I blush for shame,
So kindly be indulgent.'
But fierce and bold
In fiery gold
He glories all effulgent.

I mean to rule the earth
As he the sky.
We really know our worth
The sun and I.

Observe his flame,
That placid dame
The moon's celestial highness;
There's not a trace
Upon her face
Of diffidence or shyness:
She borrows light
That, through the night
Mankind may all acclaim her!
And, truth to tell,
She lights up well,
So I, for one, don't blame her!

Ah, pray make no mistake.
We are not shy.
We're very wide awake,
The moon and I!

Another perfect matching of music to words that lingers in the memory long after the song is sung.

By this time we are not surprised to find The Lord High Executioner's effort 'to make the punishment fit the crime'; his 'little list' is peculiarly English peccancy.

'The last literary work of Gilbert's life', Dark and Grey remind us, 'was to be the re-writing of the story of *The Mikado* for children,' from which they quote a little-known version:

As some day it may happen that a victim must be found
I've made a little list – I've made a little list,
Of inconvenient people who might well be underground,
For they never would be missed – they never would be missed.
The donkey who of nine-times-six and eight-times-seven prates,
And stumps you with inquiries on geography and dates,
And asks for your ideas on spelling 'parallelogram' –
All narrow-minded people who are stingy with their jam,
And the torture-dealing dentist, with the forceps in his fist.
They'd none of them be missed – they'd none of them be missed.

There's the nursemaid who each evening in curlpapers does your hair
With an aggravating twist – *she* never would be missed –
And tells you that you mustn't cough or sneeze or yawn or stare,
She never would be missed – I'm sure she'd not be missed.
All those who hold that children shouldn't have too much to eat,
And think cold suet pudding a delicious birthday treat,
Who say that little girls to bed at seven should be sent,
And consider pocket-money isn't given to be spent,
And doctors who on giving you unpleasant draughts insist –
They never would be missed – they'd none of them be missed.

In the quintet, the critic is nearly lulled by Gilbert's very conformist opening:

> See how the Fates their gifts alot
> For A is happy – B is not.
> Yet B is worthy, I daresay,
> Of more prosperity than A.

At this point Gilbert goes off on his old game of anything for a rhyme:

> Yet A is happy!
> Oh! so happy!
> Laughing, Ha! ha!
> Chaffing, Ha! ha!
> Nectar quaffing, ha! ha! ha! ha!

A very gleeful glee? Yes. But also a very slap-happy prosodist.

But no sooner does one condemn Gilbert the wilfully sloven song-maker, than one comes on yet another stroke of description that delights, even dazzles one. Such is Ko-Ko's description of Katisha – Gilbert's usual stalking-horse, the ageing spinster, seen through Ko-Ko's woeful eyes:

> The flowers that bloom in the spring
> Tra la,
> Have nothing to do with the case
> I've got to take under my wing,
> Tra la,
> A most unattractive old thing
> Tra la,
> With a caricature of a face!

No 'vision of roses and wine' Katisha, but how that unexpected 'caricature' zings out.

But against this should we not measure Gilbert's feeling words for Katisha?

> Hearts do not break;
> They sting and ache
> For old sake's sake:

Here the satirist is heard at his most human.

Sullivan, for superb measure, throws in a quasi-madrigal – a pastiche of a treasurable beauty, to match Gilbert's:

> Brightly dawns our wedding day;
> Joyous hour we give thee greeting! ...
> Whither, whither art thou fleeting?
> Fickle moment, prithee stay!
> What though mortal joys be hollow?
> Pleasures come, if sorrows follow:
> Though the tocsin sound, ere long,
> Ding Dong! Ding Dong!

> Yet until the shadows fall
> Over one and over all,
> Sing a merry madrigal,
> A madrigal!

This is arguably the loveliest song to be found in all Gilbert and Sullivan's more lyrical numbers.

Leslie Baily suggests that Gilbert based his popular and evocative 'Tit-Willow' number on an old English poem by Nicholas Rowe (1674–1718).

This is what Rowe wrote:

> To the brook and the willow that heard him complain,
> Ah, Willow, Willow,
> Poor Colin sat weeping and told them his pain,
> Ah, Willow, Willow; ah, Willow Willow.
> Sweet stream, he'd cry sadly, I'll teach thee to flow;
> And the waters shall rise to the brink with my woe,
> Ah, Willow, Willow.

Gilbert's version goes:

> On a tree by a river a little tom-tit
> Sang 'Willow, titwillow, titwillow!'
> And I said to him, 'Dicky-Bird, why do you sit
> Singing "Willow, titwillow, titwillow"?
> Is it weakness of intellect, Birdie?' I cried,
> 'Or a rather tough worm in your little inside?'
> With a shake of his poor little head he replied,
> 'Oh willow, titwillow, titwillow.'

'The March of the Mikado's Troops' is the only truly Japanese music (orchestrated for English musical instruments) in the whole piece.

Having launched *The Mikado* in London, Sullivan was to sail for New York on 20 June 1885. But a Gilbertian squall blew up before he could wave a debonair farewell. Gilbert fell out with D'Oyly Carte. As the months passed, the relationship of Gilbert to Carte was to decline into the great carpet row and the ensuing lawsuit. But the present storm blew up between them some time before that catastrophe.

The field of responsibility between the creative partnership and the managerial was laid down squarely among them; Gilbert and Sullivan were to preside over everything on the stage, Carte was responsible for everything in the house, including *impressage*. Gilbert now decided that Carte was taking upon himself too large a share in the running and managing of the Savoy operas.

He held that their contract in no way implied equal management by the three men in the Savoy Theatre. Daily meetings of the three men over every detail would be impossible.

'I cannot see how you and Sullivan are part managers of the Theatre any more than I am part-author or part-composer of the music.'

On 1 June Gilbert saw red:

... As you decline to permit me to have any voice in the control of the theatre that Sullivan and I have raised to its present position of prosperity and distinction, and point out to me that, by our agreement, I am merely a hack author employed by you to supply you with pieces on certain terms, I have no alternative but to accept the position you assign to me during the few months that our agreement has got to run. Henceforth I will be bound by its absolute and literal terms. If this course of action should result in inconvenience or loss to yourself, you will do me the justice to remember that it is of your own creation.

'Your note grieves me more than I can say,' wrote Carte. 'Must a dramatic author be considered a "hack" if he does not arrange the number of stalls in the theatre where his opera is played? ... If I could be an author like you, I would certainly not be the manager. I am simply the tradesman who sells your creations.'

Gilbert, in the face of Carte's reasonable, not to say flattering communication, now tried to drum in Sullivan. If Carte were left alone to run them all, he might ruin them all, was the gist of his theme!

Carte, still forbearing, wrote to Gilbert:

'Of course you run this risk. But my reply is that I stand the whole risk of pecuniary loss.' The three partners, points out Baily, shared the profit of the operas equally, but not the losses.

Sullivan managed to maintain his position on the rim of the tea-cup, and for the time being the little storm had blown itself out. But it was not entirely without effect for him; for while it lasted it blew Sullivan closer to Carte. This did nothing to improve Gilbert's mood, nor did the fact that the Press for the *Mikado* was on the whole warmer towards Sullivan than to him.

And Gilbert was not the only one to ruffle the Savoy water; word had reached the triumvirate that an American pirate, Duff by name, meant to produce *The Mikado* on Broadway and was raring to fight a lawsuit to prove that American Law would give him the right to do it.

D'Oyly Carte arranged to present the piece at the Fifth Avenue Theatre, a kind of home from home to the Savoy combination, in the middle of October, but when he realised that it was Duff's intention to steal a march by opening in mid-August, Carte put as many spokes in Duff's chariot wheel as he could. More, he sent a letter to the Cunard Line marked 'Very Private', booking fifty passages.

An agent of Duff's came to London to buy Japanese costumes from Liberty's but when the store realised that the order for costumes was none of Carte's ordering, they refused to sell them. Off went Duff's agent to Paris, but Carte had sent an agent ahead of Duff's agent to buy up every Japanese costume in Paris. 'I don't mind how much money I spend to smash Duff,' D'Oyly Carte declared.

Besides, there were to be American, Australian and Berlin productions, and various touring companies sent out from the Savoy. The costumes would not go to seed – not even sunflower seed.

Carte wrote to Stetson, of the Fifth Avenue Theatre, in New York: 'The moment you let me know when Duff proposes to open, I will swoop quickly across with my company and be before him.'

With fifty cloaks and fifty daggers, Stetson's cable came. So, at the end of the next day's rehearsal, Carte informed the cast that they were not going on tour in England, as they had supposed, swore them to secrecy and intimated that relatives would not be welcome to see them off at ship or station. Two nights later the company slipped out of London by the boat-train for Liverpool. The Company breakfasted together at a small commercial hotel, where none of them was known (all fifty of them! Not easy, one would have thought) and were conveyed to the waiting Cunarder *Aurelia* by special tug. Before the passenger tender went out, the Savoyards were battened down in their cabins trying to accustom themselves to their newly assumed names. D'Oyly Carte was on the ship's books as Henry Chapman.

When, the voyage over, the *Aurelia* docked at Staten Island at midnight on 16 August, their agent climbed aboard by way of a rope ladder (cloak and dagger to the end):

'Is anything known in New York?'

'Not one word.'

If Duff's posters announcing his opening at the Standard Theatre, a week later, gave rise to qualms in D'Oyly Carte, they must have been nothing to the qualms raised in the enemy when they discovered that the fully-rehearsed company they had supposed at a safe three thousand miles away were in New York.

The Savoyard *Mikado* was duly unveiled on Broadway and its success was 'immediate and triumphant'. One of the oddest manifestations was the decoration: in any New York home of artistic pretentions there was a Mikado Room.

Sullivan did not linger in New York. Had he not promised himself to visit brother Frederic's orphans in the West? In New York the thermometer had climbed and clung to 100° in the shade. Sullivan relaxed with some American friends, went to a play or so, supped at Delmonico's, then westward ho! to the little family almost before New York knew he had landed there.

At Salt Lake City a friend showed him around:

We drove about the town for a long time [he wrote], saw all the Brigham Young family houses ... went to the great Tabernacle and played for an hour on the great organ, a really good instrument (three manuals etc.) made by a local Morman. The next day (Sunday) I went to the Tabernacle to Service. The hymn-tune was my arrangement of St Ann's tune! ...

'I arrived at San Francisco Monday morning. I saw all I could, and should have enjoyed my stay there very much but for the ceaseless and persistent manner in which I was interviewed, called upon, followed and written to. ... Went through Chinatown with a detective, Devitt, a great character, saw the Theatre, and went into the vilest dens. Got home at 1.30.'

At Los Angeles, he found his brother's children healthy and, considering the loss that had so recently put them into mourning, reasonably happy. He picked up the family *en bloc* and took it for a wonderful tour through the Yosemite Valley.

But while on his trip Sullivan learned that D'Oyly Carte's case against the plagiarists and pirates had been heard and failed in New York: the test case had been heard by Justice Divver, of New York City, a strong Tammanyite. His decision, says Baily, included a classic ruling: 'Copyright or no Copyright, Commerical Honesty or Commercial Buccaneering, no Englishman possesses any rights which a true-born American is bound to respect.'

The legal situation was one that might have been created by Gilbert – 'So *The Mikado* is open to everyone – free to be played by every miserable penniless scoundrel in the States!'

At the end of August, Sullivan returned to New York. *The Mikado* was doing big business at the Fifth Avenue, the rival *Mikado* was at pains to make, as it were, stalls meet. D'Oyly Carte was in his element.

He arranged to give a gala: 'September 24th: House crammed with a fashionable audience. Bouquets given to all the Ladies. Very bright and spirited performance. Great enthusiasm. And I had to make a speech.'

It was this speech, published throughout the United States, that in the end brought into being a revision of the Copyright Laws of America.

Sullivan, making his speech from a box, said:

Although I have made it a rule through my life never to address the public when I appear before them in an artistic capacity [Oh, Arthur – what about that speech on behalf of the excellence of the Crystal Palace concerts given from the platform on site?], I am impelled to break my rule to-night. ... We should have been grieved indeed if you received first impressions of our work from a spurious imitation – an imitation in which the author's intentions are ignored for the very good reason that the performers don't know what our intentions are, and in which the music, through having been patched up from a pianoforte arrangement, must necessarily be mutilated, and a misrepresentation of the meaning of the composer ... tonight, you see our work exactly as we intended it should be performed.

It may be that some day the Legislation of this magnificent country may see fit to afford the same protection to a man who employs his brains in Literature and Art as they do to one who invents a new bear-trap, or who accidentally gives an extra turn to a screw, doing away with the necessity of boring a hole first. On that day these unfortunate managers and publishers, who, having no brains of their own, are content to live by annexing the brain properties of others, will be in an embarrassing and piteous condition. Like Hamlet [sic], their occupation will be gone. ...

While Sullivan is receiving the warm applause of the American audience from his box, and D'Oyly Carte is charging the windmill of American Copyright, Gilbert had remained in London to keep an eye on the Savoy production. This gave him many a delicious opportunity to come the heavy on a number of the diversions that inevitably creep in on a long run of a play. Every now and then William Schwenk would pop into the pit, gallery or the dark of a box to check up on discipline. One evening, Rutland Barrington, who had borrowed four shillings from Jessie Bond to pay a cab fare, was paying her back in pennies, half-pennies and stamps, which he handed to her one by one, on stage, unseen by the audience – not so Gilbert, whose beady eye missed little. Rutland Barrington was severely reprimanded.

George Grossmith was also keel-hauled, much as follows:

'I am told, Mr Grossmith, that in last night's performance when you were kneeling before the Mikado, he gave you a push and you rolled over completely on the floor.'

'Yes. You see in my interpretation. ...'

'Whatever your interpretation, please omit that in future.'

'Certainly if you wish it – but I got a big laugh by it.'

'So you would if you sat on a pork pie.'

Hesketh Pearson relates that Gilbert forbade 'the intermingling of the sexes in one another's dressing-rooms during the interval'. The word spread. Soon all theatre-going London talked of 'The Savoy Boarding School'.

Yes, there was much to occupy Gilbert during Sullivan's absence in America.

By the end of October Sullivan had returned to London but only to find that there was nothing to do so far as light opera was concerned.

The Mikado was playing to full houses every night at the Savoy. Three companies toured it in the provinces. The music percolated everywhere – Mayfair drawing-rooms, village halls, Military Bands, organs in the streets and no doubt musical boxes all gave it.

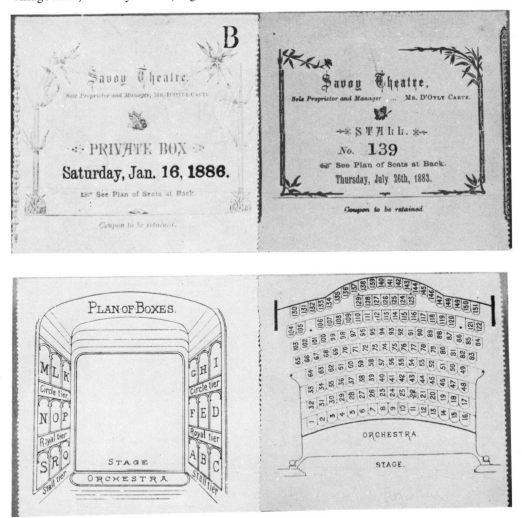

The front and back of tickets for the Savoy.

In vain the touchy Japanese tried to get it stopped – might as well try to stem ginger. It 'spread like a flame' in America and Australia. It was given – in English – in Berlin.

Sullivan wrote to the future Kaiser to ask his opinion of it, and received a reply in English:

Potsdam

Dear Sir

For the moment I am unhappily unable to fulfil your wish because I am just recovering from a very serious and rather dangerous attack of ear-ache, which compels me to stay at home and keep quiet. But as soon as I shall be able to stir to go to Reichenhall, I shall visit *The Mikado*.

To-day the first performance will be viewed by my parents and all my sisters [to say nothing of 'his cousins and his aunts'!].

I hope that for the arrival of the Crown Prince they will have 'polished up the handle of the big front door', for he might have been a Roosian etc but he is a Proosian!

Clearly there would be no immediate need to create a successor to *The Mikado*. But Gilbert was becoming fidgety. He wanted to occupy himself with a new libretto, and sent a letter to Sullivan as soon as he arrived in London: 'I don't like to ask you to reconsider the (as it seems to me) admirable plot I proposed to you last year. I content myself with assuring you that I see my way right through it, to as complete a success as we ever achieved.'

The Lozenge had raised its ugly head again to the uneasiness of Sullivan. The feeling between the two men had been congenial and generous – at least on Sullivan's side – for the success of *The Mikado* had drawn them together. He firmly believed that failure lay in this plot which, like King Charles's Head on a Lozenge, kept turning up.

At the end of a desperate week he wrote begging Gilbert to put 'The Lozenge Plot' in some comfortably distant 'pigeon-hole!'

8

Ruddigore and The Yeomen of the Guard

The January of 1886 came in cold and comfortless. On a snowy morning Gilbert fought his way to Sullivan's house to bring him the idea for *Ruddigore* or *Ruddygore* as first they spelled it. It was a re-working of Gilbert's piece *Ages Ago* written eighteen years earlier for *The Gallery of Illustration*.

They sat there, these two, the windows banking up with snow, 'trying to unravel the skein of a plot which hovered between them in the empty air'.

Silva – Sullivan's man – appeared.

Who wanted lunch?

The pair were totally absorbed.

Silva reappeared. The partners gave in to the inevitable – but they talked plot as they ate.

There was no immediate need for *Ruddigore* – even Gilbert admitted this. The official Japenese breeze over *The Mikado* had blown itself out. The world conquest was complete. Queen Victoria had sent for the music. Henry Irving had declared it to be 'the greatest triumph of light opera, British or foreign, in his memory'. Massenet wrote to congratulate 'A Master'.

But Sullivan was committed to write a new work for the Leeds Festival in October. He told Gilbert quite frankly that he would write that piece before setting in motion *Ruddigore*.

February came and was gone. Still he had not settled on a serious subject. Then Joseph Bennett called on him with an idea for a libretto based on Longfellow's *The Golden Legend*. The idea appealed to Sullivan from the very outset and he gave Bennett £300 for the libretto. Yet even when the writing of *The Golden Legend* was in his hands, he did not settle to work. He attended a few race meetings; he went about London with Liszt – indeed, he took the aged Abbé to a smoking concert given by the Royal Amateurs Orchestral Society for which the Duke of Edinburgh ('a triumph: a triumph') usually led the first violins, which Liszt announced was 'charming, charming'.

Gilbert soon became impatient with Sullivan's swanning.

The Prince of Wales was pressing Sullivan to go to work, too, but this was to set Tennyson's Ode which had been written for the forthcoming Colonial and Indian Exhibition.

Sullivan noted in his diary: 'After much hesitation I consented to do it. How am I to get through this year's work?'

A light opera, an Oratorio, a hymn, and the year already warming to summer. 'Do they think me a barrel-organ? They turn the handle and I disgorge music of any mood to order!'

In vain did the London Season sing its Swanning Song. Work had turned him into something very like a recluse. He did not emerge until: 'August 25th: Last day of work! At it all day for the introduction and solo in 2nd scene. Got it at 5 pm scored it and finished at 7.45. Thank God.'

The Golden Legend was home and dry.

But 'Most people suffer and get well again. I suffer and don't,' he wrote to Alexander MacKenzie.

When, in October, Sullivan rehearsed the Oratorio at Leeds, Dvorak was rehearsing his *Ludmilla* there. When, on 15 October *The Golden Legend* was first given, the audience stood on their chairs and waved programmes and hats. More remarkable still, his orchestra and choir pelted him, from the platform, with flowers. It must have been some compensation for working through the pain. And another panacea was on its way, according to the distinguished musician Stanford's diary: 'I heard Humperdinck say to Sullivan, after a very smooth reading of his new work, that he supposed that there were many foreigners in the band; and Sullivan was able to say "Not one!" with a not altogether non-triumphant smile.'

The Press was positively abject before Sullivan's golden achievement. *The World* went so far as to hail him as the English Mozart.

The sharp voice of posterity can be heard in *A History of Music* by Dr Ernest Walker (one of the present writer's professors):

The Martyr of Antioch ... alternates between dullness and vulgarity and sometimes attains both at once. *The Light of the World* has hardly enough vitality even to be vulgar. ... In *The Golden Legend* Sullivan no doubt pulled himself together to some extent. ... But for the best-known English composer, in the very prime of life, and putting forth his full powers, *The Golden Legend* is, as a whole, a melancholy production.

A few days later, Gilbert was already writing to urge on Sullivan:

I congratulate you heartily on the success of the Cantata which appears from all accounts to be the biggest thing you've done.

I have just finished the libretto subject to any alterations you may suggest ['Do they think me a barrel-organ?'] and I shall be in town for good. I don't expect you will want to turn to our

RIGHT Six sides of a programme for *The Mikado* in 1886, decorated with scenes from previous operas.

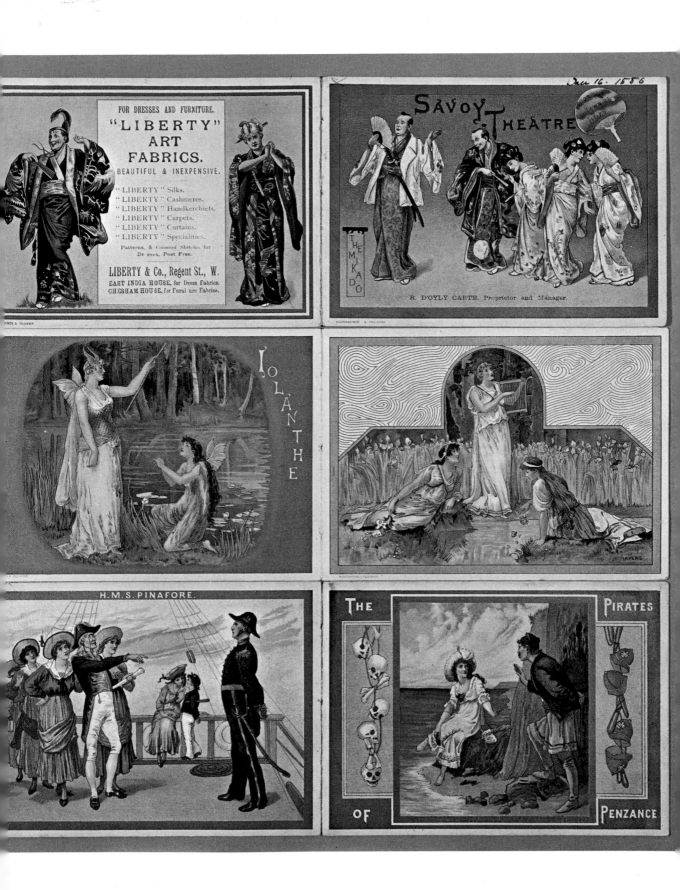

work at once without any immediate rest, but if you do, I can come up any day and go through the MS with you.

One can hear the hard-working composer's groan.

Gilbert duly turned up, the libretto of *Ruddygore* or *The Witch's Curse* completed and tucked underneath his arm. They decided to present the piece at the end of January 1887, if poor old Sullivan could only have the music finished in time. On such a piece of bungled plot-making one would have thought that even that pair of optimists would have turned their backs. But the piece is not altogether without felicities, perhaps particularly by Gilbert the lyricist and wit, as distinct from Gilbert the plot-weaver.

The usual midnight oil for Sullivan. The usual meticulously precise rehearsals, the frettings and fumings from Gilbert and: 'January 22nd, 1887: Production of *Ruddygore* at Savoy. Very enthusiastic up to last twenty minutes, then the audience showed dissatisfaction. Revivications of ghosts etc very weak. Enthusiastic reception.'

That might depend on what is read into the word 'enthusiasm'.

'Hisses at a Gilbert and Sullivan First Night!' This was the news that met the unbelieving eyes of readers of *The Times* on 24 January 1887. 'Gilbert and Sullivan's new operetta Ruddygore ... a most unfortunate name, by the bye. ...'

Even the *Atlantic Ocean* flashed the news 'THE FIRST FLAT FAILURE: THE GILBERT AND SULLIVAN OPERA NOT A SUCCESS.'

The *New York Times* in its Sunday edition (23 January) reported: '... There were shouts and cries such as: "Take off this rot! Give us back *The Mikado*!"'

One critic present in London, wrote perceptively: 'It is the misfortune of Messrs Gilbert and Sullivan that they are their own rivals, and every new work makes their task harder.' (*Pall Mall Budget*.)

The Daily News printed three separate reports of the event, one of which ran: '... In the absence of Royalty [alas! poor Arthur!], the Lord Mayor (Sir Reginald Hanson, looking rubicund and jolly) and the Lady Mayoress occupied the Principal Box on the left-hand side of the House. Lady Hanson wore an exquisite toilette and some remarkably fine diamonds.'

The choice of title was a matter for general comment. Gilbert wrote: 'We have a sort of superstition about never fixing our titles until just before the opera is produced. It is not easy to get a good title. I daresay I had half a dozen for this, printing them in block letters to see the effect on the eye. We finally fixed on *Ruddygore*. We only changed *Titipoo* [sic] to *The Mikado* at the last moment.' (*The Pall Mall Budget*.)

By 2 February the offending title was spelled *Ruddigore* in the earnest hope it would take the curse off and the Victorian British were placated.

The first act was a delight, says Reginald Allen: 'Everything sparkles with the flashes of Gilbert's wit,' said *The Times*.

'One of Mr Gilbert's happiest efforts,' said *The Illustrated Sporting and Dramatic News*.

One critic, however, saw more than reached the general eye: 'At the second encore, the Hornpipe was somewhat marred by the inability of the orchestra to pick up the tempo, whereat Sir Arthur was obviously – and audibly – irate.'

LEFT Music covers for *The Mikado* and *The Gondoliers*.

A DISTRESSED WAITER

C.G. JOLLIFFE

SIR GEORGE MORRISON
TOWN CLERK

A.C. MACKENZIE
AUTHOR of the
Story of "SAYID"

Mʳ F. KING

Mʳ ANTONIN DVORAK

ALDⁿ FRED R. SPARK. hon

Mʳ BARTON MᶜGUCKIN

Mʳ Eᵈᵂ LLOYD

Mᵈᵉ ALBANI.

Mᵈᵉ PATEY

Mʳ SANTLEY

SIR ARTHUR SULLIVAN.

ALFRED
BROUGHTON
CHORUS
MASTER

Ruddigore ran for 288 performances and Gilbert announced that the eight-month run put £7,000 in his pocket, and many other dramatists would be glad of such a failure.

LEFT Sketches at the Leeds Music Festival of 1886.

'Richard D'Oyly Carte
Simply hadn't the heart
To tell them he found *Ruddigore*.
An excruciating bore.
A cartoon by Nicolas Bentley in the *Sunday Telegraph*, 1974.

The sea air blows freshly across the harbour of Rederring, much as though the gales of *HMS Pinafore* had blown themselves into a fresh breeze by the time we arrive at 'the only village in the world that possesses an endowed corps of professional bridesmaids, who are bound to be on duty from ten till four'.

The sea-faring Richard's briny song, with its allusion to 'She's only a poor Mounseer', 'A poor parley-vous' and its 'But to fight a French fal-la! it's like hittin' of a gal', gave offence to the French at ambassadorial level. They considered it an insult, and tried to have the play taken off. One of Gilbert's most dazzling patter songs follows in Act I:

> My boy you may take it from me,
> That of all the afflictions accurst
> With which a man's saddled
> And hampered and addled,
> A diffident nature's the worst. ....
>
> If you wish in the world to advance
> Your merits you're bound to enhance
> You must stir it and stump it
> And blow your own trumpet
> Or trust me you haven't a chance.

To which Sullivan attaches a splendid rhythm but a wretched tunelessness. He does better, though, in the ballad that follows: 'The battle's roar is over, O my love.' It finds Gilbert lyrical in form and apt for vocal working. Mad Margaret's *scena* finds Gilbert

again at his most quasi-lyrical, Sullivan a trifle sluggish:

> Cheerily carols the lark
> Over the cot.
> Merrily whistles the Clerk
> Scratching a blot.
> But the lark
> And the Clerk
> I remark
> Comfort me not.

Gilbert in semi-serious mood finds happy expression in the madrigal of which the section that follows is an accomplished example:

> Leaves in autumn fade and fall,
> Winter is the end of all
> Spring and summer teem with glee
> Spring and summer then for me
> Spring is green fa la la
> Summer's rose fa la la.
> It is sad when summer goes
> Autumn's gold fa la la
> Winter still is far away.
>
> In the springtime seed is sown:
> In the summer grass is mown:
> In the autumn you may reap;
> Winter is the time for sleep.

Sullivan's setting, too, is accomplished but little more, though this is a *genre* which should have suited his talent well.

But of course it is only a matter of time before Gilbert falls from rhymer's grace:

> Oh happy the blossom
> That blooms on the lea
> Likewise the opossum
> That sits on a tree.

In the words – or very nearly – of the poet; 'Oh! Mr Gilbert, Mr Gilbert, Oh!'

However he soon obtained the present writer's ready forgiveness for his list-song in Act II – a list of curses that would win the stoniest heart:

> Coward, poltroon, shaker, screamer,
> Blockhead, sluggard, dullhead, dreamer,
> Shirker, shuffler, crawler, creeper,
> Sniffler, snuffler, wailer, weeper,
> Earthworm, maggot, tadpole, weevil,
> Set upon thy course of evil

LEFT Music cover for the *Ruddigore* Quadrille.

> Lest the King of Spectre-land
> Set on thee his grizzly hand.

It takes the present writer back in mind to the Elizabethan 'Fool! Strumpet! Eel's tongue! Thou vile standing tuck!' A clear case of *autre temps – autre* curse.

If Sullivan has reduced his music to little more than a *façon à faire*, Gilbert commits a crime against rhyme in: ... satyr (pronounced sayter)
>> ... first rater
>> ... theayter.

The present writer finds it extraordinary that he should stoop so low not to conquer. One has a sneaking fondness, however, for Gilbert's glimpse of Mad Margaret as a District Visitor:

Sir Despard: A District Visitor should learn to eschew melodrama. Visit the poor, by all means, and give them tea and barley-water, but don't do it as if you were administering a bowl of deadly-nightshade. It upsets them. Then when you nurse sick people, and find them not so well as could be expected, why go into hysterics?
Margaret: Why not?
Sir Despard: Because it's too jumpy for a sick-room.

But *Ruddigore*, considered melodically, is a dreary piece.

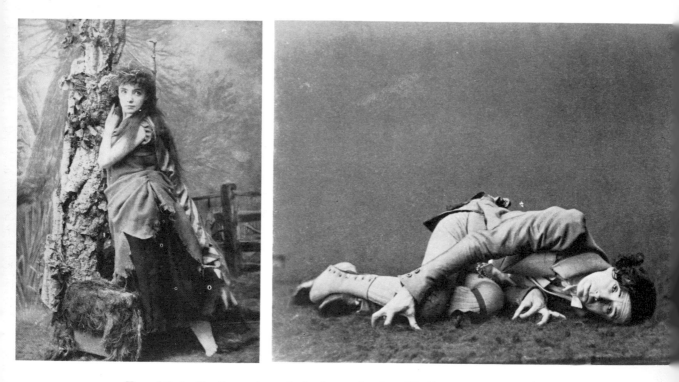

Two of the leading Savoy singers in the first production of *Ruddigore*: Jessie Bond as Mad Margaret and George Grossmith as Robin Oakapple.

RIGHT A page of illustrated criticism of *Ruddigore* from *The Illustrated Sporting and Dramatic News*, 5 February 1887.

OUR CAPTIOUS CRITIC.

ON "RUDDYGORE."

I HAVE heard all and seen some five-sixths of the New and Original Super-natural Opera in two ac's, entitled *Ruddy-gore; or, the Witch's Curse*, written by Mr. W. S. G lbert, composed by Sir Arthur Sullivan, and produced by Mr. R. D'Oyly Carte at the Savoy Theatre. The reason I did not see the remaining sixth was that on the parting of the curtain, cruelly likened by one of my neighbours to a couple of hearthrugs I discovered that from the box where-in I was seated that proportion of the stage was utterly in-visible. I do not think, though, that I lost much, and at any rate saw quite enough for criticism, whilst I was able to listen without hind-rance to words and music. Very good

music too, but all the same presenting to that of the com-poser's preceding operas the strong family resemblance which is characteristic of the wicked barcnets of Ruddygore them-selves. It opens with an overture as varied as one of those masterpieces of the Dutch *cuisine* in which sweets, sours, sharps, salts, and spices are blended together in a way more startling than grateful to the unaccustomed palate, and peters out in a final chorus which affords a striking exemplification of the family resemblance spoken of.

This strong family resemblance extends to other things. I have, I trust, too often ex-pressed in these columns my admiration for Mr. W. S. Gilbert's writ-ings to lay myself open to the imputation of ultra captiousness in pointing out a falling off in *Ruddygore*. Mr. Gilbert's dramatic fare is excellent of its kind, but its staple, as we have learned perforce, is strangely limited. The joint we have en-joyed hot from the spit may still be relished when presented cold with pickles. But when we find it persistently

served up again, now spiced with curry, now hashed with onions, now minced into rissoles, and now heated with sauce, our palled palate revolts at it. *Ruddygore* in more ways than one recalls the "resurrection pie" of our school-boy days. Not only does the author offer us a *rechauffé* of his own work and bestow upon the *plat* a title at which the squeamish affect to sicken, but he has further chosen to dig up the bones of long buried melodrama to make a cockshy of. He

has elected to burlesque a form of entertainment, the recollec-tion of which only survives in the memories of the oldest play-goers. Better surely have let the bones aforesaid rest in peace beneath the monumental stone erected over them by the late Mr. H. J. Byron in the shape of *The Rosebud of Stinging Nettle Farm*. Mr. Gilbert's very workman-hip, if inimitable, is getting monotonous. It begins to suggest the misdirected

mechanical mastery of the Chinese carver, who by patient skill produces a series of concentric balls, curious rather than

Mr RICHARD TEMPLE AS
SIR RODERICK MURGATROYD

beautiful and of no use whatever. His "crankness" as the Americans would style it, is getting crystallised. The mirror he elects to hold up to nature has a surface akin to that of a

Mr. DURWARD LELY AS
RICHARD DAUNTLESS.

Chappuis reflector, and the resulting images are as distorted as the phantasmagoria of the defunct gallanty show. His characters are getting into the habit of addressing one another

Mr RUDOLPH LEWIS AS
OLD ADAM GOOD-HEART AND ALSO
THE POSSESSOR OF A GOOD VOICE

in sentences which sound paradoxical and yet are but pla-titudinarian.

In sundry other matters in *Ruddygore* the same jarring rift mars the harmony of the lute. There has been a great flourish

made about the hyper-accuracy of the military uniforms of the Georgian era, and yet a sailor of Nelson's day appears with the name of his ship in gilt letters on the ribbon round his hat. My memory, tor, of the tars of melodrama whom it is sought to burlesque goes back to Mr. T. P. Cooke and Mr. E. F. Saville, but I c nnot recollect either of them being thus labelled. So, too, the

headgear worn by Despard Murgatroyd in the second act should surely, to be in keeping with his pantaloons, have been of beaver in lieu of glossy silk. It is still more startling to find the ghostly Sir Roderick, who has been dead ten years, and whose portrait may have been painted as many more before his decease, presented in a garb at any rate contemporaneous, if not indeed posterior in date to that worn by one of his colla-teral descendants. The licence of burlesque may excuse the put-ting of references to Mr. Algernon C. Swinburne and Mr. William Morris into the mouth of a farmer of the days when

George the Third was king. The resemblance in metre and music between the legend of the curse and the time-honoured ditty relating to Guy Fawkes, the "prince of sinisters," may be purely accidental or flatteringly intentional. To rescuscitate a picture gallery of ancestors as in *Ages Ago*, to give prominence to a chorus of bridesmaids as in *Trial by Jury*, to revive recol-lections of "Willow waly" by "Hey but," and of the mansuetude of the Pirate King by the mercifulness of the Tom Tit, may be ex-cused on the plea that every man has a right to do what he likes with his own, even at the risk of serving it up *ad nauseam*. But to deliberately serve up the bygone music hall drolleries of the dancing Quakers in a new and original opera is to go rather too far.

MISS
LEONORA
BRAHAM
AS
ROSE
MAYBUD.

As Robin Oakapple, alias Sir Ruthven Mur-gatroyd, Mr. George Grossmith duly stirs it and stumps it. In the second act he scowls like a despot assailed by dyspepsia, spurns the stage like a graffled gamecock — and may take the well-known lines addressed to Sempronius as his con-solation for these endeavours. Mr. Durward Lely as the man o' warsman, Richard Dauntless, pipes shrilly, dances a horn-pipe effectively, and as a substitute for eating banknote sandwiches or frying gold repeaters pitches his jacket care-lessly into space, regardless of the anachronistic gilt buttons

Miss JESSIE BOND
AS
MAD MARGARET
AND
Mr RUTLAND
BARRINGTON
AS Sir DESPARD
MURGATROYD.

Mr GEORGE GROSSMITH AS ROBIN
OAKAPPLE.

adorning it. Mr. Rutland Barrington has fairly astonished me by rising from indifference, and showing himself, as Despard Murgatroyd, capable not only of presenting, but of ably sustaining two distinct characters, the first

At the end of February Sullivan went to Monte Carlo in search of what was clearly needed, sun, but leaden skies presided over the jewelled limpet, clinging to the three *Corniches*, and driving rain greeted him each morning. Outdoor exercise being out of the question, he searched his baggage for a little work. He completed his song, 'Ever', and went to bed at two in the morning.

Not been very long asleep when at 6 am was awakened by a tremendous shaking of the house, increasing in intensity – realised at once it was an *earthquake*. Ten minutes afterwards, another shock – short. Everyone terrorstricken. Women rushing about and into the open-air in their night-dresses. At 8.30 another short shock. The first was the worst – it made me feel quite sick.

But the earthquake produced an incident that Sullivan always narrated with great relish. In the panic which followed the first and longest earth-tremor he put on his dressing-gown and hurried downstairs to the portico of the hotel. There happened to be staying in the hotel at the time a certain *grande Dame* 'of considerable proportions who wore a blonde wig'. As Sullivan waited, shivering, the lady scurried past him. Gone the gold hair. Gone the dignity. Gone the elaborately jewelled gown from Paris. Gone with the earthquake. The only raiment she wore was a red flannel petticoat and chemise. She rushed madly to a monkey-puzzle tree and tried, poor lady, to climb it.

Meanwhile Gilbert was blaming Sullivan for the music in *Ruddigore* in general and the ghost scene in particular: 'I fancy he thought his professional position demanded something grander and more impressive than the words suggested' (he further declared that it was like introducing fifty lines from *Paradise Lost* into a farce – say, Charley's Aunt?). And while he was resenting the inevitable friendly inquiry:

'How's Bloodygore going?'

'You mean *Ruddigore*?'

'Same thing.'

'Indeed? Then if I say I admire your ruddy countenance – which I do – it means that I like your bloody cheek – which I don't!'

Sullivan, in mid-March, had removed himself from Monte Carlo to Naples where he took to his bed, to lie through the hours in deepest agony, with a doctor keeping watch night and day. Packages of letters arrived for him from England. They could only be answered by telegram, for he lacked the strength to write. At last the doctor gave him leave to get up, but forbade him to travel. He got up and travelled straight back to Monte Carlo. But only for five days' rest. Having survived the journey he had been forbidden to take, Sullivan set out for Paris and Berlin.

For some time *The Golden Legend* and Berlin had been floating in the air – now the occasion was ripe. The German Emperor would be ninety on 22 March. Sullivan arrived in Berlin on the Emperor's birthday in a driving snow-storm. He spent the rest of the day trying to reach the singer Pattini who was to sing 'Elsie' in his Oratorio. But the jostling, rejoicing crowds beneath the snow-quilted roofs were so vast and ebullient that, weakened as he was, he judged it better to give up and make his way back to the hotel. There he sat at his window watching the torch-light procession.

Sullivan did not know Pattini, but he did know that it was essential that there should be no hitch in a Command Performance at the Court of a nation which had produced the giant, Beethoven.

Did he have some forebodings when he met Pattini? 'A little soubrette bright little voice, but does not give me the notion of singing Elsie.'

But a little high German swanning soon gave his thoughts a happier turn. The Prince of Wales was in Berlin for the Emperor's ninetieth birthday celebrations, naturally enough. Sullivan supped with Bismarck; he played the pianoforte at a 'wax-work show' given by the Berlin aristocracy, where the Queen of England's daughter, the Princess Victoria, posed as Yum-Yum in 'der Mikado'.

But all his forebodings returned when he held a full-dress rehearsal of *The Golden Legend*.

The next night – disaster:

March 26th Saturday: Went to Opera House to look after arrangements and rehearsed with Pattini, who was very uncertain in her entries, and very shaky in her time. Called at Friedebergs and ordered some jewellery for the principal artists. Dined quietly at home [so one would hope!] went at 7 to the Opera; at a quarter past was ready – Pattini wasn't. She kept me ten minutes, then appeared without her gloves. I went on, and was cordially (not the English warmth) received by a crowded and brilliant audience. All the Royalties there. The performance itself is now a matter of history, alas! Everyone worked well and everyone sympathised with me – it was the most agonising evening I have ever spent. The audience was very patient, very kind to me. The last chorus created a great effect, and I was recalled enthusiastically three times.

To leave Berlin with the impression of his newest serious work under the cloud of the wretched Pattini was a flaw Sullivan would not suffer easily. As it happened, Albani was at Antwerp. He sent a frantic telegram. She replied that she could not go to Berlin for a week. But she could come then. Sullivan dashed off to see Count Hochberg and 'the high dignitaries of the Emperor's Court'. They agreed to give *The Golden Legend* another chance. Albani arrived the following Saturday, but with no time to rehearse.

April 2nd, Saturday: Music with Princess [Victoria] in the afternoon. 7.30 second performance of *Golden Legend* in the Opera House. Full House. [Oh D'Oyly Carte thou shouldst have been with him at this hour!] Royal Family all there. Very good performance. Albani superb. Duet encored. Great enthusiasm and ovation at the end. Supped with Gye and Albani afterwards. Gave her a kiss and a diamond bracelet.

Well, they do say that diamonds are forever.

April 12th, Tuesday: Saw Prince and Princess off at 7.45 am. Being Princess Victoria's birthday I took her a basket of roses at 10. Met all the Royal Family standing on landing listening to the Kaiser Franz regimental band playing [guess what?] *Mikado* in the courtyard. Prince of Saxe-Meinigen sent for the Bandmaster and introduced him to me. After them came the band of the 'Currassiers' and also played *Mikado* – same selection. The Crown Prince chaffed me. Stayed till 12 looking at the flowers etc in Princess Yum-Yum's room.

Back in England Sullivan withdrew into his composer's shell to write the Ode for what *The Times* was to call 'the fiftieth year of a reign prosperous and glorious beyond any recorded in the annals of England', and in order to do this, he had to dismiss all thoughts of other kinds of music from his mind. His mind – not Gilbert's, which was still playing with variations on the lozenge.

For the next few months the collaborators saw nothing of one another but when the Jubilee summer had ended Gilbert started writing what he at that time called *The Tower Warden*. His decision to give burlesque a rest, at least for a time, may perhaps have been influenced by a paragraph in *The Sporting Times*, which ran: 'A *real* comic opera, dealing with neither topsy-turvydom nor fairies, but a genuine dramatic story, would be a greater novelty than anything we are likely to see during the present dramatic season.'

Sullivan wrote: 'Gilbert told me that he had given up the subject over which there had been so much dispute [charm and clockwork] and had found another about the Tower of London. An entirely new departure. Much relieved.' Almost one can see the diary nodding complete agreement. The present writer cannot share Sullivan's enthusiasm. *The Yeomen of the Guard* is like a sun-ray, or perhaps not so much a sun-ray, more a porcupine, with odd – very odd – characters, and pieces of plot, sticking out all over it.

Gilbert, asked once what gave him the idea of *The Yeomen of the Guard*, say Dark and Grey, explained that, 'while waiting for a train on a railway platform one day, he noticed a poster of a beefeater advertising The Tower Furnishing Company, and this set him thinking':

Dear Sullivan

The more I think of it, the more I am convinced that 'The Beefeaters' is the name for the new piece. It is a good, sturdy, solid name, conjuring up picturesque associations and clearly telling its own tale at once: 'The Tower' is nothing. No one knows but a few that Beefeaters were called Tower Warders. . . .

The revival of *HMS Pinafore* was once again drawing the town. It had also drawn a letter from Lord Charles Beresford:

The Admiralty
14.12.87

My dear Arthur

I was perfectly delighted with *Pinafore* last night. Quite excellent. You told me to tell you anything I saw which offended the eye of an expert. I do it. Don't be X [sic]. They are minor details but make the difference in perfection and not absolute perfection.

1. All the men's trousers are VERY BAD, they don't fit, and appear to be made of drill or calico, and not plain honest scrubbed duck which always fits and sets well.
2. The ratlings want squaring, and for good effect ought to be squared every night or morning after a performance.
3. One or two of the blue-jackets' stripes and badges ought to be put on higher up the arm and not in the joint of the elbow, most are in the right place.
4. Your Marines are far too young in appearance, and tend to depreciate the most valuable and splendid corps. (The Stage has an enormous amount of sentiment attached to it, which should be guided the right way.)

5. Manning Yards VERY BAD. Men should stand up and look proud of themselves, heels together, and hands interlocked across each other on the life line.
6. Rigging should be set up tauter.

These are a few details. The rest is quite excellent.

Yours ever

Charlie

One wonders if Sullivan ever found the courage to show 'Charlie's' letter to Gilbert, who had given the revival his habitual careful direction. Indeed, he had taken immense pains over the details. He had designed new sets. He had ordered new costumes and he advised Carte 'not to buy lanyards for the Jack Tars from the usual theatrical suppliers because he had found an old salt who will knot them elaborately, 30 of them, for 2/- each'. He had also suggested a new scene-painter: 'I think Emden will be the best person to employ to do the whole thing – he paints well enough. Bruce Smith says that if he don't paint the whole scene people will think he can't paint – well, people will be right – he can't.' No, Gilbert would not have been amused by Lord Beresford's broadside.

On Christmas Day Gilbert, with D'Oyly Carte, called on Sullivan and read the libretto aloud. The plot appealed strongly to Sullivan, in both background and content. Gilbert thought the *Yeomen* was the best thing the partnership wrote. The two minds were as much one as was in either of them to be.

In January 1888 Gilbert gave Sullivan seven numbers to set during his usual Mediterranean winter. He had gone to great lengths while preparing the new piece, prowling around the Tower in search of atmosphere, and even reading Shakespeare – which, for him, called for a great effort. 'If you promise me faithfully not to mention this to a single person, not even to your dearest friend, I don't think Shakespeare rollicking,' he confided to Grossmith.

'Shakespeare is a very obscure writer,' he said to another friend. 'What do you make of this passage:

' "I would as lief be thrust through a quicket hedge as cry Pooh to a callow throstle"?'

The friend thought it perfectly clear:

'A great lover of feathered songsters, rather than disturb the little warbler, would prefer to go through a thorny hedge. But I can't for the moment recall the passage. Where does it occur?'

'It doesn't,' said Gilbert, 'I have just invented it – and jolly good Shakespeare, too!'

Gilbert had long cherished a feeling that Shakespeare's clowns were wet and whey-faced (though how he could maintain this in the face of the clown in *Lear* is a matter for non-prejudicial examination). He was determined to settle the matter once for all with a clown he created for Grossmith, a Dagobert-the-Jester-like creature, Jack Point. But the complete libretto did not reach Sullivan until 8 June, and in a very fluid state.

During the four-month separation between the two collaborators, Sullivan had been taken gravely and painfully ill. He went to convalesce and generally sort himself to his beloved Monte Carlo, and on to Algiers. 'We are having very bad weather down here, continual rain for the last two or three days,' Sullivan wrote to Madame Ardini: 'Then there is the usual motley crew of gamblers, *cocottes* etc. I shan't stay much longer'. ...'

He now felt that he must let Gilbert know that he wished to devote himself to serious music. Here's a how d'ye do! Was Arthur playing hot and cold? Not, one thinks, consciously. For Baily, by way of illustration, gives a poignant cutting which was to be found among Sullivan's papers when he died: it was from *The Magazine of Music*'s notice of *The Mikado*, and by keeping it, Sullivan proved the importance he attached to it:

We venture to question whether Sir Arthur Sullivan is quite doing justice to himself by continuing to write in this style. There is, of course, no doubt that it pays, while symphonies *don't*; but there is also no doubt that enduring fame and a place among the great composers cannot be gained by a long course of setting verses of refined burlesque to music, pretty and graceful, but of a character that must of necessity be ephemeral.

These considerations Sullivan grappled to his soul with hooks of steel, in the pretty jewelled undulations of Monte Carlo from where he wrote to Gilbert to explain the reason for his decision to write no more light opera.

Gilbert replied:

I can't for the life of me understand the reasons that urge you to abandon a theatre and a company that have worked so well for us, and for whom we have worked so well.

Why in the world are we to throw up the sponge and begin all over again because *Dorothy* has run 500 nights? The piece that we are engaged upon has been constructed by me with direct reference to the Savoy Company: Every member has been fitted down to the ground [and into the ground?] and now that the piece is half finished you propose to scatter the company, abandon the theatre and start anew with a new company in, I suppose, a new theatre. The best composer, and, though I say it, the best librettist in England working together. We are World-known, and as much an institution as Westminster Abbey – and to scatter this splendid organisation because *Dorothy* has run 500 nights is, to my way of thinking, to give up a gold-mine. What is *Dorothy*'s success to us? It is not even the same class of piece as ours. Is no piece but ours to run 500 or 600 nights? Did other companies dissolve because *The Mikado* ran 650 nights?

But Sullivan had convinced himself that *Dorothy* had proved that other men could write light opera, whereas, he had assured himself, only Arthur Sullivan could write serious music. Time would tell – indeed time has told, ungrateful old man that he is. Gilbert ended his letter with unusual tact: 'I hope you've been lucky at the Tables. Try my system, it's very simple. Back red until it turns up twice in succession, then back black till it turns up twice – then back red and so on. I tried it a dozen different times, with Napoleons, and always won.'

This temperate – and very clever – letter from Gilbert, who was not given to stalking his prey but rather to knocking him down on sight, brought Sullivan round.

Carte, too, sent a contributory letter: 'Gilbert has been to *Dorothy* to see Miss Tempest at my request. I was quite satisfied to engage her, as I promised you in my letter from Naples, for a limited or at any rate for an undefined period. However, G having seen her has only confirmed his former objection to her and does not like her at all. He says that she "screeches".'

There were to be squalls between the partners, both before and after *The Yeomen of the Guard* was achieved.

Carte and Sullivan had hit on a project of grand proportions. Their plan was to build a new and larger theatre. Gilbert, in the other scale, did not agree on such an outlay. The scheme might have received Gilbert's assent but for the fact that he had – yet again – fallen out with D'Oyly Carte.

By some misunderstanding, Gilbert, the martinet, had not arrived for a rehearsal of a revival of *The Pirates of Penzance* at the Savoy. The company and the orchestra wasted an hour hanging about waiting for him. When he did arrive, he was in a very ill humour and berated Carte publicly 'in a way', the Manager complained, 'you might adopt if I were either incompetent or had not the interest of the theatre at heart'.

Gilbert called Carte 'dictatorial' – he should have known if anyone knew!

They took to postal fisticuffs. Carte sent two wires to Sullivan, the first on 22 March to Marseilles, the second on 24 March to Monte Carlo.

The first wire read:

SERIOUS ROW WITH AUTHOR DO NOT REALLY SEE HOW THINGS ARE TO GO ON YOU MUST STICK TO ME PRESENT REVIVAL ARTISTIC SUCCESS BUT NO MONEY DO NOT BELIEVE ANY OTHER REVIVAL WILL BE MUCH BETTER. MY CHANCE OF RUNNING PRESENT ESTABLISHMENT SEEMS TO BE TO RUSH ON NEW PIECE IF THIS IMPRACTICAL MUST TRY TO LET THEATRE . . .

Carte's second effort was more consoling.

ROW MADE UP ALL IS PEACE FOR THE MOMENT WILL WRITE DO STAY AT MONTE CARLO TILL I COME HOPE TO START END OF NEXT WEEK

Three weeks later Sullivan and Carte returned to London together: 'April 12th 1888: Went to Savoy Chapel at 11.30 to be best man to D'Oyly who married Helen Cowper-Black, otherwise Lenoir.'

Helen Lenoir, who had been for many years the secretary of D'Oyly Carte, married him in April 1888.

In the following weeks Sullivan sat to Sir John Millais for the portrait that hangs in the National Portrait Gallery. On 8 May, however, Queen Victoria, having heard *The Golden Legend* at the Albert Hall, revived the serious musician in Sullivan: 'You ought to write a Grand Opera, Sir Arthur; you would do it very well.' Once again Arthur was a house divided within himself.

The nearest he got to it in 1888 was writing the incidental music for Irving's *Macbeth* for the Lyceum in December, by which time Helen D'Oyly Carte would have laid the foundation stone for the new English Opera House (the Palace Theatre) at Cambridge Circus, in the presence of Gilbert and Sullivan.

Sullivan began composing *The Yeomen of the Guard* in July 1888 at Fleet in Hampshire and by the middle of August Act I went into rehearsal at the Savoy. Then, once again, dissension broke out between author and composer – pure routine.

Sullivan found that part of Act II was unyielding musically, and asked Gilbert to rewrite it. Gilbert growled that it was 'late in the day to begin making changes', but he would do what he could.

In the event he soon whipped them in and the second Act was in rehearsal before Gilbert had written the dialogue or Sullivan had composed a note of music for the rest of it.

Mercifully, for Sullivan was by no means at the top of his forces, it was not until the final stages in September that he resumed his habit of working far into, if not all through, the night.

Sullivan, it seems, had one fad only, when composing, and that was his J pens. And, Gilbert-like, he would write to the makers and suggest that if they put on a piece here, or take off a piece there, it would be an even greater pen. The intrusion of people into his work-room in order to discuss domestic matters did not disturb him at all, says his nephew. 'It did not spoil the sequence of his thoughts, nor destroy his mood.' He would lift himself – carefully – out of his mood when the intruder came in, and as carefully replace himself in it when he was alone again.

He would talk to his nephew when he happened to be sitting in his room, and compose as he talked, all the while smoking cigarettes from a long holder. He invariably carried a tear-the-leaf note-book in his pocket, which he would produce in some crush or other, and draw quietly aside to jot down some musical idea that had occurred to him. In his room he would draft out a sketch – an outline, one supposes – of the theme. He then added the vocal parts, and usually did not complete the orchestral treatment till the players were actually rehearsing the vocal parts.

Only once, say Sullivan and Flower, during their long partnership, did Gilbert suggest an air to Sullivan: this was Jack Point's 'I have a song to sing, O'. It had been giving Sullivan trouble for some time. He told Gilbert that it was being a nuisance. Gilbert, who loved his sea-going yacht and everything appertaining to the sea, insisted that his crew should sing sea-shanties which he would join in. It was one of these shanties, running through his head while he wrote the lyric, that gave him the rhythm.

Sullivan asked him to hum the tune. He caught the lilt of it at once. 'It was the only time in your life', he told Gilbert afterwards, 'that you wrote words and music.'

Sullivan, though not so celebrated for wit as Gilbert, exercised a felicitous turn of phrase after the fashion of his day. Once he fell from a punt into the Thames, to emerge without his eye-glass but with a brand new *bon-mot*. 'I've always been a contrapuntalist,' he observed.

The new Savoy Opera was scheduled to open on 3 October 1888. But Sullivan was faced with a great deal of work. Meeting him in March 1889, Vernon Blackburn said of him:

He was a very sick man: *The Yeomen of the Guard*, he told me, was written amid circumstances of great difficulty. He was ill, he was troubled, he was melancholy [living with Jack Point was enough to make the stoutest heart melancholy, one might think], he had taken unto himself some of the gloomy thoughts of the world; and the most famous song in the whole opera, 'I have a song to sing O,' cost him infinite pains in the construction.

He returned to the toils of musical creation, taking time off on 11 September to go to Hereford to conduct a performance of *The Golden Legend* in the Shire Hall: 'Crammed house. Very good performance, only Band *rough*, a lot of fossils amongst them.'

Up to the very last day of the rehearsals Gilbert was uneasy about the opening of the opera. He felt that the comical element was too long delayed. On the morning of the opening he sent a letter to Sullivan by messenger:

I desire before the production of our piece to place upon record the conviction that I have so frequently expressed to you in the course of rehearsal, that unless Meryll's introduced and wholly irrelevant song is withdrawn, the success of the first act will be most seriously imperilled.

Let me recapitulate:

The Act commences with Phoebe's song, *Tearful in character*. This is followed by entrance of Wardens. *Serious and martial in character*.

This is followed by Dame Carruthers' 'Tower' song – *grim in character*. This is followed by Meryll's song – *sentimental in character*. This is followed by trio for Meryll, Phoebe and Leonard – *sentimental in character*.

Thus it is that a professedly Comic Opera commences.

I wish moreover to accentuate the hint I gave you on Friday that the Wardens' Couplets in the Finale are too long, and should be reduced by one half. This, you will observe, is not 'cutting out your music', but cutting out a *repeat* of your music. And I may remind you that I am proposing to cut, not only your music, but my words.

Right or wrong, what a time Gilbert picked to deliver this ill-judged broadside!

It was only a few minutes before Curtain Up that author and composer could meet to discuss the merits of the matter. Poor Sullivan who had not wanted to compose the piece in the first place turned, of course, to his diary:

October 3: Tired and nervous. Crammed house – usual enthusiastic reception. I was awfully nervous [certainly his partner had done little to calm him!] and continued so until the duet 'Heighday' which settled the fate of the Opera. Its success was tremendous; three times *encored*! After that everything went on wheels, and I think its success is even greater than *The Mikado*. Nine Encores.

'There is no limit', wrote one critic, 'to what these cunning fellows can do.' There was certainly no limit to what Gilbert felt he could do. The present writer, however, could almost – not quite – forgive him for the sake of the neat and elegant little song that he thought too Rabelaisian for polite Victorian ears in mixed company and so cut it even before Sullivan set it. We are indebted to Leslie Baily for introducing it to us:

Shadbolt (to Phoebe):
The kerchief on your neck of snow
I look on as a deadly foe –
It goeth where I may not go,
And stops there all day long!
The belt that holds you in its grasp
Is, to my peace of mind, a rasp!
It claspeth what I cannot clasp
(Correct me if I'm wrong).

The bird that breakfasts at your lip –
I would I had him in my grip,
He sippeth where I may not sip,
I can't get over that!
The cat you fondle, soft and sly,
He lieth where I may not lie!
We're not on terms, that cat and I!
I do not like that cat.

Every Gilbert and Sullivan Opera had started with an opening chorus, Reginald Allen points out, but this one was to be 'different' from the very outset, and the company's smallest principal, tiny Jessie Bond, opened the opera alone on the stage. Since it was Jessie Bond who bore the brunt of Gilbert's first-night jitters, let us look at the nerve-ridden Gilbert, on the occasion of the first night of *The Yeomen of the Guard* or *The Merryman and his Maid* through the eyes of its soubrette:

I remember the first night of *The Yeomen* very well. Gilbert was always dreadfully over-wrought on these occasions, but this time he was almost beside himself with nervousness and excitement. ... I am afraid he made himself a perfect nuisance behind the scenes, and did his best, poor fellow, to upset us all. ... [It will not be forgotten that Phoebe was out there on the stage alone, waiting for the curtain to rise and trying to compose herself.] But Gilbert kept fussing about. 'Oh, Jessie, are you sure you're all right?' Jessie this – Jessie that – until I was almost as demented as he was. At last I turned on him savagely: 'For heaven's sake, Mr Gilbert, go away and leave me alone, or I shan't be able to sing a note!' He gave me a final frenzied hug and vanished.

For the rest of the Gilbert story let us go to *The Sunday Times*: 'It is well-known that nervousness prevents Mr Gilbert ever sitting through one of his own works. ... Consequently on Wednesday night, during the progress of *The Yeomen of the Guard*, he might have been seen in the stalls at Drury Lane, watching *The Armada*. ... He turned up in time for his call, though.'

An 'unregenerate reporter' from the *Sporting Times* wrote:

RIGHT Music cover to Bucalossi's arrangement of airs from *The Yeomen of the Guard*.

THE YEOMEN OF THE GUARD LANCERS

By P. BUCALOSSI.

On Airs from Gilbert & Sullivan's Opera.

LONDON,
CHAPPELL & Co. 50. New Bond Street W.

The First Night at the Savoy is apt to be a solemn function. Many of the merry deadheads one ordinarily chats with are conspicuous by their absence, and their places are occupied by long-haired music critics who glare at you, if you move half an inch, and who exclaim 'Ssh!' on the slightest provocation. Last Wednesday was no exception to the rule: and as the show was not over till 11.30, and there was but one interval for stretching one's legs – it may be imagined that the occasion was somewhat of an ordeal. ...

The Standard, in a column-long piece, expressed pleased surprise that 'our perennial little soubrette sang, alone on the stage', what Thomas Dunhill was to call 'an exquisite piece of lyrical music tinged with a mood of quiet regret, halting here and there that the singer may breathe the most musical of sighs. Was this quite serious, or should they be ready for a comic twist, carefully disguised? But Jessie left the stage after her last "Ah me!" weeping so ... she did not get the "bad laugh" that must have been ready, trembling on so many lips.'

'Sir Arthur Sullivan has never written anything more delicately melodious and elegant than this, in fact he has never equalled it and probably never will.' (*The Morning Advertiser*.)

Gilbert, notes Reginald Allen, did not fare as well as Sullivan in the 'morning-after press'. Virtually every critic, it seems, mentioned the similarity of plot to that of *Maritana* (which in turn derived from *Don César de Bazan*, a French play by d'Ennery). *Punch*, in particular, seized on the opportunity: *The Beefeater's Bride*: or, *The Merryman and his Maritana*, it carolled, 'by the unknown team of Sulbert and Gillivan'.

The Times wrote:

Mr Gilbert is in his way a genius, and even at his worst is a head and shoulders above the ordinary librettist. In the present instance he has not written a good play but his lyrics are suave and good to sing and, wedded to Sir Arthur Sullivan's melodies, they will no doubt find their way to many a home where English song is appreciated.

To sum up; Sir Arthur Sullivan's score is fully equal to previous achievements, and the success of the piece will no doubt be largely due to it.
Selah!

One imagines that it is more or less generally agreed that five works, *Iolanthe*, *HMS Pinafore*, *The Mikado*, *The Yeomen of the Guard* and *The Gondoliers*, show the talents of Gilbert and Sullivan interlocking most successfully together. That is to say Gilbert may be at his best and most wittily fluent in *The Mikado*: Sullivan may be at his most melodious in any one of them. The quintet of operas work, and work triumphantly, for what, after all, is a flaw here, a false accent there? Certainly it is interesting to see Sullivan the melodist fighting the material of medieval shadow and his own low spirits, in *The Yeomen of the Guard*.

There is a certain boldness in opening an opera – even a comic opera – on a solo for a solitary soubrette.

Both sail through this hazard: 'When maiden loves she sits and sighs.' But immediately after this, Gilbert gets up to his old tricks:

Advertisements in the Savoy programmes illustrated with
pictures of Phoebe and Jack Point with Elsie.

181

> Tower Warders
> Under Orders
> Gallant pokermen
> Valiant sworders.

A lazy final word in the rhymed place I find hard to pass uncensored. Again:

> The screw may twist
> And the rack may turn
> And men may bleed
> And men may burn

sounds oddly in a woman's voice, however deep or dramatic the contralto of Dame Carruthers. One would have thought a man might have sung it. Take:

> Is life a boon?
> If so, it must befall
> That Death, whene'er he call
> Must call too soon.
> Though fourscore years he give
> Yet one would pray to live
> Another moon
> What kind of plaint have I,
> Who perish in July?
> I might have had to die
> Perchance, in June!

> Is life a thorn?
> Then count it not a whit!
> Man is well done with it,
> Soon as he's born.
> He should all means essay
> To put the plague away:
> And I, war-worn
> Poor captured fugitive
> My life must gladly give –
> I might have had to live
> Another morn.

It will seem sacrilegous, to the dyed-in-the-wool Gilbert and Sullivan *aficionado*, to suggest that this suckling-like, most lyrical of all Gilbert's lyrics, which could well be anthologised, might also well be re-set by some Lennox Berkeley. Sullivan's music for it seems more to reflect the stout-hearted soldier marching through it, than the poet.

Of course Gilbert could write a smooth line with a point to it, when he took the pains. None better. But so often he wriggles out of the strong corset of prosody which keeps a jealous guard on lyricists and throws the burden on Sullivan's shoulders, as stiff and unyielding, in the matter of tempo and give-and-take, as those of a martinet. In that near

THE YEOMEN OF THE SAVOY.

Alfred Bryan's caricature of Gilbert and Sullivan on guard.

perfect song, perfect, that is, for the purpose, 'Were I thy bride', Gilbert mars his own effect with an imperfect line, considered lyrically (indeed in performance I have heard it rectified, with or without Gilbert's approval, I do not know) to 'Then all the world beside'.

Were I thy bride
Then the whole world beside
Were not too wide
To hold my wealth of love –
Were I thy bride.

Signs of Verdi, in *Il Trovatore* can be heard in:

The prisoner comes to meet his doom:
The block, the headsman, and the tomb.
The funeral bell begins to toll –
May heaven have mercy on his soul!

with bell of doom off, and full choral honours – fair enough in a composer whose musical influences are stronger than his talent for original composition. 'Up and down and in and out' is a clever example of how a composer can quicken the pace by a slight adjustment and so heighten the tension – here it is done on the end of a line – very deft and musicianly.

Gilbert obliges with some genial and very accurate advice from the Merryman to his amateur colleagues:

There are one or two rules,
Half a dozen maybe,
That all Family fools
Of whatever degree
Must observe if they love their profession.
If your master is surly, from getting up early
(And tempers are short in the morning),
An inopportune joke is enough to provoke
Him, to give you, at once, a month's warning. . . .

throws a gleam of truth on both, say, the Elizabethan jester and the fool of the Victorian family.

Then if you refrain, he is at you again,
For he likes to get value for money.
He'll ask then and there, with an insolent stare
If you know that you're paid to be funny –

And not only Victorian family:

It adds to the tasks
Of a Merryman's place
When your principal asks
With a scowl on his face
If you know that you're paid to be funny?

Poor fool!

Gilbert however wrote a melodist's dream of a quartet to which Sullivan added a librettist's dream of a setting:

Strange adventure Maiden married
To a groom she's never seen
Never, never, never seen.
Groom about to be beheaded
In an hour on Tower Green ...
Groom in dreary dungeon lying
Groom as good as dead or dying
For a pretty maiden sighing,
Pretty maid of seventeen. ...

It is strange indeed that this unlikely-looking lyric should have blossomed into Sullivan's lovely madrigal. Or maybe one has stumbled on the secret of that melodist's genius – to transmute to gold and silver what in some other alchemist's music might have been dross.

The morning following the first night Sullivan received a letter from his old chum, 'A triumph! A triumph!'

HMS Alexandra
Nanplin
28th September 1888

My dear Sullivan

I have never had sign of life from you since I left England, but no doubt you have been so busy that you have forgotten me altogether.

You will remember two years ago my asking you to send me some music for the Sultan's band, notably among it selections from your operettas. HIM is so pleased with the music that he questioned me much when I was at Constantinople the other day as to the composer, and requested me to forward to you the enclosed decoration as a mark of his appreciation. ...

I think that about the favourite piece in the *repertoire* of our band on board here is your music to Henry VIII! I like it better every time I hear it.

Yours very truly

Alfred

The year was drawing to a close and Sullivan was about to go abroad for a little sun, when Henry Irving invited him to write the incidental music to his forthcoming *Macbeth*.

If Irving's outline of what he wanted was brief, it was also more than a little vague:

My dear Sullivan

Trumpets and drums are the things *behind scenes*.

Entrance of *Macbeth, only drum.*

Distant march would be good for Macbeth's exit in 3rd scene – or drum and trumpets as you suggest.

In the last act there will be several flourishes of trumpets.

'Make all our trumpets speak,' et.

Roll of drum sometimes.

Really anything you can give of a stirring sort can be easily brought in.

As you say, you can dot these down at rehearsals – but one player would be good to tootle, tootle, so that we could get the exact tune. I'm at present moment with the 'blood-boltered Banquo' who's really making a most unreal shadow of himself.

Ever yours

H. Irving

Early in December Sullivan went to the Lyceum with the completed music and began to rehearse with the orchestra. Until then Irving knew nothing of what he had written.

Macbeth was to open on 29 December and it was not until Boxing Night that Sullivan finished the scoring – eleven hours' work. There could be only two full rehearsals, but Sullivan had a grip on the orchestra and Irving was delighted.

December 29th 1888: Left at 7.15 for the production of *Macbeth* at the Lyceum Theatre:

Words by Shakespeare

Music by Sullivan

Produced by Irving.

Great success! Author, composer and stage-manager called enthusiastically.

Only the two latter responded!

Is this the Wicked Uncle dragging away one of the Babes to be killed? No, it is only Macbeth bringing on Sir Arthur Sullivan to receive the congratulations of the Audience.

A *Punch* cartoon on Irving's Lyceum production of *Macbeth*, with music by Sullivan, in 1889.

RIGHT Sullivan painted by Millais in 1888.

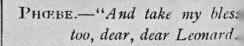

A PLOT

TO SAVE A HEAD

REPRIEVE.

FAIRFAX

PHŒBE.—"And take my bles:
too, dear, dear Leonard.

LEONARD.—"And thine, eh?
Humph! Thy love is :
born; wrap it up, les
take cold and die."

9

The Gondoliers

In the early weeks of 1889 Sullivan's view of where his future lay, hardened. He was tired of jumping the same old light-operatic hurdles. He really felt he had mastered the medium and he longed for fresh symphonic fields to conquer. Nor had he forgotten Queen Victoria – what Victorian could – and her attempt to turn his talents to Grand Opera.

January 9th 1889, called Carte, then Gilbert. Explained to latter my views as to the future, *viz.* that I wanted to do some more dramatic work on a larger musical scale, and that of course I should like to do it with him if he would, but that the music must occupy a more important position than in our other pieces – that I wanted to get rid of the *strongly marked rhythm* and *rhymed* couplets, and have words that would give a chance of developing *musical* effects. Also that I wanted a voice in the *Musical* construction of the libretto. He seemed quite to assent to all this.

But, of course, they never knew with Gilbert. Sometimes he would fly off the handle then and there; but at others it would take time for the full force of someone else's point of view to dawn; but once he examined any departure from his ordered schemes, an explosion followed.

These views of Sullivan's were no surprise to him. He had more than once felt uneasy about the siren voice of serious music that haunted Sullivan in the still of the night – those still nights he was not working through. Sullivan wrote to Gilbert that he was quite decided that his next work should be 'a major work of dramatic and serious purpose, before contemplating anything else', and he hoped Gilbert would write it with him. Gilbert answered temperately enough:

LEFT Leonard, Phoebe and Sergeant Merrill, from the first production of *The Yeomen of the Guard*.

Dear S

I have thought carefully over your letter, and while I quite understand and sympathise with your desire to write what, for want of a better term, I suppose we must call 'Grand Opera', I cannot believe that it would succeed either at the Savoy or at Carte's new theatre, unless a much more powerful singing and acting company were got together than the Company we now control. Moreover, to speak from my own selfish point of view, such an opera would afford me no chance of doing what I best do – the librettist of a grand opera is always swamped in the composer.... We have a name, jointly, for humorous work, tempered with occasional glimpses of earnest drama. I think we should do unwisely if we left, altogether, the path which we have trodden together so long and so successfully. I can quite understand your desire to write a big work. Well, why not write one? But why abandon the Savoy business? Cannot the two things be done concurrently? If you can write an oratorio like the *Martyr of Antioch* while you are occupied with pieces like *Patience* and *Iolanthe*, can't you write a grand opera without giving up pieces like *The Yeoman of the Guard*? Are the two things irreconcilable? As to leaving the Savoy, I can only say that I should do so with the profoundest reluctance and regret. [Gilbert had burned his fingers badly when, in November 1888, a few weeks after mounting *The Yeomen of the Guard*, he wrote a play, *Brantingham Hall*, which failed at the St James's Theatre. Gilbert knew well, therefore, what he was writing about the Savoy.] I feel convinced that it would be madness to sever the connections with the theatre.

If you don't care to write any more pieces of the *Yeomen* order, well and good. But before launching a grand opera remember how difficult we have already found it to get effective singers and actors for the pieces we have already done. Where, in God's name, is your Grand Opera soprano who can act? [Aye, there's the rub.]

... The best librettist of the day is Julian Sturgis. Why not write a grand opera with him? *My* work in that direction would be, deservedly or otherwise, generally pooh-poohed.

Yours truly,

W.S.Gilbert

Gilbert, it is clear, wanted the Savoy partnership to continue. Sullivan longed to be shot of it.

12th March 1889

My dear Gilbert

I confess that the indifference of the public to *The Yeoman of the Guard* has disappointed me greatly, as I looked upon its success as opening out a large field for works of a more serious and romantic character. If the result means a return to our former style of piece I must say at once, and with deep regret, that I cannot do it. I have lost the liking for writing comic opera [did he really ever have it?]. ...

But now we must decide, not argue. You say that in a serious opera, *you* must more or less sacrifice yourself. I say this is just what I have been doing in all our joint pieces, and, what is more, must continue to do in comic opera to make it successful. I am bound in the interests of the piece, to give way. Hence the reason of my wishing to do a work where the music is to be the first consideration – where words are to suggest music, not govern it, and where music will intensify and emphasise the emotional effect of the words. ...

Back came the answer from Boomerang Gilbert.

19th March 1889

Dear Sullivan

Your letter has filled me with amazement and regret. If you are really under the astounding impression that you have been effacing yourself during the last twelve years – and if you are in earnest when you say that you wish to write an opera with me in which the 'music shall be the first consideration' – by which I understand an opera in which the libretto, and consequently the librettist must occupy a subordinate place – then there is most certainly no *modus vivendi* to be found that shall be satisfactory to both of us.

You are an adept at your profession and I am an adept in mine. If we meet it must be as master and master – not as master and servant.

Yours faithfully

W.S.Gilbert

A week later, Fencer Sullivan feinted again:

27th March

My dear Gilbert

I was so annoyed at your abrupt letter to me that I thought it wiser not to answer it without a few days' delay. . . . I write therefore only to say that it seems to me a silly and unnecessary thing for you and I to quarrel over a matter that can really be so easily arranged, and that I really don't think my requests are unreasonable.

All I ask is that in the future, (1) my judgment and opinion should have some weight with you in the laying out of the *musical situation*, even to making important alterations after the

A page from Sullivan's score of *The Gondoliers*, showing part of the tenor song 'Take a pair of sparkling eyes'.

191

work has been framed, because it is impossible sometimes to form a right judgment until one begins to work at the number or situation itself; (2) that I should have a more important share in arranging the attitudes and business in all the musical portions, and, (3) that the rehearsals should be arranged in such a way as not to weary the voices, and cause everyone to sing carelessly and without regard for tune, time or account. . . .

If you will accept all this in the spirit in which I write, we can go on smoothly as if nothing had happened, and, I hope, successfully. If not, I shall regret it deeply, but, in any case, you will hear no more recrimination on my part.
Yours sincerely
Arthur Sullivan

Fencer Sullivan had modified his stance from never wanting to write a light opera again, to writing another given his conditions. But back came the Boomerang, highly indignant:

31st March '89

Dear Sullivan
. . . I say that when you deliberately assert that for 12 years you, incomparably the greatest English musician of the age – a man whose genius is a proverb wherever the English tongue is spoken – a man who can deal *en prince* with operatic managers, singers, music publishers and musical societies – when you, who hold this unparalleled position, deliberately state that you have submitted silently and uncomplainingly for 12 years to be extinguished, ignored, set aside, rebuffed and generally effaced by your librettist, you grievously reflect, not upon him, but upon yourself and the noble art of which you are so eminent a professor.
Yours faithfully
W.S.Gilbert

All through March Sullivan, as was his habit, went to the Riviera in search of sun, with Gilbert's letters, as though released from a bow, darting after him. Letters flew between Gilbert and Sullivan. Of course it was the age-old trouble between librettist and composer as to which should come first, the chicken or the egg? And to this there is no answer that satisfies both. Something's – someone's – got to give. One wonders what schizophrenia sets in when one man writes both words and music – a Cole Porter, say, an Irving Berlin, a Stephen Sondheim?

Carte, the dove of peace – of other people's peace, that is – talked the whole thing over with Gilbert, and then met Sullivan in Paris to talk the matter over with him. With the bait of a Grand Opera at his new theatre he persuaded Sullivan to start work at once on another comic opera for the Savoy on the old lines.

Dove D'Oyly had entirely won Sullivan over. Pat came the unexpected letter to Gilbert:

. . . I am quite prepared to set to work at once upon a light or comic opera with you – provided of course, that we are thoroughly agreed upon the subject.

I am enabled to do this all the more willingly since I have now settled to write an opera on a large scale . . . to be produced next spring. I have my subject [Ivanhoe] of my own choice and my collaborator; also an agreement with Carte to keep the new theatre for me for this purpose, and not to let it to anyone else before then. In this manner I can realise the great desire of my life, and at the same time continue a collaboration which I regard with a stronger sentiment than that of pecuniary advance.

On 9 May Sullivan wrote in his diary: 'Long and frank explanation with Gilbert; free and outspoken on both sides. Shook hands and buried the hatchet.' A few days later he wrote to Gilbert:

I understand from Carte that you had some subject connected with Venice and Venetian life, and this seemed to me to hold out great chances of bright colours and taking music. Can you not develop this with something we can both go into with warmth and enthusiasm, and thus give me a subject in which like *The Mikado* or *Patience* – we can both be interested?

And so *The Gondoliers* were born of a love-hate match.

Sullivan's spirits had never been better, his morale never higher. He stayed with the Prince and Princess of Wales at Sandringham. 'I was most cordially welcomed by the P. and Pcess of Wales and all the Royal Family,' he assures his diary. 'All the five children were there, also the Empress of Germany and her three daughters. It was the first time I had seen Her Majesty since the Emperor's death. She looked so sad, and I was quite touched by her affectionate greeting of me. Before dinner we had the phonograph' – Sullivan had taken a phonograph, the latest miracle, to Sandringham – 'to amuse the royal children'.

A few days later: 'February 12th: Went by the Prince of Wales's "special" with HRH, Clarke and R. Sassoon in the saloon. Very cold. Special boat (*Empress*) brought us over to Calais, excellent supper. Private Room. Left by ordinary mail for Paris.'

At the end of March Sullivan left for Venice in search of atmosphere for *The Gondoliers*. 'The city entranced him, the churches, the *campanile* with its wonderful views. Only the music at the Opera', says his nephew, 'disappointed him.' A disappointment this most consciously English of the *fin de siècle* English composers could bear, one feels. Still, to his musician's ear it was to be deplored: 'Went to the Rossini theatre to hear *Norma*. Norman and Adallini, both about 40, with worn-out voices. Tenor like a butcher. . . . Band rough, chorus coarse.'

He returned to London early in June.

'June 8th: 2.30 Gilbert came and read sketch plot of new piece. Bright, interesting, funny and very pretty.'

Gilbert sent the numbers as he wrote them to Sullivan to set. The full work would not be ready until 3 October.

Throughout the latter part of summer, Sullivan had been working at Grove House, Weybridge. 'He would', says his nephew, 'compose a couple of numbers, then not touch the work again for a week or more. The planning of *Ivanhoe* beckoned him away, as a lure to a tassle-gentle.'

Sullivan lingered on contentedly at Weybridge; rowing, walking, composing a song at mood. The Duke's song, and that of the Grand Inquisitor in Act I were, it seems, written in a morning. 'Thank you gallant Gondolieri' was composed and framed at a single sitting.

But now the lazy summer was over, and except for the days spent at the Leeds Festival, which he conducted in October, he dedicated the whole of the autumn to *The Gondoliers*.

'October 12th, Leeds: Last concert. Superb performance of *The Golden Legend*. The finest I have ever heard. Afterwards the enthusiasm was indescribable. ... All over at last. Saw the band off by the "special", then home to supper and quiet.'

November came. Sullivan adjusted his calendar to the customary nightwrite. The new piece was not due to open until 7 December – a vista of midnight oil lay ahead. The piece – again according to custom – did not achieve the dignity of a title until five days before the first night:

THE GONDOLIERS

or

THE KING OF BARATARIA

From his long-suffering diary I select a few entries:

November 4th: Too tired to go to rehearsal. Wrote *four* numbers: Finished at 4; to bed 4.15.
November 9th: Began scoring. 32 pages.
November 15th: Very seedy all day. Scored No. 10.

And so on – seedy or (comparatively) healthy until:

November 26th: Rehearsal on stage 11.30 till 4. Dined at home and went to Haymarket
            Theatre to see *A Man's Shadow*. I am out of prison at last!

But there would still be intensive work right up to and during 2 December.

He had finished and by some miracle had escaped a serious breakdown. 'None of the operas had been composed at such terrific pressure as this one.' Even Gilbert, noting the effect on Sullivan's health, urged that the piece be postponed. 'Sullivan merely smiled, and all through the night the light in his study burned till dawn.' Traditionally rosy-fingered.

At rehearsals his demeanour was the same. No irritability: only inexhaustible patience, sympathy, consideration.

'December 7th: Quiet all day. Went to the theatre at 8.35. Of course crammed house [of course!] a great reception. ... We have never had such a brilliant first night. It looks as if the opera were going to have a long run, and be a great success.' Almost one can sense the diary touching wood.

An enthusiastic Gilbert wrote the following day: 'I must thank you again for the magnificent work you have put into the piece. It gives one the chance of shining right through the twentieth century with a reflected light.'

'Don't talk of reflected light,' Sullivan replied, warmly: 'In such a perfect book as *The Gondoliers* you shine with an individual brilliancy which no other writer can hope to attain. If any thanks are due anywhere, they should be from me to you for the patience, willingness and unfailing good nature with which you have received my suggestions, and your readiness to help me by according to them.'

While they are congratulating themselves and one another, let us see what the Press has to say about *The Gondoliers*:

'A great success', proclaimed *The Sunday Times* of 8 December 1889 in a headline. 'From the time the curtain rose there reigned in the Savoy Theatre but one steady atmosphere of contentment – contentment with the music, the dances, the piece, the

RIGHT Rutland Barrington and Courtice Pounds as the gondoliers in the first production, 1889.

scenery, the dresses and not the least of all, with the talented and loyal members of Mr D'Oyly Carte's company.'

'*The Gondoliers*', gloated *The Globe*, 'is one of the best, if not the best, of the Gilbert and Sullivan operas.'

'It is not an Opera or play; it is simply an entertainment – the most exquisite, the daintiest entertainment we have ever seen,' encored *The Echo*.

The New York Herald's London Correspondent announced to the waiting New World: 'The popular composer surpasses all his previous efforts, and W. S. Gilbert proves that he has lost none of his pleasing talent.'

'Mr W. S. Gilbert has returned to the Gilbert of the past, and everyone is delighted. He is himself again,' agreed *The Illustrated London News*.

'Mr D'Oyly Carte was flitting about in front bearing the assured air of coming triumph', espied the *Daily News*, and it went on to record: 'Facing each other in the opposite stage boxes were Mrs Mackay and Mrs Ronalds, each with a large party.' Both were American, rich and social beauties.

While the *Topical Times* turned *voyeur* with: '. . . the chorus wore comparatively short skirts for the first time, and the gratifying fact is revealed to a curious world that the Savoy chorus are a very well-legged lot.'

Sullivan himself, as quoted in *Home News* (before the opening night), groaned: 'There is a good deal more work in it than there was in *The Yeomen* for nearly all the numbers are rapid. You will hear very little slow music in it. Of course the result is that there are more pages in the score. Two minutes *Allegro* means perhaps twenty pages, but', he approved, 'with an *Andante* movement you would only use about six.'

But only a week after the opening Gilbert was writing to Alfred Austin (later Poet Laureate): 'Many thanks for your kind congratulations. The piece is ridiculous rubbish and is, accordingly, hailed as a masterpiece.'

What about that reflected light so confidently forecast to 'shine through the twentieth century' in his letter to the man who had lit it? What indeed!

Christopher Hassall, in his *Biography of Edward Marsh* quotes a letter from Marsh, at that time an undergraduate and Music and Drama Critic to the *Cambridge Observer* who has this to say of *The Gondoliers*: 'It is fairly well performed, except by the hero, who is grotesque, and the heroine, who sang one particular false note which burst into the chorus as a comet might have burst into the solar system and shook the entire audience to the roots of its diaphragms. As for the opera itself, both music and words are perfect.'

In fact, I would say that in *The Gondoliers* both men could indulge their talents – Gilbert, his for the unexpected throwaway reflection:

> Jealousy yellow
> Unfortunate fellow

(and what a wealth of meaning that casual word 'unfortunate' defines) and the 'list' songs – those passages of patter in which one can feel him spring to life – and Sullivan's unfailing bent for pastiche. In spite of his bad health and lagging spirits, *The Gondoliers* is one of his most bubbling scores; the source of the 'innocent merriment' which Gilbert

The quintet in the first act of *The Gondoliers* in the 1889 production.

and Carte looked for in him.

In the all-Italian number, simply but explicitly, librettist and composer have caught the humility and diffidence of the double-yoke gondoliers, whom the flower girls hail as 'Cavalieri', in their deprecating correction 'Gondolieri', and the modesty of the girls, hailed by the gondoliers as 'Signorini', a title disclaimed by their gentle, 'Contadini'. A perfect disclaimer which crystallises their place in the plot and their essential characterisation in two words. Who else could have hit on a more clear and economical device?

Economy has been Gilbert's watchword in this piece, even in the list songs, and Sullivan seems to have given these more than his usual melodic attention. Refusing for once to be content with marking the rhythm and giving them, for the greater part, an invention of their own.

The entrance of the Duke of Plaza Toro:

> And His Grace's Duchess true
> And His Grace's Daughter too –
> And His Grace's private drum
> To Venetia's shores have come

soon becomes the cue, however much against Sullivan's grain, of the dreaded quick number with its attendant shower of notes to be written down:

> And if ever, ever, ever
> They get back to Spain
> They will never, never, never
> Cross the sea again.

197

The sudden quickening of the music gives something of the sparkle of the sun on the waves.

The Duke, one of the most successful characters within the canon, spurs on Gilbert to a pithy exposure that leaves His Grace without a last Charge to stand on:

> In enterprise of martial kind,
> When there was any fighting,
> He led his regiment from behind –
> He found it less exciting
> But when away his regiment ran
> His place was to the fore O

(We will allow him that O because of the excellence of the lyric otherwise)

> That celebrated,
> Cultivated,
> Underrated,
> Nobleman,
> The Duke of Plaza Toro!
> In the first and foremost flight [we will ignore the ignoble ha! ha!]
> You always found that knight . . .
> When to evade Destruction's hand
> To hide they all proceeded
> No soldier in that gallant band
> Hid half as well as he did.
> He lay concealed throughout the war
> And so preserved his gore, O
> That unaffected,
> Undetected,
> Well-connected,
> Warrior,
> The Duke of Plaza Toro.'

Then, once again to a mood that Herrick could have caught:

> . . . Thy cold disdain
> It gives no pain –
> 'Tis mercy, played
> In Masquerade.
> Thine angry frown
> Is but a gown
> That serves to dress
> Thy gentleness.

The present writer suspects that Gilbert's 'angry frown' was but a gown that served to dress an intermittent gentleness, but suggests that his friends had to dig a bit to find that gentleness.

Again Gilbert is adept at finding a day-by-day phrase and batting it to Sullivan who finds a happy musical equivalent:

A taste for drink, combined with gout,
Had doubled him up for ever.
Of *that* there is no manner of doubt –
No probable, possible shadow of doubt,
No possible doubt whatever.

by its very matter-of-factness is halfway to a chuckle without further effort.
Onwards to Gilbert in satiric vein – Herrick with a wink, as it were:

Why should we in vain endeavour,
Guess and guess and guess again?
Life's a pudding full of plums,
Care's a canker that benumbs.
Wherefore waste our Elocution
On impossible solution,
Let us take it as it comes!

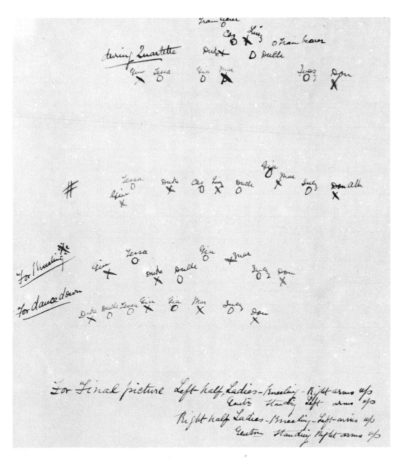

Gilberts' plan and notes for the finale of *The Gondoliers*.

Charming? And a smile into the bargain.

But alas! Trouble in paradise! The wretched Gilbert, just as we are about to open our arms and cry 'Come home, Librettist, all is forgiven,' comes up with

> Bridegrooms all joyfully
> Brides, rather coyfully . . .

One blushes for him. Granted coyfully may be a word, but it is not the right word.

But to a happier lyric.

'When a merry maiden marries' brings out the best in the lyricist and – bearing in mind the *genre* for which he is writing – the composer. Particularly happy is the magical compression of the thought *'Ou sont les neiges d'antan?'* into:

> Every kind of trouble goes
> Where the last year's snows have gone.

Onwards ever onwards to the Quartette, which is one of Gilbert's happiest characterisations:

> *Gianetta:* Then one of us
> Will be a queen
> And sit on a golden throne
> With a crown instead
> Of a hat on her head
> And diamonds all her own!
> With a beautiful robe of gold and green,
> I've always understood;
> I wonder whether
> She'd wear a feather?
> I rather think she should!

Gianetta; sister-under-the-skin to Eliza Doolittle.

The final word on nepotism rests with Gilbert. 'For everyone who feels inclined', sing the double-breasted kings-apparent 'as one individual':

> Some post we undertake to find
> Congenial with peace of mind
> And all shall equal be.
> The Earl, the Marquis and the Dook,
> The Groom, the Butler and the Cook,
> The Aristocrat who banks with Coutts,
> The Aristocrat who cleans the boots,
> The Noble Lord who rules the State,
> The Noble Lord who scrubs the grate,
> The Lord Bishop orthodox,
> The Lord High Vagabond in the stocks. . . .

Gilbert's views on the social set-up are clear for all to read:

> When everybody's somebodee
> Then no one's anybody.

The Gondoliers is given before Queen Victoria and the
royal family at Windsor Castle in 1891.

If Sullivan had written *Don Giovanni*, we may depend upon it that the old bathroom
rouser, 'Take a pair of sparkling eyes', would have been his serenade for the Don,
though it is baffling how Gilbert could have so debased his talent as to write:

> Take a tender little hand
> Fringed with dainty fingerettes

Sullivan, prince of *pasticheurs*, produced a charming *Cachucha* which combines style with economy. Indeed, in the middle eight or 'release', as we say in the Charing Cross Road, he captures magically the majesty of Spanish shoulders moving through the dance. Gilbert's contribution to the classic eight bars is:

> Clitter – clitter – clatter
> Pitter – pitter – patter

The next Quartet:

> In a contemplative fashion
> And a tranquil frame of mind,
> Free from every kind of passion
> Some solution let us find.

If only Gilbert could have taken his own words to heart!

Another composer's dream of a lyric follows the librettist's instructions:
March. Enter procession of Retainers, heralding approach of DUKE, DUCHESS AND CASILDA. All three are now dressed with the utmost magnificence:

> With ducal pomp and ducal pride
> (Announce these comers,
> O ye kettle-drummers)
> Comes Barataria's high-born bride,
> (Ye sounding cymbals clang!)
> She comes to claim the royal hand –
> (Proclaim their Graces,
> O ye double-basses)
> Of the king who rules this goodly land.
> (Ye brazen brasses bang).

One is a little dubious about brasses, however brazen, banging, for the cymbal has been ruled out having been used in the fifth line to clang.

A point-number follows:

> To help unhappy commoners, and add to their enjoyment
> Affords a man of noble rank congenial employment.
> Of our attempts we offer you examples illustrative;
> The work is light, and, I may add, it's most remunerative!
> Small titles and orders
> For Mayors and Recorders
> I get – and they're highly delighted!
> MPs baronetted
> Sham Colonels gazetted
> And second-rate Aldermen knighted.

Gilbert, thou shouldst be living at this hour!

10

The Quarrel

So, like *Pinafore, Iolanthe* and *The Mikado, The Gondoliers* proved to be a work suited to both highly-charged talents. It was too bad, therefore, that it should lead to litigation between, on the one hand, battling Gilbert, and on the other, wily old D'Oyly Carte and unwilling Sullivan.

It began with a letter from Gilbert to Sullivan who had gone swanning in Monte Carlo, Brussels and Milan for some weeks to rest before applying himself to the serious business of writing *Ivanhoe* with Julian Sturgess.

Gilbert had just returned from a little swanning on his own account in India:

My dear S

I've had a difficulty with Carte.

I was appalled to learn from him that the preliminary expenses of *The Gondoliers* amounted to the stupendous sum of £4,500!!! This seemed so utterly unaccountable that I asked to see the details, and last night I received a résumé of them. This includes such trifles as £75 for Miss Moore's second dress, £50 for her first dress – £100 for Miss Brandram's second dress (this costly garment has now, for some occult reason, been sent on tour).

... But the most surprising item was £500 *for new carpets for the front of the house*. I pointed out to Carte that we (you and I) were, by our agreement, liable only for repairs incidental to the performances ... He angrily maintained that we were jointly liable for all upholstery in front (a contention that would justify him in entirely redecorating and upholstering the theatre a month before we left the theatre for ever and charging us with two-thirds of the cost although the goods would at once become his property) – and emphatically declared that nothing would induce him to adopt any other view. ... I replied that I *was* dissatisfied, and he said 'Very well, then; you write no more for the Savoy – that's understood' or words to that effect.

I left him with the remark that it was a mistake to kick down the ladder by which he had

risen – a sentiment which I hope will meet with your approval on general principles. . . . I am sorry to bother you with this long letter, but I am sure you will agree with me that it is absolutely necessary that a distinct understanding should be arrived at, if we are to work for Carte again. Always truly yours,
W.S.Gilbert.

As *The Star* of 13 May was to comment: 'When Mr. Gilbert does quarrel with anybody they know it.'

Carte's defence, at a later meeting, was that Gilbert had overestimated the cost of the wretched carpet, which, in any case, was rightly charged as a necessary wear and tear expenditure of the tri-partnership, and that the excessive production costs of *The Gondoliers* were due to Gilbert.

Both men had been at the simmer on and off for a long time. Now their wrath boiled over.

Sullivan was obliged, since he was the owner of the third share of the Gilbert–Sullivan–Carte profits and expenses, to state his views on the carpet concern. He felt it was a legitimate charge under the heading of wear and tear and said so in his diary.

Sunday April 27th: Gilbert came to see me in the morning, and brought with him a paper containing the heads [sic] of a new agreement to be made between us three. . . .

Saturday, May 3rd. Wrote to Gilbert. I cordially agreed with him that it would be better to have a new agreement. . . . But I thought it might be better to let that stand over until the necessity of writing a new piece for the Savoy Theatre should arrive.

Sullivan's prudent suggestion to give the disputants time to cool off supplied the red rag to Gilbert's bull. He replied on 5 May: 'The time for putting an end to our collaboration has at last arrived. . . . I am writing a letter to Carte – of which I enclose a copy – giving him notice that he is not to produce or perform any of my libretti after Christmas 1890. In point of fact after the withdrawal of *The Gondoliers*, our united work will be heard in public no more.'

Sullivan must have been conscious that with Carte's commission of the serious opera he had so longed to write, his immediate future lay with him. Then, too, he was a sick man once more, for whenever he was at outs with Gilbert, he suffered severe physical pain. Gilbert, too, was not in a good state of health, his rage being equalled by his gout. Carte was suffering from the strain brought on by Gilbert and overwork, and, suggests Pearson, 'an ailment known as Swollen Head, to which successful men in control of others are frequently prone'.

Sullivan, still trying to pour oil on the troubled waters, wrote to Carte: 'Over and over again I have said laughingly but earnestly, I will write twenty more operas with Gilbert if he will always be so nice and ungrudging in his concessions, and as ready to help me as he has been from the beginning to end in this piece.' *(The Gondoliers.)*

As might have been foreseen, Gilbert brought in his solicitors. Then he demanded that Sullivan should back up his insistence that Carte should produce theatre accounts for the past years, but Sullivan replied: 'I have no grievance – no dispute, and I have raised no question which would justify me at this juncture stepping in with the demand that the Savoy accounts should be kept in a different manner.'

By now the carpet quarrel was being watched with awe in two continents.

Poor Sullivan was indeed in a dilemma. Not only was Gilbert pressing him to sue Carte, but Carte was pressing him 'to desert Mr Micawber'; and on 13 August he received a pained note from D'Oyly Carte: 'If you are not going to back me up thoroughly in the trouble, then it is hard and I feel disheartened for the first time and in a way that nothing else could make me.'

The Savoy profits were paid to the partners every quarter; but the storm over the April accounts had caused them to be suspended pending a settlement. Carte's solicitors advised him not to discharge the July account until the previous one was settled. Gilbert, being Gilbert, issued a writ at once for his share in the July profits. Carte sent a cheque for £2,000. Gilbert scrutinised the nightly returns and claimed an additional £1,000. His solicitors discovered a serious discrepancy in the recent accounts. Gilbert applied for a Receiver to be put into the Savoy Theatre. After some postponements – due to Gilbert's gout which was being treated at Carlsbad – the case came to court. Gilbert's share of the profits, on eight operas in eleven years, had been £90,000. ('Human nature' observed *The Musical Times*, 'cannot stand such prosperity without arriving at the point where it is prepared to make a *casus belli* out of a carpet.') Carte's excuse for not paying Gilbert his due made 'an unfavourable impression'. He was ordered to pay the £1,000 Gilbert claimed, immediately, and any balance due on the July quarter to be paid within three weeks. His point gained Gilbert lost no time in writing to Mrs Carte to suggest a reconciliation. He suggested, too, that an arbitrator should be appointed to settle the remaining points between them. Mrs Carte agreed to meet Gilbert to 'talk things over'. But the effect of Gilbert's admission that he had spoken to her husband while he was in a rage and made several unwarrantable charges was somewhat offset by his insistence that all the accounts, from the very beginning of the partnership, should be scrutinised. The olive branch that he held out to Sullivan, who as part of the Savoy partnership, had been joined with Carte, had sprouted an unaccustomed thorn or two. Sullivan replied:

I solemnly believe that you plunged without forethought into these disastrous proceedings in a fit of uncontrolled anger greatly influenced by the bad health you were suffering from. I have not yet got over the shock of seeing our names coupled, not in brilliant collaboration over a work destined for world-wide celebrity, but in hostile antagonism over a few miserable pounds.

The implication that Gilbert's gout had been chiefly responsible for the legal proceedings provoked a tart rejoinder:

... I cannot help reminding you that if, *after the discovery of an error of £1,400 in four months'* accounts, Carte had consented to my examining the books of the past years (into which it is reasonable to suppose that other errors of equal importance may have crept) *no legal proceedings would have been taken. ...*

Meanwhile Gilbert was buying a commodious and handsome house, 'Graeme's Dyke', a name which he promptly changed to 'Grim's Dyke', on the Harrow Weald, built from the designs by Norman Shaw, selling the London house where he and his wife had given so many children's parties, at which he was the biggest and most excited child present, 'acting in charades, playing hide-and-seek, conjuring all sorts of marvellous things out of hats and pockets, and organising everything with as much absorption as he put into his theatrical productions'.

In 1890 Gilbert bought his final home, Norman Shaw's Grim's Dyke, a large house on the Harrow Weald.

And Sullivan was trying to settle his mind to the heavy work of composing his *magnum opus, Ivanhoe.*

He retreated to Grove House, Weybridge, to work on it, but without the peace of mind in search of which he had taken refuge from town. He was deeply disturbed by the recriminations attendant upon litigation.

'May 17th, 1890. Took up first Act of new opera *Ivanhoe,* and began it. Didn't do much.'

September came, but very little of the opera was written. 'How awfully slowly it goes,' he complained to his diary. He became obsessed and driven by two lines of thought – first the absolute necessity of writing at his best, and that quickly, for time was drawing on and the more he thought about *Ivanhoe,* the more numb his creative brain felt. Clearly he was afraid of the long-awaited project; and then the wretched carpet and its all too public consequences.

He allowed his love of the river to keep him from his desk. He rowed. He walked through the fields. He went to the village fair. He kept his diary, but for weeks on end it recorded only his hours of work and his health – 'October 1st. Seedy all day. October 3rd. Interrupted. October 5th. Scoring all day. Wind (heavy). October 6th. Tired and much interrupted.'

On 15 October another blow fell in the form of a letter from Gilbert. When the Savoy accounts were being investigated, Sullivan had sworn an affidavit that there were legal expenses still outstanding that Gilbert had authorised. Gilbert had sworn the opposite and had since managed to prove his point. He now demanded that Sullivan should write 'a distinct retraction' of the affidavit since it 'in effect, charges me with perjury'.

Sullivan was perhaps foolish not to go into the matter there and then. But *Ivanhoe* was on his mind, and possibly he felt, with the Duke of Plaza Toro, that he who fights and runs away may live to write – or of course run – another day. Besides: 'December 13th: Put last note to score. *Absolutely finished*. Thank God. December 31st: *Poor old Tommy died during the night*. He came to me in November 1882, from Edward Hall, from whom I claimed him as "assets" for the £7,000 lost through his firm. Never will be seen such a dear, loving intelligent dog again.' This was a loss indeed.

In January 1891, Gilbert published his *Songs of a Savoyard*, dedicating it to Sullivan, who wrote to him on the 28th of that month thanking him for 'such a graceful and flattering compliment' and hoping he would come to the first performance of *Ivanhoe*. 'I should take it much to heart if you were not present so please come.'

But if Sullivan thought the dedication was a sign that the time had come for dischords to modulate into concord, he was soon to be disillusioned. Two days later back came a blasting. Gilbert reiterated the wrongs which had forced him into litigation and the question of the affidavit. He continued:

... In a friendly letter to you I drew your attention to the admitted facts. ... In the course of an evasive reply, you curtly forbade me to make any further reference to those legal proceedings under peril of forfeiting your personal friendship. In reply to your expressed wish that I should be present on the occasion of the first performance of your new opera, I have only to say that I shall be happy to accept your invitation, if before tomorrow evening, I receive from you an admission that the statements of which I complain were made under mis-information.

Sullivan replied the next day, 31 January, the very morning of his first night:

My dear Gilbert

I thought that bygones were to be bygones [Optimist!] ... Forgive me for saying that I can neither apologise nor retract. ... You speak of my evasive reply to your letter. I thought my reply was pretty straightforward, inasmuch as I gave you details of the matters upon which my affidavit was founded, and refused, as I do now, to admit that I was wrong. Surely, my dear Gilbert, you can afford to let things rest as they are now, and let us forget the past. Let your presence at the theatre tonight be an intimation that you are as ready and willing as I am to think no more of what has happened, and to allow nothing to disturb our old friendship.
Yours sincerely,
Arthur Sullivan
PS I have been in such a drive today I could not write before. The enclosed stalls are not what I should have liked to send you, but the Royalties have taken two boxes out of six.

'I must say,' Sullivan wrote to a friend, 'that I look upon *Ivanhoe* as the most important work I have yet written.' The disappointment must have been the more intense when he found that in spite of a respectful press it was not the success of which he had dreamed. But on 31 January 1891, the sky above the New English Opera House was blue and gold, and only two furious clouds floated on Sullivan's horizon, each cloud inscribed: Yours truly, W. S. Gilbert.

January 31st, 1891. Lovely day. Three letters from Gilbert, two answered. Went to the theatre at 7.40. Tremendous crowd outside. At 8, Prince and Princess with Pcss. Victoria and Maud and Duke and Duchess of Edinburgh ['A triumph! A triumph!'] entered their box ... at 8.5 I entered. Tremendous reception by brilliant audience. ... Went up after the first Act to the Prince's room; he and the Duke came and smoked cigarettes in my room afterwards. Great enthusiasm; everyone called. I went on with Sturgis. Gave all the stage-hands five shillings each, afterwards. Home at 4.

The first cloud had floated in from the Harrow Weald:

January 31st

Dear Sullivan

I am sorry that you have not accepted my offer. I have asked neither for an apology nor a retraction. I ask simply for an admission that the statement in your affidavit – that the profits for the quarter could not be ascertained because there were legal expenses still outstanding connected with an action I had authorised – would not have been made if you had known that these costs had been discharged in full five years ago (as in point of fact they were). If you will give me this I will use the stalls with the utmost pleasure.

Yours truly,

W.S.Gilbert.

The second cloud was attended by thunder and lightning and was sent on the same day, but from Belgravia:

Dear Sullivan

... You deliberately swore that the costs in Russell v. Carte were still unsettled and by so swearing you defeated me and put me to an expense of £400 costs. I have it in Stanley's own hand that all the costs in that action were settled five years ago, and so have you.

I decline your stalls.

Yours truly,

W.S.Gilbert

To one old hand at collaboration there seems to be no possible excuse for Gilbert's two-fold eruption on the very day of the opening of *Ivanhoe*, unless to be so seething with jealousy, rage and a sense of injury, as to go a little mad at that moment, should be held to be an excuse.

On the following day a more temperate tone came through Sullivan's letter-box but still reiterating the same demand that Sullivan should admit that his affidavit was made in error. Sullivan wearily replied that this was not possible and the matter rested for three months. On 28 May Gilbert returned for the last time to the carpet quarrel, suggesting that as Sullivan would benefit from the readjustment of the accounts consequent on Gilbert's litigation, he might wish to 'share with me the costs of the action by which it was brought about'.

The first night programme of Sullivan's opera, *Ivanhoe* to a libretto by Julian Sturgis.

In the face of this piece of total effrontery, Sullivan was silent. But the partnership was never to lose the scars of battle. The wretched carpet had put an end to trust.

However, a letter of a more comforting kind had been sent by the Princess Louise three days after *Ivanhoe* had opened:

The Queen wishes me to write and tell you with what pleasure she sees in the papers of today that your opera met with such a success on Saturday.

It is a particular satisfaction to her, as she believes it is partly owing to her own instigation that you undertook the great work.

What a joy it must be to you to feel that your work is so satisfactorily completed; pray let me congratulate you on this, your greatest triumph.

D'Oyly Carte had built his 'new Theatre at Cambridge Circus' as though it were a brimming-over cornucopia of architectural goodies. *Ivanhoe*, remembers Sullivan's

The Royal English Opera House, built by D'Oyly Carte, opened in 1891 with Sullivan's *Ivanhoe*. It is now the Palace Theatre.

nephew, was 'an orgy of splendour'. 'Nothing that is asked for is refused in any department,' Sullivan wrote during rehearsals. 'The only care Carte seems to have is that everything should be of the best.' And failure though the opera ultimately was, it seemed for a time that opulence was going, as we say, to pay off:

My dear Friend
Come un forte guerriere you have won the great battle, and not only should musical art congratulate you on having given it a modern masterpiece, but your country should be proud of you, because you are one of the national glories. ... I spent an unforgettable evening.
Your old devoted friend,
F. Paolo Tosti

In the event *Ivanhoe* ran for five consecutive months, but Carte had expected it to equal *The Mikado* and had banged the big drum far too loudly in all the pre-run publicity fanfares – as George Bernard Shaw said in *The World*: 'It really does not do to spread butter on both sides of the bread.' Sullivan was disappointed but Gilbert had a private opinion; 'He's the sort of man who will sit on a fire and then complain that his bottom is burning.'

Freed from Sullivan's restraint, Gilbert regurgitated 'the lozenge plot', dissolved it into liquid – a potion – arranged for Alfred Cellier to do the music, and called it *The Mountebanks*. On 9 May 1890, immediately after the break with Sullivan, he wrote to Horace Sedger, who was to down the managerial draught.

Sedger wished to publicise the new piece as another *Dorothy* (the kind of musical play that had one foot in the door to unhouse the Savoy Operas). 'I must protect both Cellier and myself from the calamitous effects of popular cheap gush,' barked Gilbert.

He was to continue to berate Sedger and, inevitably, to threaten him with solicitors. He was to badger Cellier who was already at death's door, though to be fair to Gilbert he may not have known that death stood so close to Cellier. But he did know that he was working with a very sick man. And if one cannot be reasonably humane to the people who share one's work, one perhaps might pause and ask oneself if one deserves that work.

It may have been that his falling-out with another collaborator served to endear the first one to him. Be the reason what it may, early in October, Tom Chappell, the publisher, told Sullivan that Gilbert was seeking 'a complete reconciliation' with him – after the differences between them had been submitted to arbitration.

Whether it was that their publisher was persuasive, or that time had healed all – or nearly all – or even that faced with the run of an opera that was grinding to a slow halt, or for all of these reasons, Sullivan prepared his creative soul to go through the prickly thicket of working with Gilbert again:

So far as I am concerned the past is no more thought of, and I am quite ready to let bygones be bygones, and to meet you at all times in the most friendly spirit, provided that the disagreeable events of the past eighteen months are never alluded to. I say this in good faith, and I hope you will meet me in the same spirit.

Gilbert replied:

... It is perhaps **unnecessary** to assure you that all feelings of bitterness have long since passed from my mind, but there remains a dull leaden feeling that I have been treated with inexplicable unfairness by an old and valued friend with whom I have been *en rapport* for many years, and with whose distinguished name I had had the good fortune to find my own indissolubly linked wherever the English language is spoken. ...

Typically, on the day before they had arranged to meet, Gilbert wrote to repeat the grievance he had against Sullivan in the matter of the affidavit yet again. Clearly the affidavit had become his King Charles's Head. '... Our renewed co-operation could scarcely be carried on successfully unless we undertook it with our minds purged of all sense of grievance. ...'

Came the 12th; and at the end of the day Sullivan's diary was able to sigh with relief. 'October 12th 1891: Gilbert came (by appointment) at 12 – stayed till 2. Full reconciliation and shook hands.'

But one wonders, did it last?

11

The Last Curtain Falls

On 4 January 1892 the Gilbert and Cellier *The Mountebanks* was presented at the Lyric Theatre. The liquidated Lozenge plot did little to attract a new public to the work; nor, one imagines, did the names chosen by the librettist for the characters in this Sicilian brew: Ravioli, Spaghetti, Elvino, Risotto. As to his lyric technique, the first couplet the present writer's affronted leaf-through stopped at was:

> Now all you pretty visitors who haven't paid, stand you aside
> And listen to a tragic tale of love, despair and suicide.

'*You* aside', however emphasised, did not, does not and will not rhyme with suicide.

Since Gilbert and Sullivan were both engaged in other work, it was agreed that they should not write another opera together until their desks were clear: 'Dear Sullivan,' wrote Gilbert in the autumn of 1891, '. . . I *must* write and produce at least one libretto during this time. That I would infinitely rather do this in collaboration with you, goes without saying – *but write I must. . . .*'

Sullivan meant to winter in his beloved Monte Carlo working on *Haddon Hall*, the new opera he was to write with Grundy as and when the mood took him, and swanning sunnily at other times. But he could not leave town until after Christmas. At the particular request of his old friend Lord Tennyson he had first to write the incidental music to *The Foresters*, which Augustin Daly was to present with Ada Rehan as Maid Marian. Sullivan thought the title 'colourless' and begged Tennyson to change it to *Maid Marian* but the poet, intractable as ever, refused to do this.

Sullivan wrote to Daly: 'I have done the best I could with the music for Lord Tennyson's play, but it is after all not very satisfactory to have to write music which, whilst it is merely incidental to the play, at the same time requires proper and adequate interpretation.'

Carte tried to coax Sullivan towards setting a piece by J. M. Barrie – *Jane Annie* – but without success.

When he left for Monte Carlo at the end of December 1891, Sullivan was indeed a very sick man. Throughout January and February he dragged himself to his desk between throes of agony.

Gilbert sent him a new libretto – *The Happy Valley* – as though to encourage him to press on through the pain. But he grew worse. There were times when he was only semi-conscious. They sent for his nephew. Word flew through London that Sullivan was dying. He himself was convinced of it. Queen Victoria telegraphed for news of him. The Prince of Wales, in Cannes, sent his own surgeon to confer with the doctor by his bedside. But somehow he rallied, pulled round, came home, albeit carried onto the cross-channel steamer by four sailors.

Time passed. He drove, says his nephew, in Battersea Park, went to Lord's to sit in the sun and watch cricket, stayed with the Prince and Princess of Wales at Sandringham. But still his brain was not ready to work and he remained unusually weak. 'How slow it all is,' he wrote.

However, somehow *Haddon Hall* was finished: 'September 4th 1892: Conducted first performance of new opera *Haddon Hall* – crammed house – reception immense – quite unnerved me. All went well – last act enormous success, called afterwards with Grundy. Gilbert came round to see me in my room. . . . Home dead tired – to bed!'

Christopher Hassall in his biography of Edward Marsh says: 'In November he heard Sullivan's latest work, *Haddon Hall*, with a libretto by Sidney Grundy, and found nothing to enjoy but the Highland Fling. "There is one Gilbert and Sir Arthur is his prophet."'

Sullivan's entry in his diary on New Year's Eve read: 'Saw New Year in, hoped and prayed that it might be a happier one for me than this last, half of which was lost through my illness. *Health* is the secret of happiness.'

Back in August 1892 Sullivan had written to Gilbert, who was by then at work on the early stages of *Utopia Limited*, suggesting that theirs should be the piece to replace, when the time came, *Haddon Hall*. After a certain amount of polite skirmishing over their renegotiated terms Gilbert wrote to Sullivan urging him on.

But the summer of Gilbert's discontent was also the summer of Sullivan's lassitude, and two months passed and still Gilbert received no answer. Gilbert wrote again: '. . . it is impossible for me to concentrate myself upon a plot unless I know who is going to set it to music. . . .'

Sullivan wrote from Brighton to say he would be in London 'for a day or two' on the 29th and added, 'Will you let me know if and when you are coming up to town and want a chat?'

A little of Gilbert's native tartness crept into his reply: '. . . if I want a chat with you! Certainly, if *you* want one with me. That is to say if we both want one with each other. . . .'

A note from the Jockey Club Rooms at Newmarket appointed a day and time, but, warned Sullivan, he would not be able to start work until February.

> Livermore Park,
> Bury St Edmunds
> 3rd November, 1892.

My dear G

    I was in hopes that our conversation on Monday last had settled everything comfortably for the future, but your letter to Carte, a copy of which he sends me this morning, has I fear put fresh difficulties in the way. ... The organisation of the Savoy Theatre is changed since you were there, and the personnel is different; so as Carte and I are responsible for this, Carte and I must have the entire control. ... I am ready and willing to modify my arrangement with Carte so far as regards its financial conditions, so as to let you in on equal financial terms. But for expenditure, accounts, etc. you must trust to my judgment, accuracy and honour. ...
Yours sincerely,
Arthur Sullivan

Only a born, bred, and dyed in the wool optimist could suppose for a moment that Gilbert would bow a meek head to this:

Dear Sullivan

    ... you omitted to disclose to me, at our meeting, that I was to be a financial leper – debarred from all right to examine into the propriety of your expenditure and the accuracy of your calculations, and waiting patiently at the stage-door [oh! exquisite image!] for such a sum or dole as you and Carte may fling at me as my share of the profits. ...

Gilbert reading *Utopia Ltd* to the cast at the Savoy Theatre. Sullivan and D'Oyly Carte sit beside him.

Eighteen packed lines follow in Hesketh Pearson's book reciting Gilbert's well-known wrongs which I will spare the reader here. And if these wrongs are familiar, by now, to the reader, how infinitely more familiar must they have been to poor convalescing Sullivan. How he must have come to dread Gilbert's hand-writing.

Letters went backwards and forwards for another two months as the terms of the new collaboration were painfully hammered out. At last, on 19 January, Sullivan was able to write to Gilbert from Roquebrune:

... Now I think there is nothing in this letter to prevent your packing your portmanteau and starting at once. I urge this because I can take you in from now till February 3rd. On that day some other friends are coming for three weeks who will take all my spare bedrooms, so that I couldn't give you a room. Leave as soon as you can – don't take *the club* train. Take the 11 am to Paris (or the 10 am from Charing Cross) and come on by the *Rapide* arriving at Roquebrune where *all* trains stop, the afternoon. Bring warm things, for though the sun shines, it is pretty cold. Bring also (concealed in great-coat pockets etc.) your own cigars, as it is impossible to get a decent one here. Send me a wire: 'I arrive such a day.'
Yours ever,
A.S.

From Roquebrune Gilbert wrote to 'Missus':

Dearest Kits,
... the reading went off *most successfully* – both Sullivan and Grove enthusiastic – declaring it's the best plot I've done. We have arranged all business matters on a satisfactory footing. This is a pleasant house standing in an orange garden close to the sea – everything very nice and comfortable and informal. AS extremely pleasant and hospitable and much disappointed that I leave as soon as Sunday. We went to the Casino yesterday – I won fifty francs – we played billiards afterwards, and in the evening cribbage – for franc holes .... the weather is lovely – like warm June weather in England. Wild strawberries ripe, and oranges to be had for the picking. ... Probably be home Thursday evening. I'll wire to Guerany to have a fly ready, so don't trouble to send.
Goodbye, old lady – no end of love from
Your affectionate
Old Boy

When Gilbert left Roquebrune after an agreeable visit, he wrote to Sullivan from Grim's Dyke: '... I arrived here all right, last night, after a beastly passage, and three tiresome days in Paris. I send you Cook on Billiards – the study of that work has *made me what I am in Billiards* and if you devote 6 or 8 hours a day to it regularly, you may hope to play up to my form when you return. ...'

Sullivan's first task on tearing himself away from some pretty sparkling swanning on the Riviera, was to compose 'The Imperial March' for the State Opening of the Imperial Institute by Queen Victoria, which, on the occasion, he conducted in full levée dress. On 19 June his diary records: 'Began new opera. Slow work.'

The Golden Legend was given at the Crystal Palace. Let us see what Shaw has to say about it: 'June 1893: I look with indulgence on *The Golden Legend*, because I know that the composer really loves "those evening bells" and all that sincerely sentimental prettiness, with a dash of piety here and a dash of fun there, as with Lucifer's Comic

Song with the Kneller Hall accompaniment, not to mention the liberal allowance of indeterminate meandering. . . .'

For some years Sullivan had disliked Gilbert's way of making cruelly amusing fun of elderly ladies. Now he wrote:

The part of Lady Sophy, as it is to be treated in the 2nd Act, is in my opinion a blot on an otherwise brilliant picture, and to me personally, unsympathetic and distasteful. If there is to be an old or middle-aged woman at all in the piece, is it necessary that she should be very old, ugly, raddled and perhaps grotesque, and still more is it necessary that she should be seething with love and passion – requited or unrequited – and other feelings not usually associated with old age? [Here one pauses to wonder if Gilbert equated the aged harridans in his libretti with the very young ladies who peopled his private life?] A dignified, stately, well made-up and well-dressed elderly lady is a charming feature in a piece, and can be of real service to the composer, because the music he writes for her is so well-contrasted with the youthful bustle of the other elements. On the other hand, the elderly spinster, unattractive and grotesque, either bemoaning her faded charms, or calling attention to what is still left of them, and unable to conceal her passionate longing for love, is a character which appeals to me vainly, and I cannot do anything with it. . . . I am sure you won't take offence at my plain and outspoken opinion, for I court an equally frank opinion from you on anything in my share of the work which you don't like or which doesn't fit in with your intentions.
Yours ever sincerely,
A.S.

This was followed smartly by:

Grim's Dyke
3 July '93

Dear S
. . . When I read the very elaborate sketch-plot to you at Roquebrune last January – or early in February – you expressed full and unqualified approbation of every incident in the piece. Not to take advantage of a hasty or ill-considered expression of approval on your part, I left with you a *verbatim* copy of my sketch-plot that you might digest it at your leisure. . . . Possibly I may even now have failed to grasp your intention in its completeness. Possibly you may have failed to grasp mine. Most assuredly it is not necessary that she should be 'very old, ugly, raddled or grotesque' – she may be and *should be* a dignified lady of 45 or thereabouts, and no more ugly than God Almighty has made the lady who is to play the part. Nor do I propose that she should be seething with love and passion.

In the event – was it over William Schwenck's dead body? – Lady Sophy in no way resembled his earlier scarecrows.

Sullivan was having trouble with the Finale of Act 1. For the first and only time in their collaboration Gilbert suggested that Sullivan should compose the music first, after which he would write the words: 'It is mere doggerel,' he said, 'but words written to an existing tune are nearly sure to be that. . . . You may chop this about just as you please.'

Had it been less painful, Hesketh Pearson wickedly suggests, Gilbert might have taken some pride in his gout. It was 'a gentleman's complaint; and made the victim use

217

the language of an eighteenth century country squire: "I have not been able to do anything but swear for the last eighteen days."' This, no doubt, was what made him so explosive. Even to Helen Carte, who at this time seemed able to charm him round her little finger, he could be prickly. In answer to an appeal from her for a donation to a charity for orchestral players, he went up like a Jack-in-the-Box:

I hate the orchestra. They take up a lot of paying stalls – they are the most cantankerous and independent set in the Theatre – and they play so loud my words can't be heard. Moreover, like many other high-souled and independent specimens of Nature's nobility, they are the first to come begging cap-in-hand when they are in difficulties.

Having thus blown off steam, I have much pleasure in sending five guineas for the fund.

No one made allowances for Gilbert's gout save Sullivan – and that Sullivan did is as it should be.

D'Oyly Carte mounted *Utopia Limited* in princely fashion. It cost £7,200 to put it on. A letter in August from Gilbert to Sullivan, shows his usual regard to detail:

Dear S

I quite agree with you that it is highly desirable that the enormously estimated expense of production should be curtailed, if this can be done without cramping the piece. I confess I should be sorry to lose the Gents at Arms – who always stand two at the entrance, and two at the exit of the Presence Chamber, to regulate the admission and exit of the ladies presented – and I am afraid that, without them, the ladies will have the appearance of loafing on to the stage, without any circumstance. Besides, you must remember that these four people must be dressed *somehow*, they can't go naked (unless you insist on it), and if they are put into good uniforms they will cost at least £50 apiece.

Sullivan had settled down in Weybridge for the summer to work single-mindedly on *Utopia* – the blazing summer with which 1893 had dowered England. Usually he worked for a few hours, then a row on the river. Then he would return to work again. He played tennis; rode his tricycle; and attended the occasional race meeting.

When his pet parrot played truant, he abandoned all work on *Utopia* while he tramped the lanes and meadows searching for it. 'Lost and searched for in vain,' he confided to his diary. Almost the diary blinked away a tear. The gardener's boy spied Polly at Shepperton, but the parrot flew across the river. More searching in vain, more sorrowing: 'Myself and servants all miserable at his loss. Then Polly appeared on the roof of the College at Woburn Park, Addlestone; a boy scrambled up after it, and with the bird-errant clutched in his arms trudged off to Weybridge. 'Great rejoicings. Gave the boy the reward of £2,' Sullivan noted in his diary.

D'Oyly Carte, however, was less than radiant. The new Gilbert and Sullivan *Utopia*, not being ready to take the stage at the Savoy, he had thought fit to mount *The Nautch Girl* by George Dance. It was the first time he had offered the Savoy public a work that was not by one of their twin idols. It did not draw the town. But the cartoonist had a lovely time drawing caricatures of Gilbert and Sullivan looking displeased, almost disbelieving, at an impression of 'the new Indian Idol'.

'October 7th. Production of *Utopia Limited* at the Savoy Theatre 8.15 p.m. I shockingly nervous as usual – more than usual. Went into the orchestra at 8.15 sharp. My ovation lasted 65 seconds! Piece went wonderfully well – not a hitch of any kind, and afterwards G and I had a *double call*.'

Amid a frenzy of applause Gilbert and Sullivan shook hands. The feud was over. Or was it?

Gilbert, Sullivan and D'Oyly Carte, each taking about eight guests, supped at the Savoy when Miss Nancy McIntosh, the American soprano who was Gilbert's new attraction and was appearing in London – in *Utopia* – for the first time, was the guest of honour.

'Pleasant it is', wrote Shaw in *The World*, 'to see Mr Gilbert and Sir Arthur Sullivan working together full brotherly.'

And again:

... I have only one fault to find with Sir Arthur's luxurious ingenuity in finding pretty timbres of all sorts, and that is that it still leads him to abuse the human voice most unmercifully. I will say nothing about the part that he has written for the unfortunate soprano, who might as well leave her lower octave at home for all the relief she gets from the upper one.

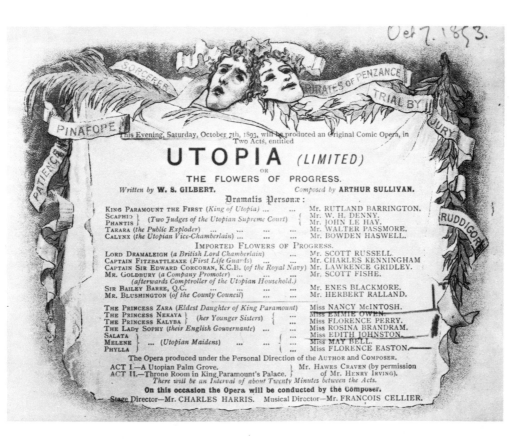

The first night programme for *Utopia Ltd*, 7 October, 1893.

This same GBS who had written plaintively – 17 December 1890: 'I was at the Gala performance of *The Gondoliers* and noticed . . . that the music was much more familiar to the band than to the composer,' and who considered *The Mikado* 'a mechanical opera'; and shrugged off Sullivan's 'Imperial March' with 'will undoubtedly have a considerable vogue in the suburbs as a pianoforte duet'.

How Shaw throws back the curtains and the blinds and lets the daylight come flooding in.

The Sunday Times weighed in with: 'It was a first night of first nights. The house was crammed with "all London" a term that means (at this season of the year) any number of critics and all who are left to represent that rather mixed community usually termed "Society".'

Among those present, noted *The Sunday Times*, were Lady Ormonde with her two daughters ('and Lady Ormonde looked very pretty in black with pale blue, and wrapped in an Indian mantle'). To which *Brighton Society* added: 'wearing some magnificent diamonds'. 'The Brazilian Minister who', continued *The Sunday Times*, 'was the guest of the ever-present Mrs Ronalds.' 'And', *Brighton Society* arrived at the climax: 'on the tier above, Madame Melba was gorgeous in dark green.'

The song for Captain Corcoran with a quotation from *HMS Pinafore* delighted the *aficionados*. After all, did it not have sanction by Mozart who quoted from his own *Figaro* in *Don Giovanni*?

'Whispers there may have been', hinted *The Daily News* 'that the pruning knife might judiciously be applied in the first Act. . . .'

G. B. Shaw summed up with:

I enjoyed the score of *Utopia* more than that of any of the previous Savoy operas. . . . The orchestral work is charmingly humorous; and as I happen to mean by this only what I say, perhaps I had better warn my readers not to infer that it is full of buffooneries with the bassoon and piccolo, or of patter and tum tum. Whoever can listen to such caressing wind-parts . . . as those in the trio for the King and the two judges in the first Act without being coaxed to feel pleased is not fit even for treasons, stratagems and spoils. . . .

Miss Nancy McIntosh, the American artist singing for the first time in England, had an impassioned speech as the Princess Zara as well as songs. She completely captivated Gilbert and went to live with him and 'the Mrs' at Grim's Dyke, as their adopted daughter and inherited it when Lady Gilbert died. Gilbert gave her private coaching. Reginald Allen calls her 'The lovely, fragile Dresdenesque Miss McIntosh'. *The Graphic* called her 'tall and beautiful' and noted that 'She looked the part to perfection.' But on the opening night she was 'too nervous to do herself justice'. After all she had never been on a stage before.

In *Utopia* some of Sullivan's writing for singers, always one of his strongest talents, can be heard at its best. And Gilbert's technique for introducing his characters on their first appearance – a technique developed in every libretto since *The Sorcerer* when the Press did not know what character was singing or which singer was who – is very much to the fore: 'O make way for the Wise Men' and 'A king of autocratic power We' from *Utopia*; 'A wandering Minstrel, I' from *The Mikado*; in Ruddigore:

Nancy McIntosh and Charlie Kenningham in *Utopia Ltd*.
Nancy was Gilbert's discovery and protegé, and became a permanent
guest at his home at Grim's Dyke.

> From the briny sea
> Comes young Richard all victorious

And in *The Gondoliers*:

Duke:	From the sunny Spanish shore
	His Grace of Plaza Tor' –
Duchess:	And His Grace's Duchess, too –
Casilda:	And His Grace's daughter, too –
Luiz:	And His Grace's Private drum
	To Venetia's shores have come *(The Gondoliers.)*

– and I defy any member of the audience, however warm and snoozy the night, not to know exactly who these exalted personages may be. And so on through innumerable first entrances in so many of the operas.

From the dialogue I cull one exchange:

King: It's a quaint world.
Phantic: Teems with quiet fun,

which given a brittle inflection might have been spoken by two characters in a play by Noel Coward. 'The rapier, not the bludgeon' is Gilbert's line in this opera, and such is his technique that he can vary the method with each work, but never the message.

In *Utopia* the message is simple, or so I take it to be. King Paramount of the heretofore perfect kingdom of Utopia, has sent his daughter to Girton to be further educated. His subjects begin to tire of perfection. The Princess Zara returns and alters all that. She turns Utopia into a second England, putting the crowning touch on it by instituting government by party – this results in a chaos well-known to us but quite unknown to poor Utopia.

Certainly Sullivan lavished some of his happiest choral writing in this *genre* on *Utopia*. The musical tone of the work is on the whole drowsy and lulling – which is not to say that it is without its brisker moments, among them the number for the First Life Guards:

> On the royal yacht
> When the waves were white,
> In a helmet hot
> And a tunic tight. ...

who blow a Pinaforian freshness, like a stiff breeze, though the scene.

Gilbert scores, too, with his plaint for a tenor:

> O Zara, my beloved one, bear with me!
> Ah, do not laugh at my attempted c!. ...
> A tenor all singers above,
> (This doesn't admit of a question)
> Should keep himself quiet,
> Attend to his diet
> And carefully nurse his digestion:
> But when he is madly in love
> It's certain to tell on his singing –
> You can't do chromatics
> With proper emphatics
> When anguish your bosom is wringing!
> When distracted with worries in plenty,
> And his pulse is a hundred and twenty,
> And his fluttering bosom the slave of mistrust is,
> A tenor can't do himself justice. ...

And the present writer, herself a rhymster on a modest scale, gleaned great pleasure from Gilbert's clever rhyming of 'Double-first in the world's University' with 'She has no one to match them in *her* city.'

Sullivan, too, comes into his own in the duet that reaches its climax, repeated, with:

> Sweet and low when all-enduring
> Are the songs that lovers sing.

222

It is hard to account for the failure of *Utopia Limited*, which has not been seen professionally played in England since its first production in 1893, for it is – for Gilbert and Sullivan – a compact, ironic and, at times, charming piece. It is still played from time to time in America but rarely heard in England, although the Amateur Dramatic Societies hold aloft the torch for Gilbert and Sullivan, and recently there has been a new recording of it from Pavillion Records along with *The Grand Duke* or *The Statutory Duel*, the last opera Gilbert and Sullivan were to write together. However, *Utopia* ran for 245 performances – a mere flash-in-the-pan when compared to the long run of *The Mikado* with its many and world-wide revivals.

Maurice Baring, in *With the Russians in Manchuria*, writes of his discovery of and pleasure in the Moscow Arts Theatre in 1904, where Chekov's plays were being acted. 'This theatre was started originally about four years ago by a company of well-to-do amateurs – under the leadership of M.Stanislavsky. They began, I was told, by acting Sullivan's *Mikado* for fun. . . .' It charms me to think that this revered Company was inaugurated by a group of amateurs in *The Mikado*.

Utopia failed, too, in New York when it opened on Easter Monday 1894. Sullivan felt in his bones that it was foredoomed to failure, as he predicted in his diary on the day it opened there.

Sullivan swanned away the first six months of 1894. In May he was fifty-two, an event he celebrated with a dinner at the Garrick Club. The Prince of Wales was among his guests.

All through his later life Sullivan loved the turf. When his work glued up, an outing at Newmarket or Ascot would bring him back fresh and clear-headed to his desk. 'Or he would compose during a morning, leave his manuscript hurriedly, like a schoolboy released from class, swallow a hasty lunch and rush off to an afternoon's racing, from which he would return and work half through the night.'

During 1894 he owned a horse in training with J. Jewitt of Newmarket. His colours – cerise and violet cap and sleeves – 'appeared at many meetings but seldom passed the post first'.

Already, three months after the production of *Utopia*, it was clear to D'Oyly Carte that the end of the run of the piece would be just around the corner. The, for those days, enormous expense of mounting the work had considerably reduced the profits of all three partners.

In a letter to Gilbert Carte said: '. . . There is no doubt in my mind that what the people want now is simply 'fun', and little else. . . . I firmly believe that if you and Sullivan would write a faintly comic piece – say, a modern farcical comedy to music – that with your united genius, we might score at least as much success as is obtained by drivelling stuff. . . .'

When *Utopia* came off, in the late spring, D'Oyly Carte put on a piece called *Mirette* by Messager.

While Sullivan was swanning away, Gilbert had found himself a delicious series of squabbles. Nancy McIntosh, in her diary, shows the seeds of one, due to flower fully later:

13 March 1894. s has written breaking off collaboration. Mr G has written.

16 March.   Mr G called afterwards to tell me a new proposition from Carte.

24 March.   Mr G saw Mr H [Henschel, her teacher of singing] and it is settled that they are to write an opera together.

7th April.   Mr G told me of H's lying letter about me and that Carte won't produce his opera and that it may fall through.

It did fall through, but *His Excellency*, with music by Dr Osmond Carr, was presented at the Lyric Theatre on 27 October 1894 under the management of George Edwardes, 'the threat', who presented *The Gaiety Girl, The Shop Girl* and many other musical comedies at the Gaiety Theatre, and *The Merry Widow, San Toy* and others at Daly's.

This storm, though still at squall proportions in Miss McIntosh's diary, branched off into two more delectable quarrels.

Gout and a falling-out with Sullivan left Gilbert in poor shape for the wear and tear of rehearsals; and such was his behaviour that even Grossmith rebelled. When finally Gilbert sent 'a stern note' five months after the opening, on the subject of gagging – a subject, incidentally, that is calculated to divide authors from actors to this day – Grossmith said: for seventeen years he had received letters of complaint from Gilbert without a murmur. During the frosty weather, when audiences had dropped, he had offered to play for nothing but instead of being thanked for helping to save a sinking ship he had received a 'disagreeable and dictatorial letter ... and I presume you think *that* was an incentive to a nervous actor to play your work properly.'

Gilbert once summed up his attitude:

With reference to gags, I am supposed to be adamantine, but this is not really so. I only require that when an actor proposes to introduce any words which are not in the authorised dialogue, those words should be submitted to me; and if there appears to be no good reason to the contrary, the words are duly incorporated with the text. I consider that as I am held by the audience to be responsible for all that is spoken on the stage, it is only right that nothing should be spoken that I have not authorised. ...

In its early days the Gilbert–Edwardes axis showed no strain. Edwardes paid Gilbert £5,000 down for the London, Provincial, American and Colonial rights of *His Excellency* for three years. However, 'the temperature of their relationship having dropped with their receipts', and a disagreement over the translation rights having burgeoned, Gilbert, up to his old games, sent Edwardes a letter detailing his objections but eventually suppressing his cruellest shaft: 'The tone of your letter may serve to frighten choristers, but I assure you it could have no other effect upon me than to aggravate any existing difficulties and to widen any existing breach.'

Edwardes lost no time in answering, also on the same day, that he had been 'most disgracefully treated'. At Gilbert's express wish he had engaged Miss Nancy McIntosh for the London and New York productions in the belief that this would influence the author to fulfil his agreement.

Gilbert's answer to this began: 'Sir: Your letter of the 13th inst is a tissue of un-truths.' ... 'It is simply untrue that you engaged Miss McIntosh for America at my

RIGHT The opening scene of *The Yeomen of the Guard*, taken from the first production.
OVERLEAF Percy Anderson's costume designs for the first production of *The Yeomen of the Guard*, with strips of the original material.

PHŒBE, (Singing).

"When maiden loves, she mopes apart,
    As owl mopes on a tree;
Although she keenly feels the smart,
She cannot tell what ails her heart,
        With its sad 'Ah me!'
    'Tis but a foolish sigh—'Ah me!'
    Born but to droop and die—'Ah me!'
            Yet all the sense
            Of eloquence
Lies hidden in a maid's 'Ah me!'"

ACT I

Julia

WILHELM
82

The GRAND DUKE.

W 82

express desire. You told me that you were most anxious to send out as many of the original company as you could induce to go. ...'

Some sort of equitable arrangement must have been patched up for, kept in their correspondence, is a wire from Gilbert: 'I UNDERSTAND PIECE TO BE PRODUCED BROADWAY FOURTEENTH OCTOBER SHALL I BE SAFE IN TAKING RETURN BERTH IN STEAMER LEAVING SIXTEENTH OCTOBER.'

His Excellency started well. Gilbert had already made fun of the army, the navy, the law, the church, medicine, aesthetics, politics, the police, big business, the throne and, in *His Excellency*, the National Anthem. In a letter to Helen Carte, Gilbert wrote: '... If it had had the advantage of your expensive friend Sullivan's music it would have been a second *Mikado*.'

What, while Gilbert was passionately pursuing fresh fights in pastures new, became of our Poor Wandering One, Arthur Sullivan?

A deal of swanning race meetings, the pursuit of health and a chance dinner shared with F. C. Burnand in the late summer.

They chatted on and, in a desultory manner, speculated on the future of the Savoy now that Carte had no opera in hand to follow hard on the failing *Mirette*. Burnand suggested that they should dig out *The Contrabandista*, which they had written together in 1867. Sullivan had put some good work into it. Before they left the Garrick Club that night, the die was cast. Sullivan was to keep such music as he thought best, and to write some new numbers.

Burnand, determined to strike the libretto while it was hot, soon had a refurbished book ready. They re-named the piece *The Chieftain*: D'Oyly Carte agreed to mount it at the end of the year. They should all have known better – and particularly D'Oyly Carte. *The Chieftain* had its roots in the previous decade. And dust it down as they might, the refurbished article did not strike a note new enough to compete with fresh fashions in musical comedies. *The Chieftain*, opening at the Savoy on 12 December was, deservedly, a failure.

As for Gilbert, aged fifty-eight in November of that year, 1894, Leslie Baily quotes: 'I am a crumbling man – a magnificent ruin, no doubt, but still a ruin – and like all ruins I look my best by moonlight. Give me a sprig of ivy and an owl under my arm and Tintern Abbey would not be in it with me.' In fact, observes Baily, 'apart from gout [if only he could have been parted from it!], his health was robust.'

But Sullivan had no need, these days, to worry about finances. He was after all earning £20,000 a year and gambling heavily on the horses – moreover it is on record that he gave away money recklessly – and secretly. To learn that a friend had fallen upon hard times – if he had anything to do with the Arts – became to Sullivan a personal desolation. 'He would give, and give again, often anonymously, until the clouds had passed over.'

Having conducted his music for Comyns Carr's play *King Arthur* at the Lyceum on 12 January 1895, he left London for, as always, the Riviera.

Towards the end of summer 1895, however, Gilbert came shambling bearlike out of the wings, bringing the plan for a new libretto: *The Grand Duke* or *The Statutory Duel*, and the broken wings of the collaboration healed themselves.

LEFT On blue background, costume designs by Wilhelm for the Fairy Queen (top) and Iolanthe from the first production of the opera in 1882; on white background, costume designs by Percy Anderson for Julia in *The Grand Duke*, 1896.

River House
Walton on Thames
11th August 1895.

My dear Gilbert,

I have studied the sketch plot very carefully and like it even more than I did when I heard it first on Thursday. It comes out as clear and bright as possible. I shall be very pleased to set it, and am prepared to begin (as soon as you have anything ready for me) and have written to Carte to tell him so. There is one very important suggestion I should like to make, which, if you see your way to accept, will relieve me of a vast amount of unnecessary labour, and turn difficult situations into easy ones for me. Of course I speak entirely from a musical point of view.

How would it do to make Lisa the *principal* soprano part and make Elsa the contralto? ... See what an advantage this will be to me. In all the concerted music there would be a soprano and contralto, instead of two sopranos ... we shall have the immense advantage of having a soprano and not a contralto at the top, getting plenty of brightness.

THE NEW SAVOY OPERA A GILBERT-SULLIVAN GHOEST?

So reads the headline of the *Musical Standard*'s review of the fourteenth (and last) Gilbert and Sullivan first night: 'In Mr Gilbert's libretto one of the characters, for the

Rosina Brandram as the Baroness von Krankenfeldt in *The Grand Duke*, 1896. 'No more ugly than God Almighty has made the lady who is to play the part.'

RIGHT The stage set for Act I of *The Grand Duke*.

sake of rhyme, pronounces ghost as ghoest, and we may be pardoned if we call *The Grand Duke* a ghoest of a Gilbert and Sullivan opera. . . .' Indeed, the house seemed haunted by the departing wraiths of the two collaborators as though the Savoy Theatre was one vast crystal ball into which the gathering might gaze: 'March 7th. Began new opera *The Grand Duke* at $\frac{1}{4}$ past eight – usual reception. Opera went well; over at 11.15. Parts of it dragged a little, dialogue too redundant, but success great and genuine I think. Thank God opera is finished and out.'

Sullivan never says much to me,' Gilbert confided to Mrs Herbert Beerbohm Tree, 'and what he does say, I usually knock a lot off of [sic] for discount.'

The Grand Duke, too, was being viewed in the light of a revival of *The Mikado*, whose sturdy person had vacated the Savoy stage only three nights earlier. *The Times* set it on the line:

The Grand Duke [it pointed out, inevitably] is not by any means another *Mikado*, and, though it is far from being the least attractive of the series, signs are not wanting that the rich vein which the collaborators and their various followers have worked for so many years is at last dangerously near exhaustion. This time the libretto [*The Times* pin-pointed] is very conspicuously inferior to the music. There are still a number of excellent songs, but the dialogue seems to have lost much of its crispness.

But Desmond McCarthy, writing in *The Pall Mall Gazette*, burned his boats with, 'It may claim to stand in the front row of comic operas.'

The Sunday Times, having noted 'the jolly hornpipe tune', suggests delicately that 'It [the first Act] will stand slight condensation.' *Punch*, however, went straight to the nose with, 'About a third of the first act might be omitted with advantage.' And landed a shrewd blow with, 'Also for the conductor to catch at the slightest possible indication of a wish to encore is a mistake.'

'Mr Gilbert has stood still, but Sir Arthur Sullivan has advanced', said 'Man of the World' in *Stage Whispers*.

'Sir Arthur Sullivan has done better than his librettist,' said *The Musical Standard*, Isaac Goldberg summed it all up with: 'The last curtain had fallen on the greatest collaboration in the history of the modern stage.'

And in agreeing with him, let us not forget that the next English musical collaboration to sweep five continents was the Beatles – a collaboration which owed much to their unobtrusive musical adviser and recording manager, George Martin.

The Grand Duke was performed only 123 times, and Thomas Dunhill was later to write of it: 'In justice to Sullivan's memory, as well as Gilbert's it is to be hoped that it will never be heard again.' A granite judgment.

The plot defies polite description. Not only does it abound in sausage rolls, it takes place in the Grand Duchy of Pfennig-Halbpfennig in the market place of Spiesesaal. It is full of characters called severally Dumkopf – a theatrical manager, Dr Tannhauser – a Notary, Viscount Mentone, Julia Jellicoe – an English Comedienne, Herald – presumably a herald.

I suppose I shall be accounted a literary cad in quoting the first three lines from the opening duet by colleague Gilbert, which go:

> Pretty Lisa, fair and tasty
> Tell me now and tell me truly
> Haven't you been rather hasty?

Other writers, as we have seen, have dealt faithfully with *The Grand Duke*. Since I have had no opportunity to see it on a stage I can leave the piece and its performance to them.

'May 13th 1896: An unlucky day for me in every respect,' sighed Sullivan into his diary. No doubt the diary sighed too. It was his birthday. He was fifty-four. He was feeling very low and ill and that he had arrived at Newmarket in time to see his horse lose, did nothing to raise his spirits.

The Grand Duke, too, was in decline. A few weeks later, in June, Sullivan took to bed with influenza to add to his *malaise*. He had often told Gilbert he would write no more light opera. He said so now. Even had he changed his mind in this respect there was no libretto – Gilbert and Sullivan were never to write together again. . . .

12

The Death of Sullivan

From convalescence in Monte Carlo – where else? – Sullivan wandered on to Lucerne. Here, says Leslie Baily, in his latest book on Gilbert and Sullivan, he found 'an autumnal romance' with a twenty-year-old English girl (almost he might have been Gilbert) whom he addressed as 'Miss Violet'. Baily prints a page of a pretty Victorian writing-paper with a sketch of the town and the name of the hotel, *Grand Hotel National*. It was, he says, the first of a series of notes written to her by the smitten composer, the last of which was written on the day she had refused his proposal of marriage: 'The most miserable day of my life.' Heighdee, Heighdee, lack-a-day him, lack-a-day him! But perhaps in the end it was as well, for what would Mrs Ronalds have had to say?

Sullivan felt the time was ripe for him to write another serious opera, and with the success of his music for *King Arthur* at the Lyceum in mind, decided to adapt it, only to change his mind and decide to compose something for Yvette Guilbert; then another change of mind, no doubt with attendant heart-searchings, and hey presto! he was to write the music for a ballet, *Victoria and Merrie England*, to be mounted in the spring of 1897, for the Diamond Jubilee. When, at the end of the summer of 1896, he sought better health in the Engadine, his only commitment in sight was the ballet.

The Engadine that year was a veritable Swan Lake: 'Walked out with Royal Party all the afternoon. In the evening I had a dinner-party at the hotel: Duchess of York [later Queen Mary], Du. of Teck [her mother], Mr and Mrs Leo Rothschild, Prince Francis of Battenburg. After dinner all adjourned to my sitting-room – a little music till 12.'

And next day: 'Walked all the morning with the Royal Party – lunched with them upstairs. Gave Princess May three combs, and Duchess of Teck two. Princess May gave me a beautiful photo of herself and the children.'

To Munich: to Vienna: and on to Nauheim, where the Empress Frederick of Germany invited him to stay at the Friedricshof [Cronberg] and he accepted with alacrity ... of course. The Empress Frederick was by now 'a lonely Englishwoman in Germany' – as alone, that is, as a Royal Lady can hope to be – who found in Sullivan some link with her country and its Art. When Christmas came, the ballet, which he had planned to finish by then, was scarcely started. He was ill and could not gather the strength to drive the project through. London had been shrouded in fog. He sought relief abroad. Accordingly he took the Villa Mathilde in Beaulieu for the season. On his first day in Beaulieu he spent ten hours composing, his nephew tells us.

Sullivan conducting in 1899, the year before his death.

While Sullivan is getting down to work in the Riviera, J. L. Toole is throwing a shaft of light on Gilbert's litigatory propensities. On arriving at Grim's Dyke somewhat tardily, he observes: 'I was afraid that if I put it off any longer, you'd bring an action against me.' And while a lady, poor timid soul, ventures to ask if Gilbert has seen Irving in his latest play, and trembles under the almost magisterial rejoinder: 'Madam, I go to the pantomime only at Christmas,' Jimmie Glover gives a more clement glimpse of Gilbert:

During the Collins regime he sent me a telegram every Christmas Eve for twelve years, asking me to reserve him two seats for the dress rehearsal, 'Right behind you'. He loved to hear the children sing the comic songs, although expressing himself as doubtful as to their humour and was always interested to see the scheme of colour worked out in the pantomime. Of its comedians, he could enjoy them all – except the music-hall portion, and these he could not tolerate. ... All the stories about his being rude to people are all moonshine. ...

In the autumn of 1897 May Fortescue, an actress who had appeared in several of Gilbert's plays, tried one out in the Provinces: *The Fortune Hunter*. Gilbert, when not 'Lozenging', and so behind his times, was apt to write ahead of his times, and here he hit on the happy fancy of a character who was trying to psychoanalyse himself. While he was in Edinburgh for the tour's second disastrous week, trying 'to pull the pieces together', he sued *The Era* for saying, among other things,

Mr Gilbert's self-esteem has with advancing years developed into a malady. In his own estimation he is a kind of Grand Llama of Dramatic Literature. The mildest criticism on his work, the most gentle disapproval of one of his plays, is a crime of *lèse majesté* for which, if it were in his power, he would punish the culprit severely. ...

When Gilbert entered the witness box, in March 1898, he was examined by Marshall Hall:

'You have read what was said in the article about your bump of self-esteem. Do you regard that as written in joke or seriously?'

'I can hardly take it seriously, because I cannot suppose that anyone thinks I wish to reconstruct the universe. I am perfectly satisfied with the cosmos as it is.' (Laughter.)

Carson, who had sparred in court with Oscar Wilde, cross-examined. The laughter in court that followed Gilbert's rejoinders probably disposed the judge in the defendant's favour.

'You don't like reading hostile criticism?'

'I have a horror of reading criticism at all, either good or bad.'

Gilbert had, it emerged, a preference for reading unfavourable criticism: 'I know how good I am, but I do not know how bad I am.' (Laughter.)

Carson, having quoted some bad notices for *The Fortune Hunter*: 'You would admit that this is a formidable list of hostile criticism?'

'Distinctly. I am quite prepared to admit that the play is a very bad play.' (Laughter.)

Asked to suggest the direction of current dramatic taste, Gilbert said: 'In the direction of musical comedy; bad musical comedy, in which half-a-dozen irresponsible comedians are turned loose on the stage to do as they please.'

'Will you mention one of them?'

'Well, take the pantomime at Drury Lane Theatre with the great Dan Leno.' (Loud laughter.)

'But that only goes on a short time in the year.'

'It goes on for a long time in the evening.' (Loud laughter.)

Carson tried to get an admission that Gilbert was quarrelsome. Gilbert denied this. Was he not touchy and quick tempered? No. Well, to take an instance had he not quarrelled with Clement Scott?

'Yes, I wrote to Clement Scott nine years ago complaining of a criticism.'

'You were cool and calm?'

'Yes, calm and deliberate. I don't know my temperature at the time.' (Prolonged laughter.)

Carson, in his speech for the defence, commented so unfavourably on the plaintiff's character that Gilbert stormed out of court.

The judge's summing up contained the telling statement: 'The plaintiff, while objecting to criticism, has not been sparing in his own criticism of others.' The jury took two-and-a-half hours to agree that they could not agree, which, it seems, meant that each side had to pay its own costs.

Gilbert wrote to Maud Tree:

... The case would have been mine but for the judge, who was a monument of senile incapacity. ... My cause was comparatively trivial, but it is fearful to think that grave issues in which a man's fortune, or a woman's honour may be involved, are at the mercy of an utterly incompetent old doll. ... Carson conducted his [case] in the spirit of a low-class police court attorney.

Gilbert must have been strongly tempted to re-write the lines:

> The law is the true embodiment
> Of everything that is excellent,
> It has no kind of fault or flaw –
> And I, my friends, embody the law!

Meanwhile, back at Beaulieu:

Sunday, March 7th: Got up wonderfully fresh after having had *four* nights of hard work until 5 a.m. each morning [the diary it was, that yawned].

Wednesday, March 17th: Much worried about 'Union March'. Couldn't get it right! ...

Thursday, March 18th: Solved the 'Union March' difficulty by cutting out the Welsh!

Thursday, March 25th: ... All done now, thank God! Wired 'Finished'.

The celebrations for the Diamond Jubilee were to take place in June. But Queen Victoria was at Cimiez, for it was spring. Did not the Medes and Persians lay it down it must be Cimiez in spring and Balmoral in the autumn?

April 6th: Went to Cimiez to see Sir Arthur Bigge [Queen Victoria's private secretary] about a 'command' hymn for the Jubilee. He told me that the Queen thought it desirable to have well-known tunes sung at the service outside St Paul's, so that people could join in them if they liked, but that, as the real Thanksgiving service would be on the 20th June, it would be better I should write a special tune for that day, which might be sung in every church of the Empire: I suggested that Bishop Walsham Howe [the Bishop of Wakefield] should be commanded for the occasion ... I stayed by the Queen's invitation, to lunch with the Household and left at 3.30.

(The diary smacked its lips.)

Nine days later:

Drove to Cimiez to see Bigge. Duke of Coburg came in while I was there – I told him it was exactly 43 years since I had joined the Chapel Royal. I entered on Tuesday the 12th of April, 1854, but made my first appearance in the Chapel and sang a solo on Maundy Thursday following.

Told him I should like to play the organ on Easter Day for the Queen. I think he must have gone and told the Queen, for I got a telegram from her the next day asking me to play. Said goodbye to the Duke, who left for Coburg that night.

Easter Sunday: Lovely morning. Drove to Regina Hotel, Cimiez, to play the organ (harmonium) at service in the Chapel by the Queen's invitation. [Holy swanning, as it were.] Saw Princess Beatrice for a few minutes before service to arrange about hymns. Queen came into the Chapel at 11 (whilst I played a voluntary) accompanied by Princess Beatrice, Princess Victoria of Schleswig-Holstein, Pcess Beatrice's three children, the suite and servants. Self and Lord Rowton only outsiders. ... Queen sent me a lovely pocket-book as a souvenir of the day.

Sullivan's suggestion to the Queen that the Bishop of Wakefield should write the Jubilee Hymn went ahead. Sullivan set the words that came, as though by magic, from the Bishop, without further ado. Had not Victoria herself approved them?

One month before the actual Jubilee, *Victoria and Merrie England* was mounted at the Alhambra: 'Tuesday, May 25th: Full dress rehearsal (private) of Ballet at 1. First performance at night. Magnificent house – all the élite of London present, including Princess Louise, Duke of Cambridge and the Adolphus Tecks. Great enthusiasm. Conducted the performance myself. Genuine success.' It is on record that the piece was 'the most attractive production of the Jubilee year and made a lot of money'. It is mind-bending to speculate on what the rest of the Jubilee entertainment might have been.

The Jubilations over, the Queen sent for Sullivan. She had always considered him to be the leading British musician of her reign (which is a frightening thought when one compares his music with that of Benjamin Britten, the leading British composer of the music of Queen Elizabeth 11's reign). Had he not, by the delight of his melodies, swept Mr Mendelssohn's music from the Windsor Broadwood pianoforte? He had caught the History of England (for the Jubilee) and charmed it into notes.

'Monday, July 5th: Invited to Windsor. Went about 6. Nice little room.' He dined at 8.30 with the Household: 'After dinner was received by the Queen in the Long Corridor [sounds draughty]. Had twenty minutes conversation with Her Majesty who was most kind and gracious. After I retired, she sent me the Jubilee medal by Miss Phipps. Played billiards and smoked with the Household till bedtime.'

A month later he left for Bayreuth and the Wagner Festival: 'Put on light clothes and went to the performance of *Parsifal*. Although many points open to severe criticism, the work and performance impressed me immensely.'

Three days later.

Beginning of *Ring. Rhinegold* commenced at 5, and went on without break till 7.30. Then home to dinner. [Did the diary give a sigh of repletion?] Much disappointed in the performance; *all* of them. Orchestra rough and ragged, conducted by Siegfried Wagner. Vocalists beneath contempt. Sometimes stage-management is good, but much is conventional and childish. It is difficult to know how Wagner could have got up any enthusiasm or interest in such a lying, thieving, blackguardly set of low creatures as all the characters in his opera prove themselves to be.

And the next day:

Performance of *Walkyrie*. Very pleasant party – good lunch. Back at 3.15. Unfortunately fell asleep and didn't wake till 5 and so missed last act. Much that is beautiful in the opera – less dreary padding than in the others.

August 16th: Performance of *Siegfried*. I think it intolerably dull and heavy, and so undramatic – nothing but 'conversation'; and I am weary of Leit Motiven. [The Imperfect Wagnerite?] What a curious mixture of sublimity and absolute puerile drivel are all these Wagner operas.

August 17th: Last *Ring* performance *Gotterdammerung*. 1st Act 4 to 6. Dull and dreary. 3rd Act 8.45 to 10. Very fine and impressive.

Typically, son of his days that he was, Sullivan, who found Wagner 'dull and dreary' picked Coleridge Taylor – 'he is a *composer* – not a music-maker' he wrote after hearing *Hiawatha* – almost as his successor: 'Much impressed by the lad's genius.' Well, not for the first time, we are left with the saddening lines from *Cymbeline*:

> Golden lads and girls all must
> As chimney-sweepers, come to dust.

While Sullivan was beginning to think about a new opera – this time with Comyns Carr and Arthur Wing Pinero: 'I like it immensely. It is original and fanciful. I don't know whether it is *too* serious.' And struggling with india-rubber-like material, and finding that the libretto of *The Beauty Stone* was 'too wordy'; Gilbert was entertaining the boy who one day would grow up to be the humorist P.G.Wodehouse.

Hesketh Pearson has an apt story about him:

P.G.Wodehouse once explained why butlers, as a class, were gloomy, one reason being that 'so many of their employers were sparkling *raconteurs*'. They were compelled to hear again and again the same old story told in the same old way, with baleful effects on their constitutions. In his youth P.G. had been taken to lunch at Grim's Dyke. Half way through the meal Gilbert started to tell the sort of yarn that begins dully and ends brightly. Unfortunately the youngster, who did not think the anecdote a bit funny but knew it must be because of the teller's reputation, mistook a pause in the narrative for the moment when the joke had been reached, and discharged a hearty resounding laugh. The other guests seemed a bit puzzled, 'as if they expected something better from the author of *The Mikado*', but in duty bound made mirthful murmurs and then drifted into conversation.

It was at this point that I caught my host's eye. I shall always remember the glare of pure hatred which I saw in it. If you have seen photographs of Gilbert, you will be aware that even in repose his face was inclined to be formidable and his eye not the sort of eye you would willingly catch. And now his face was far from being in repose. His eyes, beneath their beetling brows seared me like a flame. In order to get away from them, I averted my gaze and found myself encountering that of the butler. His eyes were shining with a dog-like devotion. ... I made his day. ... I suppose he had heard that story rumble on to its conclusion at least twenty times, probably more, and I had killed it.

But that Gilbert did not see himself as the world saw him – which of us does? – was shown, half banteringly, in a letter to the distinguished actress Mary Anderson back in 1888: 'My dear Miss Anderson: Reassure yourself, *I cannot glare*, I don't know how it's done.'

Gilbert, sardonic, acid, a wit, could be concise when occasion called for crystallisation:

At a dinner, Edmund Yates, editor of *The World*, usually a talkative fellow, was particularly quiet. 'Why this religious silence?' another guest asked? 'He's probably thinking of the next *World*,' cracked Gilbert.

Asked if he felt 'out of place' in a company that included several clergymen, 'Yes. I feel like a lion in a den of Daniels,' snapped Gilbert.

'My cook gets eighty pounds a year and gives me a kipper; Sullivan's cook gets five hundred pounds a year for giving him the same thing in French.'

He thought poorly of most of his contemporary colleagues, and particularly poorly of the plays of Henry Arthur Jones. Hearing that his next piece was to be called *The Princess's Nose*, 'Hope it'll run,' he grunted.

In a letter to Maud Tree he let fly at Henry Arthur Jones's *The Tempter*, a play in blank verse which her husband, Herbert Beerbohm Tree, mounted, calling it

... gross and damnable – its literature, the literature of the servants' hall. ... O merciful father that stayst thy hand though thy rebellious children deserve the blow, save and protect us from this plague of Jones (which we have nevertheless rightly incurred for our many backslidings) through the merits of Thy beloved son, Jesus Christ, Amen. This is a form of prayer to be used in all Churches and Chapels throughout the United Kingdom and in the town of Berwick-upon-Tweed. ...

Declining an invitation to a concert given to raise money for the Soldiers' Daughters' Home he added a rider that he 'would like to see the Soldiers' Daughters' home after the concert'.

However Mary Anderson, writing about this witty, bitter, angry, kindly mixture of a man, says: 'My memories of Gilbert are sweet and bitter. He was a very kind-hearted man, but he did not want anybody to know it.'

G. K. Chesterton, comparing Gilbert to Dickens called him, 'A smaller and more sneering but equally sincere man.'

And the divinely named Miss May Fortescue bore witness to Gilbert's better self – for however monstrously he behaved from time to time, there was another face to the burly Janus – the face he showed his wife and friends in need:

... his kindness was extraordinary. On wet nights when rehearsals were late and the last buses were gone, he would pay the cab-fares of the girls whether they were pretty or not, instead of letting them trudge home on foot ... he was incapable of petty meanness. He was just as large-hearted when he was poor as when he was rich and successful. ... Gilbert was no plaster saint, but he was an ideal friend.

But back to Sullivan, struggling with his inclement libretto. Much of the composing was done on the Riviera, and his struggles rained down on the pages of his diary like leaden confetti: 'It is heartbreaking to have to try to make a musical piece out of such a badly constructed – for music – mass of involved sentences.'

The Beauty Stone was finished and ready for production towards the end of May 1898. It survived for seven weeks. 'It contained some good numbers,' wrote Sullivan's nephew, 'but the story clove its way through a forest of words. . . . But because of the difficulties he tried in vain to surmount he put in more work upon it than he did upon *The Mikado*.'

In the autumn of 1898 Sullivan conducted the Leeds Festival for the last time. For twenty years it had been his baton that carried the Festival to success. He seemed, indeed, to have become part of it:

Saturday October 8th, 1898: Leeds. Last day of Festival. After last performance the Chorus cheered me so tremendously that I suddenly broke down, and ran off the orchestra crying like a child.

When I came out of my room again *all* the Chorus were waiting for me, and I shook hands with all! Then went and had a light supper at Albani's and at 11.10 saw the Band off in their Special. Red and blue fire and cheering as usual. When at supper was surprised by a serenade by about 30 of the male chorus: I invited them in; gave them Champagne and cigars and they sang half-a-dozen pieces, retiring at 1 a.m. Went to bed tired – rather a trying day. . . .

Why should he suppose he had been to Leeds for the last time? He confidently expected, says his nephew, that he would conduct the 1901 Festival. In a letter he wrote:

In 1901 I shall have been 40 years before the public – as I date my career from the time I returned from Leipzig in 1861 and I intend making the Festival an occasion of publicly retiring from the active pursuit of my profession, and to do this with *éclat* I mean to produce a work – which I am engaged upon now – which would be, I hope, a worthy successor to the *Golden Legend*, and form a dignified close to my personal public appearances. The words are from one of the (in my humble opinion) greatest poems in the English language, and it has taken a strong hold upon me.

He had been writing to Rudyard Kipling about the setting of *Recessional* but, in the end, he decided that the measure of the lines was too intractable.

His days were running to their end; death, the anodyne of all agonies, was to claim him before the next Festival.

The old Gilbert and Sullivan operas were constantly revived by D'Oyly Carte at the Savoy. *The Gondoliers*, put on again in March 1898, had been taken off to make way for *The Beauty Stone*. When it failed so lamentably, *The Gondoliers* came back. Towards the end of the year D'Oyly Carte decided, strange choice, to revive *The Sorcerer*. Sullivan took the rehearsal on the morning of the first night and found he knew 'precious little about the piece': 'Dined at home and went to the Savoy to conduct the 21st anniversary of the production of *The Sorcerer*, originally produced at the Op. Comique 17th November 1877. Tremendous house – ditto reception. Opera went very well. Call for Gilbert and self. We went on together but did not speak to each other.' ('Oh, the pity of it, Iago, the pity of it.')

It was the last time the two men were to meet.

Sullivan, meanwhile, had been discussing a libretto with Basil Hood. 'He is such a nice fellow and so pleasant to work with.' After various false starts and illnesses and a frustrating trip to Switzerland, they settled on an Eastern subject.

The habit of work replenished the composer, as it always does. But, as is the way of such things, some days the Opera went well; on others it dragged. And, also, as is the way of such things, his spirits rose when work had gone well and sank when it had gone ill, with the inevitable inter-reaction that when his spirits were high his work responded well, and when low, his work was blocked.

He came back to England and took a house in Wokingham. Here the material seemed more pliant; the work went better. D'Oyly Carte arranged to mount the Opera towards the end of November. But Sullivan's score was not rehearsed until after 18 November: 'Finished last bit of score of new Opera to be called *The Rose of Persia*. Have been rather longer than usual over the scoring, but a good many changes and alterations made during progress may account for it.'

The Boer War broke out with a suddenness that took by surprise 'a nation long steeped in peace'. London became a city of waving Union Jacks. The Widow of Windsor took counsel of heaven. The *Daily Mail* asked Sullivan to set Kipling's 'The Absent-Minded Beggar'. It is on record that Sullivan had trouble with the metre – when did he not? Though when he did solve the prosody, he appeared to have sailed through the songs – raved, no doubt cussed, walked, gave it up, took it on again, no doubt cussed again and sweated it out. It was on 1 November that he started to work on Kipling's lines, and on 5 November: 'Finished and wrote out "Absent-Minded Beggar".' The diary must have sighed with relief.

'November 13th: Went to Alhambra to rehearse "Ab. M. Beg." with Coates and orchestra. Then to Savoy to rehearse new Opera. Conducted "Ab. M. Beg" at the Alhambra in the evening – packed house – wild enthusiasm. All sang chorus! I stood on the stage and conducted the *encore* – funny sight!' He wrote to Kipling: 'Your splendid words went, and still go every night with a swing and enthusiasm which even my music cannot stifle. It has been a great pleasure to me to set words of yours.'

The song swept the barrel-organs; tens of thousands of copies were sold for the families of soldiers' dependants. Troops marched away singing it. 'Pay! Pay! Pay!' piped up one and all. And, finally the accolade, the Queen wrote to ask the composer for a copy – almost one can see her singing 'Pay! Pay! Pay!' from the tower at Windsor.

Two weeks later the dress rehearsal of *The Rose of Persia* set in: 'November 27th: Full rehearsal (band, dresses, etc.) at theatre. Everything went smoothly, but it seemed *dull* as ditchwater. . . .'

He had underestimated his own work, says his nephew. The Savoy had been none too successful for him of late years – indeed, he had written to Helen Carte that he felt Fortune had for the time being left the house. He was continually ailing, constantly in an agony of pain, which was no help to his state of mind. Morale was at lowest ebb: 'November 29th, Wednesday. 1st performance of *Rose of Persia* at Savoy Theatre. I conducted as usual – hideously nervous – as usual – great reception as usual – great house as usual – everything as usual – excepting that the piece is really a great success I think, which is *unusual* lately.'

When *The Rose of Persia* ended its run, it was replaced by a revival, *The Pirates of Penzance*, which, in its turn, was succeeded by a revival of *Patience*.

And Gilbert? More and more he was falling prey to his infirmities. Back in 1893 his gout had been so bad that he had to rehearse *Utopia* on crutches. Now, in 1899, he helped to dig the lake at Grim's Dyke that was so tragically to see his end in the fulness of time.

My dear Dorothy,

I am not as well as a perfectly pure and blameless character deserves to be, for I have a racking cough, which is bringing me to an early grave. I always thought I should die young.

> So young – so beautiful, and yet to die!
> Oh, what a dashed unlucky dog am I! (Shakespeare.)

I am making a lovely lake 170 yards long and 50 yards wide. ... We are going to turn the water on at midnight on the 31st December. ...

(But it was not the cough that carried him off; but the lake, during the scooping-out of which he added to his ills by shovelling the wet clay.)

'I had gout all my life,' he was to say, 'until 1900, when rheumatoid arthritis came along. They eloped together – the only scandal I ever had in the family.'

Gilbert photographed in 1900.

And Sullivan? He had always had a boyish urge to invent things and this did not desert him through the years, when health, work and swanning permitted. One of his schemes was a blind which would roll itself up when a button was pressed. But for the most part his inventions rarely travelled beyond his drawing-board. However, it was at this period that he dreamed up a safety device for a carriage: 'If the horse ran away one could release the shafts [had one the presence of mind] by pulling a lever so that the horse was freed from the carriage.' He now cleverly set Invention in double harness with Swanning by taking a model to Marlborough House for the inspection of the Prince of Wales:

Took my model to Marlborough House to shew it to P. of Wales. He was thoroughly delighted with it, and shewed keen interest [reported the diary proudly]. Sent for Lord Suffield, who was in the house, to shew it him. s also thought well of it but thought it should be worked from *inside* by the occupant. [Practical fellow, s.] Both HRH and myself combatted this, as giving too much facility for nervous people. HRH promised to let me apply it to one of his carriages.

One month later: 'Went to Holmes' who had carriage ready with SSS [Sullivan's Safety Shafts]. Drove it about Portland Place. *Very* successful.' (The diary beamed.)

After this SSS faded out, driven away by the composer's return to work, no doubt. For around Christmas 1899 he went to his desk to start a work of the dimensions of *The Golden Legend*.

His imagination was fired, not so his creativity. Themes raced each other to his note-book, there never to be heard again. 'The vitality of his body was drifting away like the slow and gradual sinking of a tide – so slow – so gradual – as to be unobserved.' Agony would intervene. The last Christmas he was to share, a Christmas with a wonderful Christmas Tree, brought back other Christmases when he was young. Swanning had lost none of its mystique. Life took on an interest with each invitation and every party he was well enough to glide through.

'... I thought I was growing old,' he confided to his diary, 'But does one grow old if there is always something to interest?' Bright-eyed but bent, the diary smoothed back a grizzled forelock. He was right, of course – the spirit was – intermittently – willing, it was the body that was weak.

It is on record that the new century dawned in a mistiness that wrapped London in a wet and shining cloak.

Sullivan, contrary to his usual flight from an English winter, clung to his shell at Queen Anne's Mansions. There was little to hold him in London, yet London had never held him more closely, contained him so single-heartedly. On 2 January he attended a meeting at the Crystal Palace. There, says his nephew, he watched 'the divine horses'. But at Sydenham station on the way back, he fell between the platform and the foot-board of the train and was nearly killed. After this the future seemed to him to have been given back to him and he could see it stretching ahead, a shining ribbon he must joy to follow. So, at the end of February, he decided to slip away to Monte Carlo. Yet before March was out, he had tired of the sun. The tables no longer exercised their old fascination for him. He walked – but almost always alone. He visited Melba. He ate little for he had lost his appetite even for *gourmandise*. He wrote to Mrs Ronalds and wrote not once but twice a day and linked the letters with telegrams. Finally, too restless to concentrate he left Monte Carlo for Paris when he found, suddenly, that he was too weak to continue his journey for some days.

Did the unforseen weakness act as a warning? No: for he was unusually elated at finding himself at home in his own apartments.

'May 26th 1900: Sir George Martin and Colonel Arthur Collins came to see me. Former invited me on behalf of Dean and Chapter to write a *Te Deum* for Grand Peace Service when war is over. Consented to try and see what I could do.'

He went swanning off to Epsom and arrived in time to see the Prince of Wales win the Derby with his horse Diamond Jubilee. Hardly had he settled to work on the *Te Deum* than a request from the Emperor that he should go to Berlin to conduct one of his own operas arrived. It was a request the flattered Sullivan could hardly refuse, but the visit was not a success. He hated the production, and the Press gave him no peace. He had a long talk with the Kaiser, and a London reporter caught him off guard. The Emperor's conversation with him was published in London and came out at a tense time between England and Germany on account of the German attitude to Kruger. The Kaiser was understandably extremely angry with his guest:

June 17th: Brooding all day long over the unfortunate interview. Curse the Press and its correspondents. I cannot get over the fact that after all these years of care and avoidance of disclosing anything – even the most ordinary incidents about the Royal Family – I should have let my enthusiasm run away with my discretion, and related before professional reporters what had passed between H. Majesty and myself.

Then, too, it infuriated the Prince of Wales, and Sullivan worried over it for weeks.

In June Hood brought him the outline of an Opera, *The Emerald Isle*. 'Delightful, new and free', Sullivan noted in his diary.

He took a house at Shepperton and worked at the *Te Deum* but only to be dissatisfied with what he had done. Berlin was weighing on his mind. So was *The Emerald Isle*, with D'Oyly Carte pressing for a November opening. And then there was Ben, his new dog.

July 3rd, 1900: Ben, a handsome young collie, arrived from Manchester on approval. Thoroughbred and nice-tempered and playful. He slept in my room this night – at least, he was supposed to sleep, but he was so restless and excited, and kept me awake *all night*. At 5.15 I took him downstairs and let him out, but I couldn't tie him up anywhere, so I had to take him back into my bedroom – then I hit him with my slipper till he lay down quietly under the bed, till he was let out early. O what a night!

Ben spent two beautiful days with England's premier composer. 'He stopped the *Te Deum*. He turned the house into a turmoil. He dragged bones about over carpets. Then, with a label round his neck, and looking angelic, he was escorted to the station en route back to Manchester.' The *Te Deum* took its proper place in the scheme of things once more. But how empty the house and walks and waking must have seemed.

'July 14th: Finished *Te Deum* words and all.'

With the final draft of the work, Switzerland began to beckon Sullivan. But on 30 July: 'The Duke of Saxe-Coburg [Alfred Duke of Edinburgh] died last night – upset me terribly – another of my oldest and best friends gone.'

'August 10th: My old friend Lord Russel of Killowen, Lord Chief Justice of England, died in London at Cromwell House, after a few days' illness. Another friend gone! They go with cruel rapidity.'

And there had been George Grove. One by one the clouds were obscuring Sullivan's sun.

But Gilbert was travelling abroad in search of it.

'The pleasure of travelling abroad', writes Hesketh Pearson, 'was heightened by the young and pretty women to be met on steamers and in hotels.' But he remains strong in the belief that Gilbert's relations with them never advanced beyond the flirtatious. The trip was undertaken in the hope that it might lessen his rheumatoid arthritis.

Already back in 1898 he had taken his rheumatism to Naples and on to the Crimea, to

Yalta, '... There is a sea-side resort, Yalta, which is one of the loveliest places I ever saw.' We find Yalta mentioned often in Chekhov's letters but to him it was an exile – a health-imposed exile: in a letter written at about the same time, Chekhov exclaims, 'I am bored. The weather here is magnificent and warm, but that's only gravy, and what good is gravy without the meat.'

Sullivan, with grief in his heart, left London for Switzerland to begin *The Emerald Isle*, but: 'The hotel is full of howling and shrieking Germans.'

Not unexpectedly he moved on. But *The Emerald Isle* was slow and recalcitrant.

Between bouts of work, a little swanning. But one day, having called on the Duchess of York, he was caught in a heavy rainfall. A chill clamped close his throat. He could scarcely speak. He set off quickly for Paris. He felt that never again would he see England and home. But we breathe again. On 19 September he reached the harbour of

Sir Arthur Sullivan in the last years of his life.

his London apartments. And at the end of September he 'dragged himself to his desk': 'Tried to work – no result,' records the indomitable diary, sadly.

He went to Tunbridge Wells and on the day of his journey wrote: 'Felt very seedy all day – pain from kidney trouble. . . . Awfully nervous and in terror about myself.'

It was his inability to work that frightened him – it would! there is nothing more unnerving – and 'closed the curtains of gloom' about his mind.

'October 14th, Tunbridge Wells: Have been here just a fortnight, and what have I done? Little more than nothing, first from illness and physical incapability, secondly from *brooding* and nervous terror about myself. Practically I have done nothing. . . .'

There followed the last entry he was ever to write in his diary: 'October 15th: *Lovely day*. . . . I am sorry to leave such a lovely day.'

But he might have had to leave in June.

He returned to London but without the strength for work.

He had promised to conduct the revival of *Patience* on 7 November. Until three days before that, he really believed that he would gather his strength to do so. It was an evening full of heart-warming enthusiasm; but at the end only Gilbert and D'Oyly Carte took the call. Sullivan's music-making in this world was at an end. He was never to hear his *Te Deum. The Emerald Isle* was to be completed but by another hand.

It was the moment for complete understanding for Gilbert and Sullivan, each of the other. They had worked in the light of each other's grace. Ten days before he left 'the lovely day' for ever, Sullivan received a letter from Gilbert:

My dear Sullivan

I would be glad to come up to town to see you before I go, but unfortunately in my present enfeebled condition, a carriage journey to London involves my lying down a couple of hours before I am fit for anything, besides stopping all night in town. The railway journey is still more fatiguing. I have lost 60 lbs in weight, and my arms and legs are of the consistency of cotton-wool. I sincerely hope to find you alright again on my return, and the new opera running merrily.

Yours very truly,

W.S.Gilbert

Shortly after 6 o'clock on the morning of 22 November, with his nephew keeping vigil, Sullivan died.

Mrs Ronalds, who had been warned, waited in an agony for a cab which did not come. When at last one was procured and drove her to Queen Anne's Mansions, the blinds had already been lowered.

Grief made hearts heavy all over the world. The Queen of England sent a wire expressing her sympathy.

Eighteen years before his death Sullivan had written detailed instructions for his burial in Brompton Cemetery:

DIRECTIONS

1. I wish my body to be embalmed before burial. Let nothing prevent this being done.
2. My funeral is to be conducted in the same manner as that of my dear Mother, and if possible by the same undertaker.

3. My body to be buried in the same grave with my Father, Mother and Brother in Brompton Cemetery.

4. If can be conveniently arranged, I should like the Quartet from *The Light of the World* ('Yea though I Walk') or the Funeral Hymn from *The Martyr of Antioch*, to be sung at my funeral, the latter if there is a chorus.

It was, however, the wish of the Dean and Chapter of St Paul's that the place of burial should be changed, and the decision was only taken after the grave in Brompton Cemetery had been opened to receive him. (What a hustle and bustle and muttering of sextons that must have produced.)

The Queen herself ordained that the first part of the service for the former Chapel Royal Chorister should be held at the Chapel Royal.

And then, according to the wishes of the Dean and Chapter, the second service took place and Sullivan was buried in the crypt of St Paul's, swanning to the last, bless him.

As it so happened, the procession passed along the embankment and by the Savoy, where D'Oyly Carte was lying gravely ill at his house in Adelphi Terrace.

Two days later vandals broke into the crypt and stole all the cards bearing royal and distinguished cyphers and signatures. But Sullivan's honours they could not steal.

And Gilbert? A letter sent from abroad to Sullivan's nephew:

My dear Sullivan:

I did not hear of your uncle's terribly sudden death until three days since, or I should have written to express my personal sorrow, and my sympathy with you in the great loss you have

The funeral of Sullivan in St Pauls' Cathedral
(*The Graphic*, December 1900).

247

sustained. It is a satisfaction to me to feel that I was impelled, shortly before his death, to write to him to propose to shake hands over our recent differences, and even a greater satisfaction to learn through you that my offer of reconciliation was cordially accepted. I wish I had been in England that I might have had an opportunity of joining the mourners at his funeral.

And when, in 1905, the bust of Sullivan was about to be placed in the Savoy Gardens, Gilbert wrote to his nephew that he had heard that:

... you want a quotation from one of the libretti to inscribe on your uncle's bust. What do you say to this (from *The Yeoman*).

> Is life a boon?
> If so it must befall
> That Death whene'er he call
> Must call too soon!

It is difficult to find anything quite fitted to so sad an occasion, but I think this might do.
Yours truly,
W.S.Gilbert.

Old Savoyards round the Sullivan Memorial on the
Embankment in 1914; from left to right: George Power, Leonora Braham,
Jessie Bond and Julia Gwynne.

13

Gilbert Alone

And Gilbert without Sullivan? Gilbert, whom Quiller-Couch calls 'this neat rhymer, this neat wit, neat barrister, neat stage-manager', who, 'nursed at the back of his head a conception of himself as a great and serious dramatist – even as Sullivan, with better excuse, nursed the conception of himself as a great composer in Oratorio,' and, as we have seen, opera; did this same Gilbert ripen as time, like an ever-rolling stream, rolled on.

He found Barrie's *Peter Pan* 'feeble and silly', Shaw's *John Bull's Other Island* 'bizarre, sometimes amusing, but on the whole boring', *The Scarlet Pimpernel* 'just stupid', *When Knights were bold* 'banal', Alfred Sutro's *John Glayd's Honour*, 'well-written but immoral' and *Raffles* 'rot'. And who am I to prove he was in every case wrong?

On the other hand he held that Pinero's *His House in Order* was excellent. No, I do not think we may fear that the years, as he lived on, blunted his shafts. Arriving one day at the Beefsteak Club, Gilbert looked around. He marvelled: 'A dozen men. And I'm on terms with all of them.'

And again, when asked his view of a project:

'Sir, I view the proposal to hold an International Exhibition at San Francisco with an equanimity bordering on indifference.'

Again: of an enemy: 'I never could understand his hostility (except that he is the avowed enemy of the whole human race), until I remembered that thirty-seven years ago I introduced him to the woman who is now his wife.'

Already, back in 1893, he had become a Justice of the Peace for the division of Gore in the County of Middlesex. 'You have, I believe, studied the law as a barrister and have a sound knowledge of it?' observed the High Sheriff.

'That is so, but I hope you will not consider it an impediment,' returned Gilbert. Presumably M'lud did not.

As a magistrate, says Pearson, he combined sternness with kindness that made him, in many of the cases caused by poverty, pay the fines himself; but cases of cruelty, particularly to animals, were punished to the utmost of his jurisdiction.

One 'unhappy fellow', who had tried to commit suicide, was bound over with a warning from William Schwenk Gilbert, JP: 'If you attempt suicide again, you will be brought before us and punished for both offences, but if you succeed you will be beyond our jurisdiction.'

But many a heart will go out to him from our own times, when, as a member of the general public, he wrote a letter to the Press: 'Saturday afternoon, although occurring in regular and well-forseen intervals, always takes the railway by surprise.'

Thomas Blackwell, purveyor of jams and other preserves, complained that some workmen on the Grim's Dyke estate had damaged something on his adjoining grounds: 'I am extremely sorry,' wrote Gilbert, 'that my men should have damaged anything in your preserves. Pardon the word "preserves".'

But he was soon on friendly terms with Blackwell, which was as well, for as time passed, the Grim's Dyke grounds were turned into a kind of zoo, so passionately attached to animals did Gilbert become. Lawns, flowers, trees, bracken, rhododendrons, ferns, bee-hives – all were turned into a bee-loud glade, a sanctuary for birds and animals which were quite welcome to come into his house, too. Dogs and cats had their baskets and stools for day-time naps; they dined with the family, each having its table-cloth spread on the floor. The pekinese had their toys, taking them upstairs to bed and bringing them down every morning in their mouths (the French poodle scorned such trifles), and we are told that one of the pekes caught a burglar by barking loud and clear and continuously outside a room on the top floor. A maid went in and a man rushed out – a weather-clock springs to mind – but in sprinting to the hall and freedom, he barged into Butler and was successfully holding his own against a footman, when Gardener appeared. A three-to-one tussle took place and the noise could be heard in the drawing room, where – finishing touch – a guest was singing: 'O for the wings of a dove'. Gilbert had a splendid chat with the intruder about burgling in general, and when the police arrived, sent the burglar off to the police station in his car: 'He must be so very exhausted after the struggle.' Incidentally, 'The Mrs' kept a truncheon by her bedside at night, for fear of a repetition.

Gilbert's library, with its ever-open door to the garden, was a pet meeting-place for the animals: one of them, a fallow deer, became friendly with a donkey named Adelina (Patti), so called on account of her high notes, and they wandered the lanes together. This involved Gilbert in a number of fines, tips and telegrams. But it was not until the deer went into the library four times in one afternoon to nuzzle her nose into his hand that Gilbert gave her to the herd at Bently Priory, not far away. Four years later, tiring of her exile, the fallow deer found her way back to the library.

He kept monkeys, too, and built a substantial house for them, but his favourites were a pair of lemurs. One of the pair took a dislike to his cigar, snatching it out of his mouth and throwing it to the ground, but gradually it acquired a taste for the odorous smoke and would perch on his shoulder and try to swallow the rings. They particularly cared for Gilbert's dining-room and would go marauding there for nectarines. They would also invade 'Missus's' strawberry beds. All this Gilbert bore with the utmost good-humour, because they were animals. He expressly forbade the gardeners to kill a squirrel. The species was sacrosanct since 'his adopted ancestor', Sir Humphrey Gilbert, step-brother to Sir Walter Raleigh, went down off the Azores with his ship *The Squirrel* – a squirrel was the crest of W. S. Gilbert.

His love of animals persisted. And not only animals.

On a ship in search of health, in a letter to a friend, he stated that he had met the most beautiful red-head he had ever seen. Again, this time in 1903:

I have discovered the loveliest girl in the world. She is on the stage and quite inexperienced, but with a good deal of dramatic aptitude. I've taken her in hand, and got her an engagement for £5 a week at the Criterion, and a further engagement at the Haymarket in the autumn. Not a bad beginning for a young girl who (until she met me) had not a friend in the theatrical profession. I am sorry to say she is an ungrateful little cat, and looks upon all I have done for her in the natural order of things.

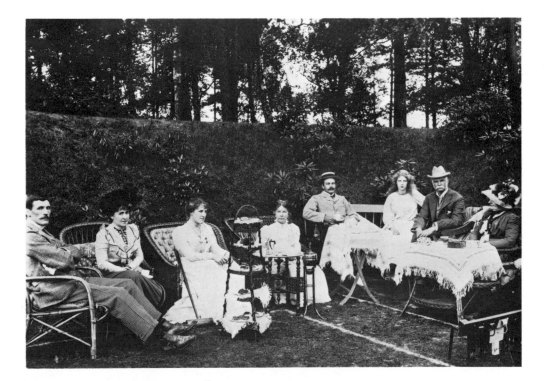

Gilbert (far right) with a croquet party at tea in the garden of Grim's Dyke. 'Missus' presides over the teapot.

Yet it should not be forgotten that biographer after biographer has said that Gilbert's partiality to young and lovely ladies was all in 'the cause of innocent merriment, of innocent merriment'.

And then there was his wretched rheumatoid arthritis: 'I am still rather Richardy (I hate the slang expression "Dicky") in the knees.'

Though he was nearing seventy he did not care to be reminded of that fact: 'Personally I'm sick of birthdays; I've had so many of them, and they begin to pall, but (such is the inconsistency of the animal man), I felt I could do with a few more.' None the less, the thought of death began to haunt his letters: 'This will be my last year on earth,' he wrote erroneously to a close friend in 1909, 'and I want it to be a jolly one and I want you to make it jolly. Live as long as you can, for when you go it will be "Adieu" (and when I go I'm afraid it will be *au Diable*). I'm told by a palmist that I am to die on the 10th July. She is a Hebrew maid; I call her the sweet palmist of Israel. ...'

In October 1902 he had bought an American Locomobile steam-car, and hard on had his first accident:

... I made my debut by spoiling a parson, who came round a dead wall on a bicycle. He was pretty badly hurt. The car was turned over at a ditch. I was pitched over the dash-board onto

Lucy Gilbert feeding a faun.

252

my head (I saw many beautiful stars of beautiful colours and was quite sorry when they vanished), and my wife was pitched very comfortably into a hedge, where she looked like a large and quite unaccountable bird's nest.

Before the year was out, he had two more accidents to report:

... we seem fated to cause disaster: On Thursday, although we were only creeping on at two miles an hour, we caused a horse, which was driven in a trap by two ladies, to shy up a bank. ... One lady was thrown out and run over, the groom was also thrown out, and the trap ran over his hand; the horses then bolted with the other lady, but was eventually stopped without damage. Happily the lady who was run over was not much hurt. She good-naturedly explained that 'it was only her legs'. ...

His steam-emitting Locomobile was followed by a 12 h.p. Napier, and he engaged 'a gentleman driver' whom he instructed never to exceed the maximum limit of twenty miles an hour, for by now Gilbert had become the Deputy Lieutenant of Middlesex and was strongly conscious of the need to keep within the law. Another Napier (16 h.p.) replaced the first. And then wham! In 1903 he and a local omnibus hurtled into collision.

He bought a Cadillac which he kept in use together with a 25–35 h.p. Darracque. In 1909 the motorist's *Cordon Bleu* was bought – a Rolls Royce (he insisted on being allowed £500 for the Darracque). The *Cordon*, however, appears to have been insufficiently *Bleu*, for in September, there was Gilbert, hollering for his money back – £1,399 11s. The car, after many upbraiding letters, was put into the order Gilbert demanded: 'Of course its condition must be permanently satisfactory.' Then, on 9 April 1910, it knocked down a woman. 'The accident was caused entirely by her culpable negligence in running from behind a stationary van.'

Again one is compelled to sympathise with Gilbert even as one reflects that the poor gentleman does seem to have been a shade accident-prone.

Gilbert's many kindnesses would fill a book. When Dickens's son-in-law C. E. Perugini came to ask for the loan of £100, Gilbert begged him to accept it as a gift, on the grounds that it was easy enough for himself to lend it, but how difficult for the other to ask for it: 'What is beyond all price', he said, 'freedom from anxiety, and peace of mind.' And following the Lloyd George Budget of 1909, with its super-tax, health insurance and dole, he sent a letter to *The Times*: 'I shall discontinue my subscriptions to all charities for the very poor and confine my donations exclusively to a class which has not come within the purview of Mr Lloyd George's humanitarian scheme, such as underpaid curates, distressed gentlefolk and poor professional men.'

Moreover, in June 1909, at last, at last, intimations of a knighthood:

21st June, 1909.

Dear Sir Henry Campbell-Bannerman

I am obliged to thank you for your offer to submit my name to the King for the honour of Knighthood. It is an offer which I gratefully accept. ...

He attended the long and secretly coveted investiture on 15 July at Buckingham Palace: '... duly tapped on both shoulders by Edward VII ...', and of course it took Gilbert to complain: '... found myself described in the official list as Mr William

Gilbert, playwright, suggesting that my work was analogous to that of a wheelwright, or a millwright, or a wainwright ... there is an excellent word "dramatist" which seems to fit the situation, but it is not applied until we are dead; then we become dramatists as oxen, sheep and pigs are transfigured into beef, mutton and pork after their demise.'

He called the title a 'tin-pot, twopenny-halfpenny sort of distinction, but as no Dramatic Author as such ever had it for Dramatic Authorship alone, I felt I ought not to refuse it.' 'A mere triviality', he called it; 'An unmeaning scrap of tinsel'. 'A reward for having brought up a family of plays without ever having had to apply to the relieving officer for financial assistance,' but the award at least removed a smouldering if un-spoken grudge, even though he declared: 'This indiscriminate flinging about of knight-hoods is making me very nervous. It's quite possible they may give one to my butler. He's a very good fellow and I'm afraid it may upset him.'

We need have no fear: in the years in which Gilbert survived Sullivan, the old Adam, like cheerfulness, keeps breaking through.

The years that were left to him were not without event. In 1908 he won £75 in a sweepstake at the Derby. Soon after he saw Maud Allan dance, and defined her art in his diary as '*dégoûtant*'. In 1909 he read a headline in an evening paper: 'Death of W. S. Gilbert in great agony', to which he added one word: 'Liar'.

'I should like to die upon a summer's day in my garden,' he wrote.

This much at least was to be granted him.

In 1899 Gilbert had a lake dug in the grounds of Grim's Dyke. Twelve years later it was the scene of his death.

Nancy McIntosh.

Besides, were there not revivals with delicious opportunities for managerial fall-outs? Without his long-time two safety valves, D'Oyly Carte and Sullivan, Helen Carte was left to take the brunt. He warred long and hard with her after she found it impossible to cast Nancy McIntosh in a revival of *The Yeomen of the Guard* in 1906. '... You have placed upon me the deepest – I may say the only – indignity ever offered me during my 40 years connected with the stage. ...'

The reproaches continued to rain down on Helen Carte.

It was not only the late unlamented Locomobile that let off steam.

Dear Mrs Carte

The cast of *The Gondoliers* is, with few exceptions, so very unsatisfactory to me that, in justice to myself, I am bound to disclaim all responsibility for it.

Helen Carte announced a revival of *The Mikado*, only to have the performance forbidden by the Lord Chamberlain. The Japanese Prince Fushimi, it seemed, was about to pay an official visit to England. Gilbert, as can be imagined, was not one to sit down under this edict. He appeared before the Committee on the Censorship in 1909 and protested.

Patience was mounted instead of *The Mikado*. On the first night, in April, he dined at the Garrick Club, went to see the performing sea-lions at the Palace Theatre and arrived at the Savoy to take his curtain.

Early in June 1908, the Lord Chamberlain having come to his senses, *The Mikado* was revived.

Helen Carte's season continued, with various revivals, for two years, which offered Gilbert plenty of opportunities to complain about: the many exceedingly incompetent people, the terrible scenery, the atrocious costumes.

On 2 February 1909 he wrote to her:

... You are not a free agent or you would never have treated me with the gross insolence and black ingratitude which have characterised the Savoy methods during the last 2½ years ... the operas have been insulted, degraded, and dragged through the mire. ... Blind and blatant ignorance accompanied by contemptible economy have characterised the productions of the past two years, and people have been engaged whom the call boy would have told you were ridiculously unsuitable. ...

'Everyone says I'm such a disagreeable man,' quoted Gilbert from *Iolanthe*, in a speech he was making, 'and I can't think why!' He seemed mildly astonished by the wave of laughter with which this was greeted. But I dare say Helen Carte could have enlightened him.

On the last day of 1908 Gilbert wrote to Edward German suggesting he should compose the music for 'a 3 Act Fairy Opera'. German readily agreed but Gilbert found it hard to interest a theatre management. Eventually C. H. Workman, who had been a performer at the Savoy, dug out some backers. After the usual squalls and tantrums, largely over Gilbert's determination that Nancy McIntosh should sing the leading role, *Fallen Fairies* was produced on 15 December 1909. The Press was not enthusiastic and the piece ran for only six weeks.

At the end of 1909, Gilbert asked Malone, manager of the Adelphi, if he would mount a revival of *Ruddigore*, but proved not to be as staunch in the defence of his late collaborator's work as he had been in the cause of the lovely Miss McIntosh. He wrote (on behalf of Sullivan's nephew and heir and his backsliding self), 'We propose to cut a good deal of the heavy music in Act 2.' One wonders if Sullivan's nephew had been consulted in this matter.

On 30 May 1910, Helen Carte asked if Gilbert wished to resume control of the Savoy operas, her rights in them having lapsed? This gave him a first-rate opportunity to be pig-headed. Naturally he availed himself of it to the full: 'The bottom has been knocked out of their value for production in London by the circumstances attending their recent revival. Many years must elapse before the operas recover their former prestige.' Helen Carte acquired the rights for a further five years for £5,000.

If Gilbert was liked – and he was – by his staff (twenty-eight in the house, twelve outside), 'The Mrs' must have been adored. By general consent she never contradicted Gilbert. She did her best to let him see only such press-cuttings as dealt tenderly with his work (a doubtful benefit to him but something of a let-off to herself and Miss McIntosh who would have had the storm loosed on them). She held his affection largely by her sympathy and understanding, and, though there were some who likened her to Agate's 'Mousey-pousy', this was generally recognised as the ideal marriage, in spite of – perhaps because of – Gilbert's weakness for very young ladies of undeniable pulchritude.

But to return to his staff: the butler was with him for twenty-six years, and three of his gardeners for fourteen, thirteen and eleven years, which speaks well for him as a master. His 'gentleman driver' drove his car for eight years. If only he could have dealt as fairly with his collaborators and friends. The only dark cloud floating over Grim's Dyke at the turn of the year, had been Nancy McIntosh's visit to Los Angeles:

23rd January 1908

Dearest Nancy

... I write this for fear you might think that I had forgotten a duty which is also a pleasure. ... I haven't any more news. My wife sends her best love and wishes for a happy new year, *which we hope and trust you will spend with us*, but we seem to see difficulties ahead. I only hope you are not going to chuck us after so many years.

Kind regards and all good wishes to your father and brother.

Your affectionate

Judge

Conceivably it was in recognition of her return to Grim's Dyke that Gilbert had written for her the ill-fated part in *Fallen Fairies*.

He had once given her his photograph, writing on the cover, says Pearson – 'For Nancy, with a heart full of love.' The devotion of 'Judge' and 'the Missus' must have been touching to behold. Her company, and indeed her help in their social scene, was a gift beyond rubies. Gilbert had once written BN (Before Nancy): 'We have a largish dance tomorrow, so the house and all in it are upside-down. Poor Kitty looks quite odd and unusual upside-down.'

On 20 May 1910, Gilbert watched the funeral of the King who had knighted him. He did not have a good view of the procession, and we may imagine that he would not have let the occasion pass without comment.

Gilbert in the dining room at Grim's Dyke.

One day a journalist who was preparing Gilbert's obituary for *The Times* arrived at Grim's Dyke. Gilbert, amusable for once, 'laughingly supplied as many details as he could remember'. He showed, reports Pearson, no lack of vitality, no loss of memory, no lessening of interest in whatever took his fancy. *And he was as prickly as ever.* This we can all believe.

If he felt depressed, the Book of Job became his balm: 'Men of my age are like trees in late autumn,' he wrote, 'their friends have died away as the leaves have fallen from the trees.' In March 1911 he estimated 'the old crumbling ruin has been propped up and under-pinned, and will, I think, stand for a few months yet.' 'Walk!' he exclaimed, when advised not to walk from Harley Street to Eaton Square, soon after luncheon, 'Of course I'll walk. I walk six or seven miles a day. I never wore a pair of glasses in my life and I still feel eighteen.' Of old age he said: 'It is the happiest time in a man's life,' then, mournfully, 'the worse of it is there's so little of it.'

Early in May 1911 he was still well enough to bathe in the lake, attend the magistrate's court and 'round up two gazelles which had taken refuge in the library'. On Sunday, the 28th, he bathed in the lake in the morning and again in the afternoon, played croquet with Nancy before and after luncheon, walked in the grounds, listened to Nancy singing after tea and took his third dip in the lake before dinner, all dutifully noted in his diary, ending in French: *'premier melon'*.

29 May filled Grim's Dyke with as sunny a day as ever Gilbert wished, flowers blooming and blazing from the borders of green baize lawn, and filling Gilbert's gardens with the buzz of bees. Fruit ripening nicely, gazelles affable.

Gilbert, in tranquil mood, called to see May Fortesque, who had been thrown from her horse in Hyde Park and was lying in her house, where Broadcasting House now stands: 'I won't ask you what you think of her appearance, for you can scarcely see her,' said her mother, as he was taking his leave: 'Her appearance matters nothing; it is her disappearance we could not stand,' said Gilbert, well up to form.

In the afternoon he went down to bathe in the lake with two young ladies, Winifred Emery and a Miss Ruby Preece. Neither could swim well. Ruby suddenly found she was out of her depth and in a panic. She called out to Winifred. At that moment Gilbert appeared: 'It's not very deep,' he called, 'don't splash.' He plunged straight in and swam towards her: 'Put your hands on my shoulders and don't struggle,' he said. She obeyed. He sank almost at once. She went under, too, but came up after a moment, to find that she could just stand. When she reached the bank, she could not see him. Gilbert had died of heart-failure. He could not stay to die in June.

Index

259